CHAINS

链锁

EDITED BY
Linda Jaivin, Esther Sunkyung Klein,
AND Annie Luman Ren

CHINA STORY
YEARBOOK: CHAINS

中美 全球研究中心
AUSTRALIAN CENTRE ON
CHINA IN THE WORLD

Australian
National
University

ANU PRESS

Australian
National
University

ANU PRESS

The China Story
中⟨國⟩的故事

Published by ANU Press
The Australian National University
Canberra ACT 2600, Australia
Email: anupress@anu.edu.au

Available to download for free at press.anu.edu.au

ISBN (print): 9781760465797
ISBN (online): 9781760465803

WorldCat (print): 1389271104
WorldCat (online): 1388686091

DOI: 10.22459/CSY.2023

Design concept by Markus Wernli; 'Chains' cover design by ANU Press, and chapter and foci openers by Chin-Jie Melodie Liu

Typesetting by Serena Ford, Chin-Jie Melodie Liu, and Xiaoyu Sun

The Australian Centre on China in the World is an initiative of the Commonwealth Government of Australia and The Australian National University

本书概要

2022

年10月，习近平在中国共产党第二十次全国代表大会上重申了「坚持对外开放的基本国策」。过去四十年来，这一政策为中国带来了经济繁荣，同时也巩固了中国共产党的政治合法性。然而，尽管中共高层一再强调「持续对外开放」，2022壬寅虎年却始终绕不开「锁链」这一话题及意象。在「清零」政策下，全国上下强制实施严厉的「全城封锁」或「小区封锁」，而上海旷日持久的封城尤为世间瞩目。新年伊始一位抖音博主意外被摄的「铁链女」视频引发了全国范围内对人口贩卖的强烈舆论谴责，围绕着性别暴力和妇女权利这一更为普遍的双重话题的讨论随之如火如荼地展开，当然也时刻被严加防范着。然而就在此年，「二十大」以降，在最高政治权力层面本来就寥寥无几的妇女代表人数越发式微，几近为零。

此外，中国在2022年面临全球供应链的危机，以及八月份由第四次台海危机引发的岛链问题。尽管亚太地区局势紧张，中华人民共和国在太平洋岛屿国家之间接二连三频出外交新猷，并庆祝与日本和澳大利亚建交50周年。岁暮年关，乌鲁木齐市一处被封锁公寓的火灾悲剧激发了民众抗议的连锁反应，为期三年的「清零」政策终于偃旗息鼓。《中国故事年鉴2022：链锁》如实记录以上及是年其它重要事件，深入阐释，以期为历史提供一明鉴。

Translation by Annie Luman Ren

Contents

CHINA STORY YEARBOOK | Introduction
CHAINS | Linda Jaivin

引言

INTRODUCTION

INTRODUCTION

Linda Jaivin

In early 2022, a vlogger passing through a village in Jiangsu province in the People's Republic of China (PRC) came across a woman chained by her neck to the wall in a freezing shed outside the home where her husband and children sat eating dinner. The video of 'Little Plum Blossom', a victim of trafficking and domestic violence, went viral, sparking widespread outrage. Before long, another kind of enchainment was dominating public discourse as city after city was shut in and shut down in service of the party-state's zero-COVID policy. As 2022 wore on, dramas erupted with supply chains and island chains and not-always-whispered critiques of Xi Jinping locking in a third term for himself as general secretary of the Communist Party of China (CPC). Censorship in the cultural sphere, meanwhile, intensified to the point that one observer remarked that China's film industry had entered 'an era of dancing in chains' 戴着镣铐跳舞的时代.[1] Even before the hanging of a protest banner on a bridge in Beijing and the deaths of ten people in a locked-down apartment block in Ürümqi sparked a nationwide chain reaction of protests, it was clear that 'chains and locks' 链锁 was the logical theme for the *China Story Yearbook 2022*.

According to the Chinese zodiac, 2022 was the Year of the Tiger. Tigers, which in China are both endemic and endangered, traditionally represent a range of things: power and predation, good luck, and protection. Countless Chinese stories, fables, and legends feature them, as Annie Luman Ren explains in 'The Year of the Tiger'. Among these are a parable from the ancient *Book of Rites* that tells of Confucius encountering a woman weeping bitterly by a grave. She tells his disciple that tigers have killed her father-in-law, husband, and son. 'Why do you not leave this place?' the disciple asks. She answers that while there are tigers there, at least there are no tyrants.

Locked Down, Breaking Out

The thirteen million people of Xi'an began 2022 in lockdown after testing revealed 127 cases of COVID-19 in that city. In February, the twenty-eight and a half million residents of Shanghai entered what for many would be more than two months of being locked in their homes. 'Big Whites'

大白 (public health workers/enforcers in white hazmat suits) and blue fences became common sights around the country. In August and September alone, more than 300 million people in over seventy cities went into lockdown. The other 1.1 billion were subjected to regimes of endless testing. The translation of a 'letter from lockdown' by a young Shanghai resident gives a taste of the many little stories unfolding behind the big ones of this extraordinary time.

When lockdowns were not in force, a universal 'traffic-light' COVID app determined citizens' individual mobility. Red indicated COVID-positive and yellow suspected contact with a positive case. Only those riding the 'green horse' *lüma* 绿马 (a homonym for 'code green' 绿码), as the slang went, could access public spaces or transport. Public security officials found the app useful for preventative policing — for example, turning protesters' app profiles to code red.

The wider uses of the COVID app reignited debates about data privacy and surveillance. Most of China's data privacy laws apply to private enterprise. Government agencies enjoy relatively free access to data on grounds of public or national security. Tsinghua University sociologist and data privacy campaigner Li Zhen 李振 maintains that the collection of data and surveillance associated with the fight against COVID-19 'has totally destroyed the past thirty or forty years of legal progress in China'.[2] In an online essay that was quickly censored, another Tsinghua academic, law professor Lao Dongyan 劳东燕, criticised general complacency about increasing levels of control and surveillance: '[M]any of those put in chains are not only not angry at losing their freedoms but are quite comfortable with it. They are like frogs being boiled in warm water.'[3]

By year's end, it became clear that complacency had limits. Reports and photographs of incidents in which the government's zero-COVID policy had led to tragedy continued to circulate, defying the censors. Among them was the story of a pregnant woman miscarrying outside a hospital that had denied her entry because she lacked an up-to-the-minute COVID test. Then there was footage of officials refusing to let residents out of a locked-down building during an earthquake, and a road accident in which twenty-seven people died when the bus forcibly transporting them to a quarantine centre in Guizhou crashed. 'We are on the bus' became a (rapidly censored) hashtag.

On 13 October, a middle-aged tech worker named Peng Lifa 彭立发 hung a banner from the Sitong overpass in Beijing demanding 'Freedom, not lockdowns, elections, not rulers, dignity, not lies'. It also called for a general strike and demanded that Xi Jinping step down. Peng's words — though rapidly censored — spread like an electric current, graffitied on toilet walls, bounced in and out of the country via virtual private networks (VPNs) and Twitter, and affirmed by a simple (and quickly banned) hashtag saying, 'I saw it'. Nationwide demonstrations erupted demanding an end to zero-COVID. Some protesters held up sheets of blank paper to symbolise all they wanted to say but could not, inspiring the phrase 'A4 revolution'. A new vernacular phrase entered the language: 'To come out of the political closet' 政治出柜.

By December, the government unchained the country from 'dynamic zero-COVID', despite serious concerns that China's healthcare system would collapse under a massive rise in cases. It relaxed the rules on lockdowns, testing, quarantine, and mobility. Dynamic zero-COVID vanished from official rhetoric and the previously ubiquitous Big Whites began vacating the streets. (Later, some of them staged their own protests over not being properly paid.) The *People's Daily* claimed that the protests ('circumstances') had nothing to do with the sudden relaxation:

> It is absolutely necessary for people to appreciate that the present optimisation of our suite of coronavirus responses reflects a forward-leaning recalibration and is not a passive reaction to circumstances. The Ten New Regulations ... in no way signal a relaxation of our COVID response ... [nor do they] signify a complete opening up or so-called 'giving in and giving up'.[4]

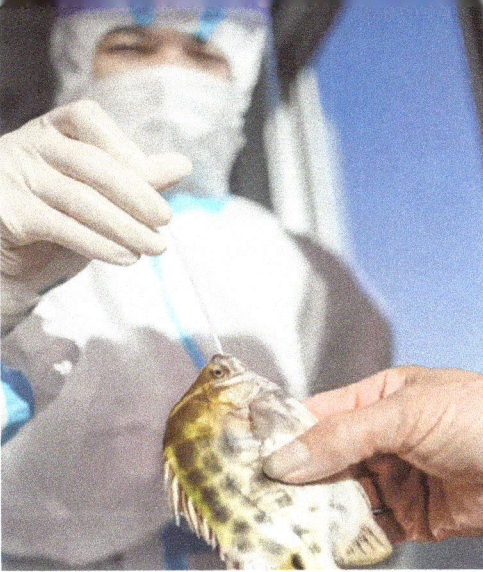

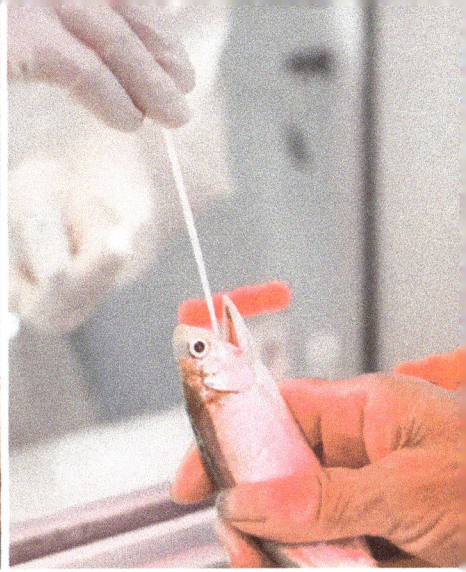

Zealous officials swab fish caught for market, provoking disbelief and mockery
Source: Taihainet

It was also necessary for the party to demonstrate that it is what it has always claimed to be: 'great, glorious and infallible' 伟大光明正确. Jeffrey Wasserstrom and William Yang look at the balance between official celebration and mass protest in 'A Year of Protests, Ceremonies, and Surprises'.

Meanwhile, by year's end, there were reports of panic-buying of fever medicines at pharmacies, patients being treated outside overcrowded hospitals, and crematorium workers on double shifts. The government censors also worked overtime to suppress any suggestion that the sudden relaxation had precipitated a public health crisis, that its vaccination drive had been less than successful (or, by prioritising workers, had failed its most vulnerable), or even that there had been more than a few COVID-related deaths, which was manifestly untrue.

Chains of Command, Chains of Supply, and Links to a Greener Future

The big political story of 2022 was the Twentieth Party Congress in October. The delegates affirmed Xi Jinping's convention-breaking third term as general secretary of the CPC. The forced removal from the congress of his predecessor, Hu Jintao 胡锦涛, after Hu became visibly agitated by something he read in the official papers on the desk in front of him, was the only discordant note in an otherwise tightly orchestrated ceremony. The terse official explanation was that Hu was suffering from a health issue. Chinese-Canadian political scientist Wu Guoguang 吴国光 remarked on the *Bumingbai* 不明白 podcast that if Hu had truly suffered a health emergency, it says something about the humanity of the top leaders that they appeared less concerned about their colleague and elder than most people would have been for a stricken stranger.[5]

Neil Thomas, in 'A Matter of Perspective: Insider Accounts of Xi Jinping and the Twentieth Party Congress', and Ben Hillman, in 'Ghosts of Mao and Deng', contribute analyses of the congress from different angles. We have also provided a simple primer on the congress, explaining how delegates are chosen, noting major personnel changes, and listing key points from Xi's official report, which was notably less sanguine than others in recent years.

Although Xi cited 'major positive results' in 'economic and social development', the extensive and often chaotic lockdowns affected everything including production, shipping and transport, and consumption in 2022. Gross domestic product (GDP) growth sank to just more than 3 percent compared with 8.1 percent the previous year.

In mid-December, the annual Central Economic Work Conference set the economic policy directions for the coming year. It pledged to improve corporate governance of state-owned enterprises to make them more fit for the market. It committed the Chinese economy to 'a high level of openness to the outside world', including expanding access to the domestic market for foreign trade and investment. Industrial priorities would include 'new energy, artificial intelligence, bio-manufacturing, green low-carbon manufacturing, and quantum computing'.[6] The conference also affirmed the state's commitment to developing the private economy. This brought some comfort to the sector sometimes referred to as '56789' because it contributes about 50 percent of the state's tax revenue, 60 percent of GDP, and is responsible for 70 percent of innovation, 80 percent of urban employment, and 90 percent of new jobs.[7]

Stimulating domestic consumption is another focus. Yet, with youth unemployment hovering around 18 percent, at least some young Chinese, whose trend towards 'lying flat' led the world in 'quiet quitting', have begun to unchain themselves from consumerism. Not so long ago, young influencers staged photogenic 'accidental' spills of their designer bags (ideally the result of a fake tumble out of a Porsche or Lamborghini). In 2022, a new generation of young people were sharing tips for saving money. These included 'stooping', which is collecting other people's discarded but usable furniture and other items, and second-hand shopping — long anathema to status-conscious Chinese consumers.[8]

In her chapter, 'The Chinese Economy: Bursting Bubbles, Terminal Troubles?', Jane Golley surveys both the state of China's economy in 2022 and where reality differs from perception. She cautions against both what *Bloomberg* economist Thomas Orlik calls 'Sinophrenia' ('the simultaneous belief that China is about to collapse and about to take over the world') and its overly cheerful opposite, 'Sinophoria'.

In 'The Untold Story of Chinese Banking and Why It Matters', meanwhile, Adam Y. Liu delves into the background of the scandal that caused thousands of angry depositors to storm bank branches in Zhengzhou, Henan province, between April and July. It is a tale that exposes both the mechanics and the hazards of financial decentralisation. In a second forum on the economy, 'Coal Supply Chains: No Bright Outlook for Australia', Jorrit Gosens examines the outlook for Australian–Chinese coal supply chains and concludes that 'energy crisis or not', the outlook is not 'bright': the Chinese government is committed to increasing self-sufficiency in coal while dampening its overall demand for the fuel. Nonetheless, China remains the biggest user of coal in the world, climate change commitments notwithstanding.[9]

There were some significant advances in strategy and planning for a greener future in 2022, including the release in June of a National Climate Change Adaptation Strategy to make China climate-resilient by 2035. In September, China's Ministry of Industry and Information Technology revealed further details of strategies for achieving carbon zero and announced pilot programs in 'green finance' for the 'green transition'.[10]

Our environment section profiles two industry sectors that are crucial for the transition. In 'Supercharging China: Cars, Batteries, and Lithium', Barry van Wyk surveys the electric vehicle industry, while Hongzhang Xu looks at China's 'green steel' and its implications for Australian iron-ore exports in 'China's "Green Steel": Unchaining from Australia'.

Women: Power Down

No-one was surprised by the gender reveal of the Twentieth Politburo Standing Committee: seven men. No woman has ever sat on the CPC's most powerful body, but it was widely noted that not a single woman was nominated to take the place of retiring member Sun Chunlan 孙春兰 on the twenty-four-person Politburo. As China hardly lacks talented women, Cai Junyi asks in 'The Communist Party of China: Where Are the Women?' about the role of women in Chinese politics and what structural and other factors inhibit their rise to the top.

Xi Jinping, meanwhile, continues to promote policies that reinforce gender normativity and strengthen male dominance over Chinese society and the economy. They exhort boys to become more 'masculine' and urge young women to uphold 'traditional values', marry young, and ideally, have three children. In the interest of promoting the birthrate, however, unmarried mothers can access the same maternity leave as married ones. In late 2021, the State Council 'outline' on women's development for the period 2021–2030 laid out a policy to reduce the number of 'non–medically necessary' abortions.[11] The authorities have also made it harder to obtain divorce, even in situations of domestic abuse, which police often do not treat seriously as a crime.

Two particularly shocking cases of violence against women in 2022 drew attention to this problem. As Joel Wing-Lun writes in 'What Have We Learned from "the Woman in Chains"?', the 'outpouring of anger' that resulted from the sight of Little Plum Blossom chained in her freezing shed 'united liberals, feminists, and nationalists in outrage'. It remains to be seen how much, if anything, will change as a result.

Pan Wang picks up the narrative in 'Violence against Women: Can the Law Help?'. The furore around Little Plum Blossom's treatment had barely died down when another egregious incident of misogynistic violence put gendered violence under the spotlight once more. One evening at a restaurant in Tangshan, not far from Beijing, a middle-aged man approached a table of young women and put his hand on one of them. After she pushed his arm away and shouted at him to leave them alone, he slapped her hard in the face. In the melee that erupted as a result, and despite the presence of witnesses, the man and his companions beat the women savagely, leaving them with horrific facial and other injuries. Yet, little was done by local authorities to bring the men to justice until the security footage was leaked online, attracting more than 4.8 billion views. Official media generally presented the incident as a problem of local gangsterism, avoiding any suggestion that it reflected broader or deeper social problems.

At the end of October, the National People's Congress announced revisions to the Women's Rights and Interests Protection Law — the first revisions in almost thirty years.[12] The product of long consultation, they addressed some of the hot issues of 2022, for the first time making it a crime to obstruct the rescue of trafficked individuals, as well as holding employers accountable for violations of women's labour and social security rights. The revised law strictly prohibits trafficking, kidnapping, and sexually harassing women by 'means such as spoken language, text, images, or physical conduct'. If a woman reports sexual harassment, the 'relevant state organ' is obliged to respond promptly and reply in writing; victims have the right to seek justice through both the criminal and the civil justice systems. Although schools and workplaces are tasked with preventing harassment, there does not appear to be any legal recourse available to victims should they fail to do so.[13] And while the law forbids employers from limiting certain roles to males or prioritising male applicants, there are exceptions 'as otherwise provided by the state'.

Feminism remains a 'sensitive' word and #MeToo a banned term, but women in China are not easily silenced. When protests broke out in late November and early December, it was widely noted how frequently young women took the lead — and the LGBTQI+ community was present as well.[14]

Erasure and Indelibility

In a report released minutes before her departure, outgoing UN Human Rights Commissioner Michelle Bachelet accused China of 'serious human rights violations' in Xinjiang, saying they could amount to 'crimes against humanity', and judged credible the numerous allegations of torture, sexual violence, and forced medical procedures. Beijing attempted to prevent the publication of the forty-five-page report, saying it consisted of smears, slanders, and 'disinformation ... fabricated by anti-China forces' and interfered in Chinese internal affairs. James A. Milward discusses the attempted erasure of Uyghur culture and Xi Jinping's visit to Xinjiang in July in '(Identity) Politics in Command: Xi Jinping in Xinjiang'.

Hong Kong courts, meanwhile, cast aside 177 years of tradition in 2022 when the territory's justice minister decided that some people charged under the National Security Law would be tried in the absence of a jury of their peers. Among those affected is publisher Jimmy Lai 黎智英, founder of *Apple Daily*, the hugely popular, now defunct, newspaper that supported the 2019 protests.

Louisa Lim discusses often overlooked aspects of Hong Kong history, weighs up the resilience of the territory's unique local culture, and offers a personal and journalistic perspective on the city's five years of prodemocracy protests in 'Dispossession and Defiance in Hong Kong'.

China's LGBTQI+ community is another group that is in danger of erasure. In 'Double-Speak as LGBTQI+ Resistance', Ausma Bernot writes about the coded language that many in the queer community use to communicate on social media.

Troubled Waters, Pacific Ties

The economic disruptions caused by lockdowns and other COVID-related controls on movement in 2022 rattled global supply chains. When Shanghai's GE Healthcare factory, which manufactures the contrast media used in medical scans, temporarily shut during the city's lockdown, for example, doctors in the United States and elsewhere had to postpone vital scans for cancer and cardiac patients.[15] The globalised economy is by nature vulnerable to such upsets; as Peter Hasenkamp of Tesla once said, 'It takes 2,500 parts to build a car, but only one not to.'[16]

Industries reliant on semiconductors include telecommunications, health care, computing, transportation, and clean energy. Taiwan produces 65 percent of all semiconductors and 90 percent of the most advanced chips. In 'Semiconductors, Supply Chains, and the Fate of Taiwan', Samuel George looks at how the location of the world's leading manufacturer of smart chips on the island affects the geostrategic calculus in both Beijing and Washington.

That calculus was tested in 2022. Like Deng Xiaoping and other leaders before him, Xi Jinping insists that Taiwan's 'reunification' with the motherland is a matter of when, not if. Yet, none of China's previous leaders has approached this task with as much urgency as Xi. The CPC is alarmed by an increasing tendency of younger Taiwanese to reject altogether the identity of 'Chinese'.[17] It is also closely monitoring the growing sentiment in Washington for abandoning its long-held policy of 'strategic ambiguity' on whether it would enter armed conflict on Taiwan's behalf in the event of a military attack by the PRC.[18]

In August, Nancy Pelosi, then Speaker of the US House of Representatives, became the highest-ranking US official to visit Taiwan in twenty-five years. Her visit prompted the 'Fourth Taiwan Strait Crisis' (the first was in 1954–55, the second in 1958, and the third in 1995–96). Arthur Ding offers a Taiwanese perspective on the events of August in 'Buckle Up: Pelosi's Visit and the Fourth Taiwan Strait Crisis'. Lennon Chang, meanwhile, in 'Psyops and Cyberwar in Taiwan', looks at Beijing's intensifying grey-zone cyberwarfare against Taiwan, which includes hacking public information screens during Pelosi's visit, denial-of-service attacks on government websites, and the active spread of disinformation. Such actions are consistent with the People's Liberation Army's recent focus on developing an 'information-based combat system'.[19]

There are many hypothetical scenarios as to how the PRC might attempt to take Taiwan by force, but in all of them the navy plays a crucial role. Edward Sing Yue Chan's essay, 'Building a World-Class Navy: The Story of China's First Aircraft Carrier', tells the fascinating story of how China acquired its first such vessel, and describes China's increased naval assertiveness in 2022, including in the Pacific. There, Beijing's new security pact with Solomon Islands set off alarm bells in Canberra and Washington. In his chapter, 'The China–Solomon Islands Security Agreement: Clear and Present Danger', Sean Kelly examines the details and implications of the agreement. Denghua Zhang, meanwhile, describes how China 'recalibrated' its Pacific policies in 2022, partly in response to the reaction to that pact, in 'Beijing Reshapes Its Pacific Strategy'.

Foreign Ties

China historically has had a complicated relationship with Russia and the Soviet Union. Czarist Russia was among the imperialist powers that contributed to China's 'century of humiliation'. The newly formed Soviet Union, however, became the first of those powers to relinquish Moscow's imperialist holdings and claims. Mao Zedong greatly admired Joseph Stalin, but detested Nikita Khrushchev. Relations between the two socialist giants deteriorated in the 1960s to the point of border war and fears of nuclear attack. Later, relations warmed, though Mikhail Gorbachev's endorsement of *glasnost* ('transparency') and *perestroika* ('structural reform') alarmed the CPC leadership of the 1980s; when the Soviet Union collapsed at the start of the subsequent decade, the party took that as a lesson. When Gorbachev died in August at the age of ninety-one, the Chinese leadership's condolences were brief and restrained.

Vladimir Putin is a different story. Xi Jinping and Putin, who enjoy an ostentatious friendship, elevated their countries' increasingly amicable relationship to what they called 'a no limits partnership' at the start of the year. Shortly afterwards — although there is no evidence that Putin revealed his plans to Xi — Russia invaded Ukraine. Alexander Korolev's chapter, 'A "No

Limits" Partnership? China–Russia Strategic Cooperation', examines China–Russia strategic cooperation in the fraught circumstances of 2022, while Kecheng Fang discusses the reaction on Chinese social media to the war in Ukraine. The PRC has tried to navigate a neutral line on Ukraine, criticising Western sanctions against Russia while being careful not to violate them itself. In September, Putin indicated that he understood China's 'questions and concerns' about the conflict, though whatever they were, neither Xi nor other PRC officials said anything about them in public, and at the end of the year, the two countries held their customary joint naval exercises in the East China Sea in the interest of regional 'peace and stability'.

China's relations with Japan and Australia have not been quite as close. In 2022, China attempted something of a reset with the latter while celebrating fifty years of diplomatic relations with both.

Japan's military and imperialist aggression against China, which began with the Sino-Japanese War of 1894–1895 and culminated in its invasion of China in the 1930s, is central to the narrative of the 'century of humiliation'. Anti-Japanese sentiment bubbles under the surface, spilling over in times of tension. In 2022, such sentiment played a role in the 'cancellation' of a popular actor.[20] After former Japanese prime minister Shinzo Abe was assassinated in July, ardent Chinese nationalists freely rejoiced online.

During the Fourth Taiwan Strait Crisis in August, five People's Liberation Army (PLA) missiles landed in Japan's exclusive economic zone — illustrating why Tokyo considers any attack on Taiwan to be a threat to Japan. In November, Japanese prime minister Fumio Kishida and President Xi held their first summit in three years. Yet, days later, Japan claimed that armed Chinese vessels had entered its territorial waters near the disputed Senkaku/Diaoyu Islands in the East China Sea.[21] By the end of the year, Japan and Australia had strengthened bilateral collaboration on security.

In 'Taking Stock at Fifty', Yi Wang and I survey fifty years of Australia–China relations, through to the ice-breaking meetings between Australian ministers and their Chinese counterparts in 2022, including that between

Prime Minister Anthony Albanese and President Xi. Geremie Barmé revisits the contentious idea that Australia could become a *zhengyou* 诤友 ('a friend who tells hard truths') to China.

This year, many stories were first commissioned for and published on thechinastory.org website, with the goal of providing timely expert analysis and background to current events, while highlighting important stories or aspects of stories that have been missed by the mainstream media. The authors of those chosen from the site for inclusion in this yearbook were given the opportunity to update them for publication. Other stories were commissioned specifically for the yearbook to cover emergent themes or major scheduled events, such as the Twentieth Party Congress. Limitations of space and resources mean that while we take a broad and multidisciplinary approach to the choice of topics, allowing both detailed reporting and broader analysis, we can never hope to cover everything that has occurred in the vast Sinosphere in any given year. The *China Story Yearbooks* together with thechinastory.org are intended to be a cumulative body of work that achieves balance and breadth over time and across platforms.

Vale

In November, the Chinese world farewelled Bao Tong, the influential Deng-era reformist who was the highest-ranking party official to be imprisoned after the protests of 1989. Bao, who had been a close associate of the purged party leader Zhao Ziyang, died at the age of ninety. Weeks later, Zhao's successor, Jiang Zemin, died at the age of ninety-six. The combination of the loss of two iconic figures of those times with the party's confirmation of Xi's third term — breaking a key convention set by the CPC under Deng — seemed to be confirmation that the first part of the Reform Era itself had passed. Hong Kong lost two of its sharpest and most iconic dissident voices as well with the passing of Li Yi 李怡 (1936–2022) and Ni Kuang 倪匡 (1935–2022).[22]

A Note from the Editors

The *China Story Yearbook* is a project initiated by the Australian Centre on China in the World (CIW) at The Australian National University. It has always been the approach of the *Yearbook* to view political and economic developments as part of a greater picture that encompasses society, personalities, and culture — a picture that is illuminated by considerations of language and history. Our ongoing reference to the China Story 中国的故事 reflects the principle set out by CIW founding director Emeritus Professor Geremie R. Barmé: China's story is not only the version portrayed by the CPC but also includes the diverse perspectives of a multitude of others, within and outside the People's Republic of China, who are dedicated to understanding the complexities of China through its language, history, culture, politics, economy, society, and most importantly, its people.

Co-editors Linda Jaivin, Esther Sunkyung Klein, and Annie Luman Ren are enormously grateful to all our contributors, to Jan Borrie for copyediting the book, to Serena Ford, Melodie Chin-Jie Liu, and Xiaoyu Sun for typesetting the book, to Melodie Chin-Jie Liu for the artwork on the internal pages, to Teresa Prowse from ANU Press for the cover design, and to the two anonymous referees for taking the time to read and comment on it before publication.

The Year of the Tiger

ANNIE LUMAN REN

In This Whirlpool of Chaotic

Jumble, 'Your World' is also

'My World'

Translated with an Introduction

by PEISHAN YANN

THE YEAR OF THE TIGER

Annie Luman Ren

'IN CHINA, THE historical attitude to the tiger is full of contradictions', observed Cao Zhenfeng 曹振峰, a specialist on Chinese folk tradition:

> The tiger is both loved and hated; it is a frightening beast as well as a protecting god; it is a sign of danger and a symbol of good luck; it causes people to flee from it but also to chase after it … Never has there been an animal like the tiger that embodies such distinct and discrepant meanings.[1]

The current geographic territory of the People's Republic of China (PRC) was once home to one of the world's largest tiger populations. In historical times, there were Siberian (or Amur) tigers in the north-east, Indochinese tigers in the south-west, Bengal tigers in the south-east of Tibet, and South China tigers across vast areas south of the Yangtze River.[2] Ancient oracle bone and bronze inscriptions are full of references to the tiger, which is often shown with its claws out, jaws wide open, and tail swinging. This clear pictorial representation of the animal was eventually replaced with the character for tiger used today, 虎,

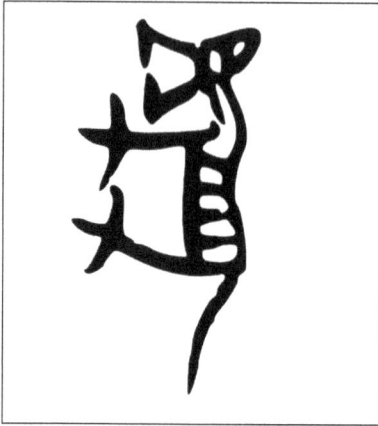

Oracle bone inscription of a tiger with its wide open jaws and a whipping tail
Source: Chinese etymology

which derives from the seal script of the Qin dynasty (221–206 BCE) and is pronounced *hu* in Mandarin in the third tone.

This modern character is made up of two symbols: 虍, meaning the pattern of the tiger's skin, and 儿, representing a person. Chi Hsu-sheng 季旭昇, a specialist on Chinese etymology, believes that the 'human' component was added to the tiger pictograph because ancient texts often compare people to tigers.[3] The character in fact stands for a 'human tiger', just like we say 'he's such a tiger!' today. In common speech, a tiger is a *laohu* 老虎. The prefix 老 means 'old' but

is also a form of affectionate and respectful address. A teacher is a *laoshi* 老师, regardless of age.

As a cultural symbol, the tiger stands for power and vigour. Traditionally, it is featured on the clothes and accessories of kings and ministers to signify their authority and courage. Today, some Chinese parents still dress their children in colourful tiger-head shoes and caps, which are believed to protect the wearer from disaster and disease. In martial arts, the *Fu Jow Pai* 虎爪派 or 'Tiger Claw School' draws its inspiration for hand-to-hand combat techniques from the ripping, tearing, pulling, and grasping movements of a tiger's attack.

At the same time, many consider the tiger a menacing predator — a harmful pest. History books abound with records of 'tiger troubles' 虎害 alongside famines and plagues. A famous story from the *Book of Rites* portrays the tiger in such a light, albeit to communicate a political message:

> In passing by the side of Mount Tai, Confucius came upon a woman who was wailing bitterly by a grave. The Master sent his disciple Zilu to

question her: 'Your wailing,' said he, 'is exactly like that of one who has suffered sorrow after sorrow.'

She replied, 'It is so. Some time ago, my husband's father was killed here by a tiger. My husband was also killed by one, and now my son has died in the same way.'

The Master asked, 'Why do you not leave this place?'

'There is no oppressive government here,' answered the woman.

The Master then said to his disciples, 'Remember this, my children. Oppressive government is more terrible than tigers.'[4]

A poster during a vigil held for victims of the Ürümqi apartment fire, a tragedy attributed to China's zero-COVID policy. The slogan 'Oppressive government is more terrible than fires' 苛政猛於火 is a wordplay on Confucius' famous statement
Source: @ShengXue_ca, Twitter

Confucius's words ring true even today. The iron-fisted zero-COVID policy of the Communist Party of China (CPC) has ushered in a new wave of migration abroad — a phenomenon playfully dubbed by netizens as *run* 润, meaning simply 'run' (though the character itself means profit or to dampen or embellish). Those who are finding ways of leaving are even considered masters of *run xue* 润学, or 'the study of running away'.[5]

Among the rich and colourful expressions inspired by the tiger, a number refer to abusers of power. The idiom *hu jia hu wei* 狐假虎威 ('the fox borrowing the tiger's might') tells the story of how a fox walked in front of a tiger, which scared all other animals away, and so tricked the tiger into thinking that the fox was the most fearsome beast in the jungle. Another expression, *wei hu zuo chang* 为虎作伥 ('becoming the tiger's servant-ghost'), refers to an old belief that those eaten by tigers turn into evil spirits, helping tigers to catch more victims. In 2022, both terms were directed against the 'army of millions' who helped to enforce China's zero-COVID policy regardless of the human cost.[6]

In the popular imagination, Wu Song 武松, the twelfth-century tiger slayer, represents an underdog defeating a much bigger, stronger adversary, like David against Goliath. This story, as told in the novel *Shui Hu Zhuan* 水浒传 (translated variously as *The Water Margin* or *Outlaws of the Marsh*), begins with the traveller Wu Song arriving at an inn near Jingyang Ridge. After learning that a man-eating tiger has been terrorising travellers, Wu Song disregards the innkeeper's warning: 'Three bowls of wine and you mustn't cross the ridge.' He knocks back eighteen bowls of wine before proceeding to cross the ridge. Drunk, he falls asleep halfway, and awakes, startled, to find himself face to face with the tiger.

An influential reader and literary critic from the Ming dynasty (1368–1644 CE), Jin Shengtan 金圣叹

(1608–1661), was struck by the lively and detailed description of Wu Song's ensuing fight with the tiger. In his notes on this episode, he draws the reader's attention to the ten different positions in which Wu Song holds his club during the struggle. The club, at a crucial moment, breaks. Jin writes: 'We are absolutely stunned and hardly dare to read on. After the club is broken, Wu Song's extraordinary power of fighting the tiger with his bare hands can be revealed. However, the reader is so frightened that his heart and liver have jumped out of his mouth.'[7]

Wu Song eventually kills the tiger and becomes a hero to the local people for 'getting rid of the menace' 为民除害. He is even awarded 1,000 strings of cash by the local magistrate. The novel does not say what happens to the body of the tiger. Tigers were then, as they are now, treasured commodities. Their pelts are eagerly sought after and, in traditional Chinese medicine, 'virtues are ascribed to the ashes of the bones, to the fat, skin, claw, liver, [and] blood'.[8] Tiger whiskers are said to be good for toothache while tiger penis, when preserved in liquor, is reputed to enhance a man's potency. Such ascribed benefits have led to excessive hunting of tigers, especially over the past century. This, combined with deforestation and loss of habitat, has seen the population of tigers decline drastically. In 2018, it was estimated that fewer than 3,900 tigers existed in the wild.[9] The Worldwide Fund for Nature honoured the Year of the Tiger by fundraising for tiger conservation, with artists including Ai Weiwei working with master weavers from the Turquoise Mountain Foundation in Afghanistan to create tiger-themed rugs for auction.[10]

From a young age, Mao Zedong was fascinated by the story of Wu Song. In a speech commemorating the twenty-eighth anniversary of the CPC in 1949, Mao declared: 'We must not show the slightest timidity before a wild beast. We must learn from Wu Sung ... Either kill the tiger or be eaten by him — one or the other.'[11]

Mao also popularised the term 'paper tiger' 纸老虎 — an idiom first used in *The Water Margin* to denote an empty threat. In 1946, when he was still in Yan'an, Mao used the term to describe hostile imperialist forces such as the US government — a thing that may at first seem as terrifying as a real tiger but can be easily defeated. In recent years, Chinese state media have, on more than one occasion, called Australia a 'paper cat' — an even more deflating variation of Mao's original metaphor.

In the jungle of contemporary Chinese politics, the tiger has become synonymous with corrupt senior officials. Mao used the expression 'hunting big tigers' 打大老虎 during the PRC's first anticorruption campaign in 1951– 1952. Half a century later, the expression resurfaced when Xi Jinping launched his major anticorruption campaign soon after coming to power in 2012. The slogan Strike Tigers and Flies Alike 老虎苍蝇 一起打 (flies being low-level officials, a lesser but more common pest) has since become a trademark of Xi's 'strongman' image. The party's tiger hunt became a nationwide sport. Just as people in the past loved to hear storytellers talk about Wu Song's conquest of the tiger, many Chinese today enjoy the spectacle of corrupt officials in prison jumpsuits confessing their sins on national television, begging for forgiveness.

The metaphor of tigers and flies so beloved of CPC leaders has its origin in an earlier anti-graft campaign headed by Chiang Ching-kuo, the son of Mao's mortal enemy and rival Chiang Kai-shek, whose government retreated to the island of Taiwan in 1949. One year before the defeat, Chiang Ching-kuo arrived in Shanghai to stabilise its economy, which had been marred by years of war, corruption, and rampant inflation. The slogan of his campaign was 'strike the tigers, don't swat the flies' 只打老虎，不拍苍蝇, making it clear that he was only after the 'fat cats' among profiteers and speculators. Unfortunately for Chiang Ching-kuo, the biggest tigers of all were among his own family and supporters. He might have 'talked tiger' but in the end he could only go after smaller game, as the cartoon by Mi Gu reproduced here suggests.

While in Shanghai, Chiang Ching-kuo reportedly led a crowd of 5,000 young army veterans singing a song called *Two Tigers* 两只老虎 set to the tune of *Frère Jacques*.[12] The same melody had previously served as the Republic of China's military anthem, Song of the National Revolution. It is unclear when tigers were first written into the lyrics of this song, but Chiang Ching-kuo was reportedly fond of it, singing it on various occasions in Jiangxi province, where he served as commissioner between 1939 and 1945.[13] It is agreed that in the context of Chiang's anticorruption campaign, the two tigers represent profiteers and communists. Yet the lyrics, which are about one tiger missing an ear and another missing a tail, could have originally been poking fun at the isolationist United States, unable to hear the cries for help of people around the world, and the Soviet Union, lacking balance and unlikely to survive.

Regardless of its political associations, the song *Two Tigers* went on to become a popular nursery rhyme loved by millions in the Chinese-speaking world. Powerful and protective, menacing and harmful, the tiger remains a complex, ambiguous figure in China's symbolic landscape. And if tigers still symbolically play the villain in the Chinese political agenda, their traditional associations are complex and live on through countless legends, myths, stories, and songs.

CHINA STORY YEARBOOK | In This Whirlpool of Chaotic Jumble,
CHAINS | 'Your World' Is Also 'My World'
| Peishan Yann

IN THIS WHIRLPOOL OF CHAOTIC JUMBLE, 'YOUR WORLD' IS ALSO 'MY WORLD'

Translated with an introduction by Peishan Yann

TRANSLATOR'S INTRODUCTION[1] The COVID-19 lockdown in Shanghai in the People's Republic of China (PRC) from April to June 2022 may seem remote for most people who only know about it from news reports, which can convey the scale and magnitude of the lockdown, but not the pain it inflicted. For China's biggest city, of approximately twenty-six million people, to descend into a full lockdown while the rest of the world was navigating away from it was incomprehensible at best. Compounded by the lack of clear and transparent communication from the authorities and the redoubling of tough, senseless measures to contain people, Shanghai residents struggled through more than two months of turmoil with little recourse. Like other Chinese cities in lockdown, Shanghai came to a halt, but it was a halt like no other as China's largest commercial engine ground to a stop, putting lives, livelihoods, and emotional and mental health at risk as the country stubbornly stuck to its zero-COVID policy, under which little else mattered.

In addition to the inconvenience and anxiety of being locked inside, and the fear of testing positive for the virus and being moved to a quarantine centre, the prolonged lockdown also prevented access to many daily necessities, including medicines, toilet paper, and even food. Hunger was real and immediate. Residents mostly relied on *tuan gou* 团购 or 'community group-buying' to procure daily essentials for entire residential compounds during the lockdown.[2] These experiences have been brought to life by first-person accounts on various Chinese podcasts, including *Stochastic Volatility* 随机波动, which is hosted by three young women, who recently read out letters from Shanghai residents at breaking point. Listeners from mainly first-tier cities aged in their twenties to mid-thirties found such downloadable podcasts that directly addressed their concerns deeply appealing, especially in long periods of isolation during the pandemic, when the intimacy and familiarity of the human voice became even more soothing and reassuring. Timely and lively discussions on the pandemic resonated with them, and they drew strength from them to bear the unbearable.

The letter translated here provides powerful insights into life during the lockdown. We hear about the discrimination suffered by nine male migrant workers crowded into a single rental unit when most tested positive for the virus, and their vulnerability in the face of their neighbours' cold indifference and cruel criticisms. Another harrowing story is that of an eighty-eight-year-old woman crying out for help and being ignored by her residents' committee as supplies of food and medicine ran critically low. But there are also glimmers of heart-warming kindness: younger residents looking out for their elderly neighbours and people feeding the stray cats in the *longtang* 弄堂 ('laneway communities').

Amid this whirlpool of chaos and uncertainty, people recorded their stories and the absurdities surrounding them. Their stories need to be heard, translated, and shared.

***

Dear *Stochastic Volatility* hosts, Zhiqi, Shiye, and Jianguo,

Most of the time, I'm inclined to assume the role of the listener and reader, very rarely willing to pick up my pen, and never have I voiced my opinions on a public platform. The power of language is all but weak. It's such a heavy responsibility as well. I have no confidence I will be able to accurately express what I've seen in words. I'm even more scared that what I say will be misconstrued and others will get hurt. So, I've always just curled up inside my shell, unable to speak.

But living in Shanghai and being a part of what may be the greatest absurdity of the twenty-first century, there is always a flag waving from a small corner in my room and that flag says, 'Cry out!',[3] protesting my silence and my failure to record what I see. So, I thought, why not write something for the *Stochastic Volatility*'s letterbox, this semi-private and semi-public space.

This is the fifth week of working from home. Objectively speaking, life hasn't been too bad. I have a source of income and know how to find information online. So, access to daily necessities is not a problem. But the familiar structure of my daily life is crumbling bit by bit. Moreover, I've a pessimistic inkling that life will never return to 'normal'.

What I'm seeing is the weakness of the individual, and this lockdown has also fully exposed what lies beneath this weakness — the absurdity that we once considered ourselves unrelated individuals.

I live in an old *longtang* in downtown Shanghai, an alleyway community with a severely ageing population. Half of its residents are younger people from outside Shanghai, the other half elderly native Shanghainese. Until a month ago, these were like two parallel worlds. I feel ashamed that I have never attempted to remove the filter from my eyes to really observe the people who live around me, the human beings who are closest to me in the physical sense, until a month ago.

When the invisible barriers built around a 'normal life' were shattered by lockdown orders, the world revealed its original shape — real people of myriad and enormous differences, all equally fallen into this whirlpool of chaos. There is no longer a distinction between 'your world' and 'my world'. Everybody is enclosed within the same fortress walls in the same physical space, in a closed circuit without an exit switch. All I can do is to record the little stories that happen in this closed circuit.

The Ones Who Lost Their Voice

There are nine of them in one unit, seven of whom have tested positive. The neighbourhood committee has not disinfected their apartment, given them supplies or conducted PCR testing. Neighbours, please take extra care to avoid them, they are going to break out at any moment!

This message suddenly appeared in my neighbourhood WeChat group.

This is the first time that I had become aware of this group of residents in my neighbourhood. Their cramped living conditions are unsuitable for self-isolation. They were not relocated to quarantine centres quickly enough and have cross-infected each other. Finding themselves in dire straits, they were robbed of a voice to cry out for help. I do not know what they look like or what they do for a living, but I do know they have been blindly condemned by the community as tenants engaged in illegal overcrowding.

Someone asked in the chat: 'Nine people in a single unit. How could they possibly like Shanghai that much? Shared rentals are such a big problem, just wait until the pandemic is over, I'll dob them in.' Another person said: 'So many positive cases and they still haven't been shepherded out to quarantine centres. Their rubbish is piling up in the corridor day by day. What are others living in the same building supposed to do?' Someone else commented: 'Everyone steer clear of them, they are coming downstairs to dump their rubbish. Rubbish accumulated from nine people. It already stinks!' Still, one person observed: 'They have not joined any *tuangou*, the neighbourhood committee has not given them any supplies either, these boys must be starving.'

As for these nine people, they had no collective voice. They did not join any community group-buying or ask anyone for help. Neither did they respond to any suspicions or accusations. No-one knows why they came to Shanghai to live in such an overcrowded rental unit. No-one knows about their living conditions, or what help they need the most right now. They are simply

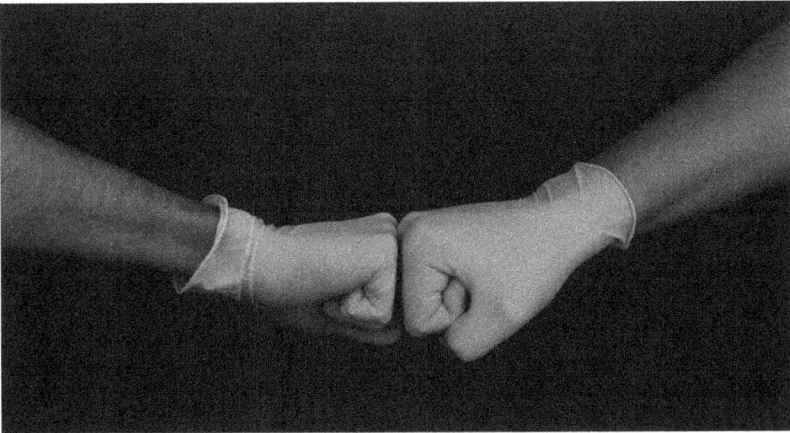

People with sanitised gloves
Source: Branimir Balogovic, Unsplash

labelled 'tenants in shared rental with COVID-19' — a collective identity that has been tossed out into the open for criticism and then dismissed.

Working by my window, I could occasionally hear shouts from the residential compound. A cry to the vast empty city, absorbed into the incessant rain that marks the change from spring to summer. I think, perhaps this is the only sound they can make, the only one I can hear.

Please Help Me!

They said that the lockdown would only last for four days. I only stocked up on some vegetables which cannot last long. The medication for a bedridden elderly person with dementia is running low. And my domestic helper has only two days' worth of medicine for her high blood pressure. I rang the neighbourhood committee this morning and they said they were busy but would ring me back in the afternoon. I waited until past 3pm and still they did not make contact. I rang countless times afterwards but the number was always busy; this went on until 6pm. The two of them will die without their medicine. I am 88 years old myself and have difficulties with mobility. I've been on tenterhooks all day and can't sleep at night. Will someone please help me!

This was another message from my neighbourhood WeChat group, posted by an eighty-eight-year-old resident. Police officers and volunteers in the community have since made contact with her and provided help. Hopefully she and her family can pull through this rough patch.

In the Weibo community page 'Help Needed for Shanghai Pandemic' 上海疫情求助, there are many similar cries for urgent assistance. I do not know how many of these pleas have been attended to, or how many of them have been swept away into this vast sea of information. Nor do I know the number of people out there who have no idea how or where to seek help.

I have no idea what I could do to help. In our residential compound, some concerned neighbours have left notices with their contact details on the ground floor of those apartment blocks mostly inhabited by senior citizens, so that those in need could reach out.

I met an old lady with silver hair when I was on my way to pick up some supplies. We stood by the side of the road watching a little black kitten eat. I asked if she had enough food at home and if she needed anything. She smiled sweetly and replied that she had enough. Everything was fine and she only wanted to come out for a stroll and see how her elderly neighbours were doing. She said that having a young person stop and show her concern had made her very happy. The old lady declined my material assistance. I am not sure if she was only trying to reassure me when she said she had enough to eat but I do hope my show of concern brought her some emotional solace.

In this great chaos, I have come to believe in the resilience of the people and have witnessed sparkles of kindness glimmering through this calamitous darkness. And yet, none of this should have happened in the first place.

Stray Cats

In my *longtang* there live around ten stray cats. In normal times, old grannies will come out and feed them at fixed mealtimes. The cats have their own food bowls and

Stray cats are a common sight in Shanghai
Source: Anna Kumpan, Unsplash

territory. But since all this huge uncertainty has swept over us, how are these stray cats supposed to live?

A week ago, I noticed their food supply had been completely cut off. Previously proud and uninterested in engaging with people, they started circling me, mewing loudly. It occurred to me that the apartment blocks where the cat-feeding grannies live were all under lockdown, and these cats had been without food for nearly a week. I opened my delivery apps and was relieved to find that while all the takeaway food businesses catering for humans had stopped operation,

a pet store was still selling cat food and could deliver. Dry cat food was out of stock of course, but limited titbits and canned food were still available. I managed to snatch up two weeks' worth of supplies. From then on in the lockdown, I took on a new routine of feeding the stray cats.

I must admit, human beings are very selfish animals. When I discovered that it was still within my power to do something for the cats downstairs, my anxiety and guilt seemed to have lifted a little. For all the talk about kind intentions, all I wanted was to avoid falling into the category of 'not doing anything to help'. What I did really was merely pick the easiest task rather than the much more difficult ones that would require more time, effort, and commitment, such as becoming a community volunteer or speaking up on behalf of those who were suffering.

Later, I discovered that in the cats' bowls, dry cat food was mixed in occasionally with the canned food I had provided. It seems there are others like me who are trying to not let the cats go hungry. I hope that neither the people nor cats living in my *longtang* go hungry.

I've written all this and still I have no idea how I am going to get through this spring. Perhaps spring has already slipped by. What I know is that such trivial stories as I have told here will continue to unfold in a ceaseless cycle, just as we will continue to experience fear, anger, despair, and helplessness. But I hope those who witness these stories don't lose the courage to record them.

I end my letter with these lines from Baudelaire's *L'Avertisseur*:

> Whatever he may plan or hope,
> Man does not live for an instant
> Without enduring the warning
> Of the unbearable Viper

From *L'Avertisseur* by Charles Baudelaire, translated by Lewis Piaget Shanks, in *Flowers of Evil* (New York: Ives Washburn, 1931)

Shanghai, 14 April 2022

Mesmalheurs

聚焦

FOCUS: THE TWENTIETH PARTY CONGRESS

THE TWENTIETH PARTY CONGRESS: A PRIMER

Linda Jaivin and M. Su

WHAT IS A Party Congress?

The Party Congress 中国共产党全国代表大会 is the most important meeting in the calendar of activities of the Communist Party of China (CPC). Since 1977, one has been held every five years. Before that, they were less regular. Delegates to the congress formalise changes to the party's leadership, review the previous five years, and set policy directions for the next five.

When and Where was the Twentieth Party Congress Held?

The Twentieth Party Congress took place on 16–22 October 2022 in the Great Hall of the People, Beijing, in the People's Republic of China (PRC).

One to Twenty

First Party Congress: 23 July to 2 August 1921, Shanghai and Jiaxing.

Second Party Congress: 16–23 July 1922, Shanghai.

Third Party Congress: 12–20 June 1923, Guangzhou.

Fourth Party Congress: 11–22 January 1925, Shanghai.

Fifth Party Congress: 27 April to 9 May 1927, Wuhan.

Sixth Party Congress: 18 June to 11 July 1928, Moscow.

Seventh Party Congress:
23 April to 11 June 1945, Yan'an.

Eighth Party Congress:
15–27 September 1956, Beijing.

Ninth Party Congress:
1–24 April 1969, Beijing.

Tenth Party Congress:
24–28 August 1973, Beijing.

Eleventh Party Congress:
12–18 August 1977, Beijing.

Twelfth Party Congress:
1–11 September 1982, Beijing.

Thirteenth Party Congress:
25 October to 1 November
1987, Beijing.

Fourteenth Party Congress:
12–18 October 1992, Beijing.

Fifteenth Party Congress:
12–18 September 1997, Beijing.

Sixteenth Party Congress:
8–14 November 2002, Beijing.

Seventeenth Party Congress:
15–21 October 2007, Beijing.

Eighteenth Party Congress:
8–14 November 2012, Beijing.

Nineteenth Party Congress:
18–24 October 2017, Beijing.

Twentieth Party Congress:
16–22 October 2022, Beijing.

Who Goes, How Are They Chosen, and What Do They Do?

A total of 2,379 people were expected to attend the Twentieth Party Congress: 2,296 delegates representing the 96.7 million members of the CPC plus eighty-three special invitees, including retired former leaders. Forty-one people sent apologies, leaving a total of 2,338 attendees.

Thirty-eight 'electoral units' 选举单位 choose the delegates in multiple rounds of referrals and reviews overseen by and subject to the approval of party discipline and inspection organs, who screen for such things as loyalty to Xi Jinping and appropriate representation of ethnic minorities. Provinces, municipalities, and regions choose nearly 70 percent of the delegates, or 1,585 delegates in 2022. The People's

The Twentieth Party Congress took place took place on 16–22 October 2022 in the Great Hall of the People, Beijing
Source: zh.wikipedia.org

Liberation Army and People's Armed Police chose another 13 percent of the total, and central party organs and state organs about 12 percent. Of the 2,296 delegates, 619 were women, or 27 percent of the total, a slight rise (2.8 percent) from the 19th congress in 2017.

The delegates' function is largely ceremonial: approving the selection of the new Central Committee and acclaiming official reports and resolutions.

Who Holds the Power?

The delegates formally approve the selection of the CPC Central Committee 中国共产党中央委员会. The Twentieth Central Committee has 205 members and 171 alternate members, with an average age of 57.2 years. Among those retiring in 2022 were Premier Li Keqiang 李克强 and Chinese Political Consultative Conference chairman Wang Yang

汪洋, though neither had reached the official retirement age of sixty-eight. Of the 205 members of the Twentieth Central Committee, 135 (66 percent) are new. Only eleven of the full members, or 4.9 percent, are women; another nineteen women are alternate members.

The Central Committee approves the appointments to the Politburo 政治局. The Twentieth Politburo has twenty-four members, only four of whom are under the age of sixty (three are fifty-eight and one is fifty-seven). The oldest member is seventy-two-year-old Zhang Youxia 张又侠, who is vice-chairman of the Military Commission.

For the first time in twenty-five years, no woman sits on the Politburo. Historically, there have only ever been six female full members and two alternates. Of those six, three were the wives or widows of top leaders. Mao Zedong's wife, Jiang Qing 江青, lost her position after her arrest as part of the 'Gang of Four' after Mao's death in 1976; she died in jail in 1991. Lin Biao's wife, Ye Qun 叶群, lost her position in 1971 when she and her husband — Mao's erstwhile 'closest comrade-in-arms' and chosen successor — supposedly died in a plane crash while fleeing China after allegedly trying to assassinate Mao. Deng Yingchao 邓颖超, the widow of popular premier Zhou Enlai 周恩来, joined the Politburo in 1977 as part of the group around Deng Xiaoping that ushered in the Reform Era; she retired in 1985. (See Focus, 'The Communist Party of China: Where Are the Women?', pp.147–152.)

The Politburo selects the Politburo Standing Committee (PSC) 政治局常务委员会. Its members are the most powerful people in China. No woman has ever sat on the PSC. The current PSC has seven ranked members of whom Xi Jinping, as the third-term general secretary and chair of the Central Military Commission 中央军事委员会, is the most powerful of all; unlike previous committees, which comprised diverse 'factions' or groups — prominently including

that which had its origins in the Communist Youth League — the new one is believed to consist entirely of men loyal to Xi personally and to his vision for the country.

No. 1: Xi Jinping 习近平, aged sixty-nine, holds the titles of CPC general secretary and chair of the Central Military Commission, among other non-party titles, including that of state chairman or president.

No. 2: Li Qiang 李强, aged sixty-three, was Xi's subordinate when Xi was party secretary of Zhejiang province. Promoted to the Politburo in 2017, he was also party secretary of Shanghai, responsible for the strict COVID lockdowns there in 2022. He is new to the PSC.

No. 3: Zhao Leji 赵乐际, aged sixty-five, is considered a member of Xi's 'Shaanxi Gang' 陕西帮. It is said Zhao's father had a personal relationship with Xi's father, Xi Zhongxun 习仲勋.

No. 4: Wang Huning 王沪宁, aged sixty-seven, has been the party's leading political theorist since the 1990s, including during the administrations of Xi's predecessors Jiang Zemin and Hu Jintao, and has been a member of the Politburo since 2012. He is one of Xi's closest advisers. Unlike the others, Wang came to prominence not as a party bureaucrat but because of his work in the Central Policy Research Office 中共中央政策研究室, a major CPC think tank.

No. 5: Cai Qi 蔡奇, aged sixty-seven, is the party secretary of the Beijing Municipal Party Committee and first secretary of the CPC Secretariat. A former subordinate of Xi's in both Fujian and Zhejiang, he has been known to call Xi 'Xi Dada' or 'Daddy Xi'. He is also said to be a fan of the television series *House of Cards* and was behind the forced eviction of rural migrants from Beijing beginning in 2017. He is new to the PSC.

No. 6: Ding Xuexiang 丁薛祥, aged sixty, is the youngest member of the PSC and the director of the General Office of the Central Committee. Dubbed Xi's 'chief of staff', he has worked under him for many years, and frequently accompanies Xi on both domestic and foreign trips. He is new to the PSC.

No. 7: Li Xi 李希, aged sixty-six, until recently the party secretary of Guangdong province, chairs the powerful Central Commission for Discipline Inspection 中国共产党中央纪律检查委员会, which prosecutes the anticorruption campaign that is one of Xi's signature policies. He is said to be a close friend of Xi's and is new to the PSC.

Reports, Speeches, and Constitutional Amendments

Xi Jinping's keynote speech was titled 'Hold High the Great Banner of Socialism with Chinese Characteristics and Strive in Unity to Build a Modern Socialist Country in All Respects' 高举中国特色社会主义伟大旗帜，为全面建设社会主义现代化国家而团结奋斗—在中国共产党第二十次全国代表大会上的报告. It took about one hour and forty-five minutes for him to read the abridged version of the report, which in full is 31,600 characters and, printed, runs to 72 pages.

The overall message of the report was that China is advancing by leaps and bounds under the leadership of the Communist Party, with Xi at the helm. It reaffirmed that the central task of the CPC is to build a powerful modern socialist country and promote the great rejuvenation of the Chinese nation.

Compared with previous reports, there were many more mentions of security 安全 (in particular, 'national security' 国家安全) and references to 'risks' and 'challenges', and none of the previously popular expression 'period of strategic opportunity' 战略机遇期.[1] There were also fewer mentions of the economy (in particular, the market and reforms) — although there were numerous references to the importance of technology.

Among the changes to the party constitution adopted by the congress was the enshrinement of Xi Jinping Thought on Socialism with Chinese Characteristics for the New Era as well as the Two Establishes 两个确立 and Two Safeguards 两个维护. The first establishes Xi as the party's 'core' and Xi Jinping Thought on Socialism with Chinese Characteristics for the New Era as the party's guiding ideology — in essence, putting Xi on par with Mao and above Deng Xiaoping and his other post-Mao predecessors. The 'safeguards', meanwhile, maintain that 'core' status in the party and the party's authority over the nation.

The line from Xi's official report that the party must 'resolutely oppose and contain Taiwan independence' was also written into the party constitution.

An Unscripted Moment

After the press had been let into the congress, Xi's predecessor, Hu Jintao, appeared visibly agitated by something in the red folders on the table before him. When Xi motioned for attendants to lead him away, Hu appeared unwilling to go, and an attendant lifted him from his seat by the right armpit. As he left, he said something to Xi and patted the shoulder of Li Keqiang; both men nodded without turning to face him. Hu's first reappearance in public was at the 6 December memorial service for his own predecessor, Jiang Zemin.

CHINA STORY YEARBOOK | A Matter of Perspective: Insider Accounts of
CHAINS | Xi Jinping and the 20th Party Congress
Neil Thomas

A MATTER OF PERSPECTIVE: INSIDER ACCOUNTS OF XI JINPING AND THE TWENTIETH PARTY CONGRESS

Neil Thomas

LAST AUTUMN SAW the return of every China watcher's favourite 'parlour game'.[1] The Communist Party of China (CPC) convened its Twentieth Party Congress, a quinquennial gathering of about 3,000 party representatives in Beijing, for a week of meetings that approved a report by General Secretary Xi Jinping 习近平, amended the party's constitution, and selected a new Central Committee (see Focus, 'The Twentieth Party Congress: A Primer, pp.41–46). The game is to guess which cadres win promotion to the elite Politburo and its top

seven-member Politburo Standing Committee (PSC). Bonus questions in 2022 were whether Xi would secure a precedent-defying third five-year term as general secretary and even revive the title of party chairman once held by Mao Zedong 毛泽东.

The results showed that even professional analysts of the People's Republic of China (PRC) can struggle to pierce the black box of the party's backroom machinations. Xi won a third term, as was widely expected, but did not become party chairman, as some experts had postulated. But Xi surprised most analysts

CHINA STORY YEARBOOK | A Matter of Perspective: Insider Accounts of
CHAINS | Xi Jinping and the 20th Party Congress
Neil Thomas

by installing a PSC and Politburo packed exclusively with his allies and loyalists, cementing a personal hold over Chinese elite politics that is unprecedented in the post-Mao era. Most observers had assumed, based on his previous behaviour and mounting policy headwinds, that Xi would retain a handful of more moderate leaders from different factional backgrounds. Yet, such figures as Li Keqiang 李克强, Wang Yang 汪洋, and Hu Chunhua 胡春华 — all linked with former general secretary Hu Jintao's Communist Youth League faction — were retired or demoted. Xi ignored decades-old norms about incumbency, retirement, and powersharing.

The 2022 congress was hardly unique in defying expectations. Experts speculated before the Nineteenth Party Congress in 2017 that Xi would make Premier Li Keqiang 李克强 retire early and would exempt his old friend Wang Qishan 王岐山 from retirement norms — neither of which happened. Many wrongly forecast that both Xi's ally Chen Min'er 陈敏尔 and Li's ally Hu Chunhua 胡春华 would reach the PSC, but both had to settle for less-senior roles as ordinary Politburo members. Errant political forecasting is hardly unique to China, but the high levels of secrecy there make predicting outcomes like this even more difficult.

In 2017, right before the Nineteenth Party Congress, Jessica Batke and Oliver Melton asked in a commentary on *ChinaFile*, 'Why do we keep writing about Chinese politics as if we know more than we do?'. They argued that Western media and China pundits project an 'air of certainty' about Chinese politics that is unwarranted given the scarcity of facts:

China's Party-state is extremely successful at controlling information. Even the most basic insights into policy deliberations and processes, leaders' intentions and views, and elite power dynamics are filtered through a sophisticated propaganda and censorship regime ... [I]n most cases, [we] depend heavily upon assumptions that paper over information gaps, or are structured in ways that exclude policy considerations and important variables ... [W]e all too often use what little we do know to make assumptions that form the bedrock of larger, more sweeping judgments.[2]

What we do know is mostly hard facts devoid of human context: the formal structure of political institutions, the officials who hold positions in these institutions, and the policies produced by these officials in these institutions. Propaganda trumpets policy outcomes as products of the scientific process of Socialism with Chinese Characteristics. Internal rules forbid members from questioning party decisions or publicising internal operations. We therefore know the what, but we usually can only speculate about the how and the why.

A major lacuna is insight from people working within the system. Typically, there are no media interviews with senior leaders, no leaks to the press about private meetings, no journalistic exposés from within or outside China about how decisions are made, and no tell-all memoirs by retired politicians. Secrecy is fundamental for a party devoted historically to revolutionary warfare and presently to authoritarian control.

Party members and public servants are expected to speak with one voice: that of the party.

Seldom does a Chinese political insider turn against the regime and manage to tell their tale. Firsthand stories of intra-party politics, especially those published in English, generate an extraordinary buzz simply because they are so uncommon. That two such accounts emerged in the leadup to the Twentieth Party Congress is remarkable. They provided a window into a hidden world, but their reception also showed how the China-watching community had yet to fully heed Batke and Melton's warning.

Insiders Out

Red Roulette by Desmond Shum 沈栋 became the most explosive book on Chinese politics for years when it hit the shelves in September 2021. Shum, mostly through the ambition and networking of his former wife Whitney Duan 段伟红 (whose looks he feels the need to disparage), made a fortune as an entrepreneur in Beijing at the height of China's 'gilded age' under General Secretary Hu Jintao 胡锦涛 in the 2000s and early 2010s.[3] His lucrative ventures — which included helping the family of then premier Wen Jiabao 温家宝 profit from the float of Ping An Insurance, demolishing villages to build the Beijing Airport Cargo Terminal, and developing the Bulgari Hotel in Beijing — both required and enabled him to schmooze with senior CPC officials. The book details the extraordinary wealth accumulated by top leaders and their families and the grubby reality of doing business in China, with official permits requiring the endless wining, dining, and vulgar bribing of party cadres.

Shum also offers glimpses of the personality politics that rumble beneath the party's well-oiled exterior. We learn, through Wen's wife, Zhang Peili 张培莉, that it was Xi who convinced the PSC in February 2012 to purge Bo Xilai 薄熙来, a Politburo member and Xi's political rival, after Bo's wife murdered British businessman Neil Heywood. Wen and then Hu concurred with Xi, perhaps eyeing their own security after the leadership transition coming that November. The only objection came from security czar Zhou Yongkang 周永康. Zhou became the highest-profile casualty of a sweeping anticorruption campaign that Xi launched shortly after taking office. But Xi still made the Wens and other 'Red Families' 'donate' their ill-gotten wealth to the state, according to Zhang. Shum, disturbed by Xi's hardline politics, saw the writing on the wall for the freewheeling China in which he had thrived, and moved to the United Kingdom.

Still, the rewards of working with the party could be staggering. Shum intimates that he exited China and his marriage in 2015 with a significant chunk of the hundreds of millions of dollars that he and Duan made from what he calls 'influence peddling' with the party elite.[4] Duan was less fortunate. She was close to Sun Zhengcai 孙政才, a rising star on the Politburo and a potential successor to Xi. Sun had given land to the couple in Beijing's Shunyi district in exchange for political favours. Duan's starring role in the Wen family's moneymaking had already put her at risk and, after Xi purged Sun in July 2017, she disappeared — almost certainly detained by party agents. While Duan's extralegal detention is reprehensible, Shum's tales of rampant graft and dysfunction serve as a convincing, if unintentional,

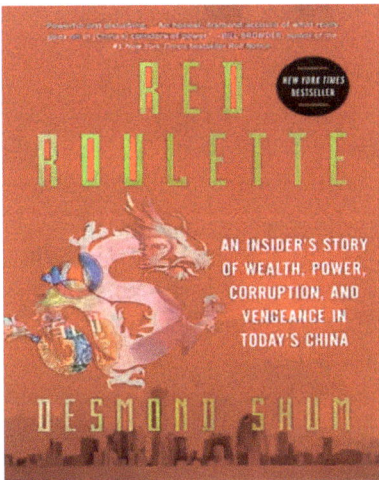

Red Roulette: the most explosive book on Chinese politics for years when it hit the shelves in September 2021
Source: Wikimedia

argument for why the party needed an anticorruption campaign, albeit one less politically selective than Xi's version.

For all his access, Shum was never a party cadre, although he held a seat on the Beijing branch of the Chinese People's Political Consultative Conference, which is part of the party's united-front system to coopt non-party groups and individuals. A view from inside the system itself comes from Cai Xia 蔡霞, a liberal-leaning professor at the Central Party School (CPS) from 1998 until her retirement in 2012.

Cai has lived in exile in the United States since her scathing critiques of Xi's 'mafia boss' mentality had her expelled from the party in 2020. She has become an outspoken Xi critic, authoring, among other articles, two essays in the influential foreign policy magazine *Foreign Affairs*, one each in 2021 and 2022.

Cai was a self-confessed 'true believer' in Marxism and in the party's ability to embrace economic and political reform to improve the lives of Chinese people. Her confidence in the party faded when Hu Jintao began reining in civil society, and then vanished completely in Xi's New Era. In her essays, titled 'The Party That Failed' and 'The Weakness of Xi Jinping', as well as other reports and interviews, Cai argues that Xi's 'one-man show' of political crackdowns, personality cult, and centralised power is leading the party and the country towards disaster.[5] She offers a rare window into such experiences as the hollow tedium of drafting party documents (in the early 2000s) and shares revealing anecdotes like how Xi's well-connected mother helped advance his career by writing to his early bosses.

CHINA STORY YEARBOOK | A Matter of Perspective: Insider Accounts of
CHAINS | Xi Jinping and the 20th Party Congress
Neil Thomas

Lessons from the Twentieth Party Congress

Shum and Cai suggested somewhat different takes on Xi's standing ahead of the Twentieth Party Congress. *Red Roulette*'s tales of bigwigs and businesspeople felled by the new regime emphasised how Xi had 'grabbed so much power' that he was the 'chairman of everything' and could become 'emperor for life'.[6] The party's capabilities were growing not only to 'maximize its control inside China', but also to 'export China's repressive system overseas'.[7] Cai was more pessimistic about Xi's prospects. Her more recent *Foreign Affairs* essay, published the month before the congress, claimed that Xi's authority 'is being questioned as never before' because 'resentment among CPC elites is rising' due to political restrictions and policy mistakes that potentially threaten China's social stability, economic growth, and international relations.[8]

Cai had argued in 2021 that '60–70 percent of the CPC's high-level officials' favour constitutional democracy, human rights, and positive US–China relations, citing her 'thirty years of contact' with senior cadres.[9] She said that Washington should 'support liberal elements within the party' to advance political reform. Her pre-congress article asserted a 'row' among top leaders that was 'breaking out into public view' because then premier Li Keqiang opposed Xi's zero-COVID policy, echoing a prominent claim made earlier that year in the pages of the *Wall Street Journal*.[10] Li 'may soon reach a breaking point' and 'stealth infighting' will intensify before the congress, Cai argued, because Xi 'may not have locked up a third term'.[11]

Both authors show how the informal politics of patronage, rivalry, and control pervade Zhongnanhai, exposing party propaganda as the shiny skin of a rotten fruit. But the outcomes of such intrigue do manifest in the formal structures of political authority and the party does tell us who is promoted, who is purged, and which ideas become policy. And the months leading up to the Twentieth Party Congress saw the continuation of pro-Xi political trends, with Xi promoting more allies, sidelining more associates of Li, and further embedding his personal leadership and policy agenda into official ideology. Li's economic stimulus measures were not a rebellion against Xi (as some observers claimed) but rather the implementation of his instructions to 'balance epidemic prevention and control with economic and social development'. Li was at best a dissembling Zhou Enlai 周恩来 to Xi's domineering Mao.

Shum's emphasis on Xi's power was ultimately more accurate than Cai's stress on his vulnerability. Her views that Xi wants 'a China-centric world order' and 'the planned economy of the Maoist era', and that a 'vicious cycle' of intensifying factional competition could push Xi to attack Taiwan, are also debatable. However, her observations that Xi wanted to 'tighten his grip' domestically and 'raise his ambitions internationally' have proved on target. Even Cai, for all her doubts, conceded that Xi would probably win a third term, although her analysis was a far cry from forecasting Xi's incredible consolidation of power.

No Proclivity for Change

An illuminating concordance between Shum and Cai is that neither foresaw Xi returning China to strongman rule. Cai was 'full of hope for China' in 2012. Like the US columnist Nicholas Kristof, who infamously predicted that Xi would 'spearhead a resurgence of economic reform, and probably some political easing as well', Cai thought the new leader 'had hinted at his proclivity for change'.[12] Shum also 'had initially been optimistic about Xi's rule', partly because he and Duan were close to Xi allies Wang Qishan and Chen Xi 陈希, a former Politburo member and head of the party's Organisation Department since 2017, and 'the general consensus in our social circle was that Xi would follow the established rules in China'.[13] Chen Xi reportedly believed that Xi would wind down the anticorruption campaign during his first term, while Wang anticipated 'large-scale privatization'.[14]

As we enter a second decade of Xi's leadership, such uncertainty about his thinking — even among his cronies — reflects a more fundamental truth about Chinese politics: even those near the top may not know what is going on.[15] The system can be opaque to insiders, too, and has been this way since the beginning. Robert

CHINA STORY YEARBOOK | A Matter of Perspective: Insider Accounts of
CHAINS | Xi Jinping and the 20th Party Congress
Neil Thomas

Loh, a 'patriotic national capitalist' who fled Shanghai in 1957 and produced the remarkable memoir *Escape from Red China*, describes officials whose lives depended on Mao's favour but who could still not read his intentions. *Prisoner of the State*, the posthumously published reminiscences of Zhao Ziyang 赵紫阳, the party general secretary purged for opposing military action to crush the Tiananmen protests in 1989, is permeated by uncertainty. In high office, Zhao was still constantly guessing what paramount leader Deng Xiaoping was thinking. Under house arrest, he never knew when he would next be allowed to receive visitors or take excursions. In the present, the more Xi controls the system, the less we will know about Chinese policymaking, and the harder it becomes to anticipate its direction.

Too often, facing this information vacuum, we in the West listen more to Chinese voices that say what we want to hear about China, including advocates for a more open economy, a shift to liberal democracy, or greater protections of human rights. Zhao's favourable comments about democracy were seen to 'offer hope' of political reform in China,[16] while Loh presciently identified the party's obsession with control. *Red Roulette* arrived during a rectification drive against big tech, reinforcing narratives about Xi's power over the private sector, while Cai's writing fed into horserace journalism about leadership splits ahead of the congress. We want to hear that everything Xi does is disastrous and that no-one likes it, because that resonates with the objections that many of us have to his policies, but it is hard even for those inside the system to know whether that is true. Yet, we can agree strongly with the moral criticisms levelled at the party by voices of conscience, and accept the factual accuracy of their personal testimony, while still engaging critically with their analytical conclusions about Chinese politics.

The Western media also at times struggle to understand the position of their interlocutors in the Chinese system. For example, *The Guardian* said Cai's words were 'potentially dangerous for the Chinese leadership',[17] *CNN* claimed her criticisms dealt the party an 'embarrassing blow',[18] and the Hoover Institution hailed her as 'an important figure from within the

Chinese Communist Party system'.[19] Cai may have had 'a front-row seat to the CPC's court intrigue', as she put it in her September 2022 article, but she was not a player on the elite political stage. Her position as one of more than 150 full professors at the Central Party School did not rank within the top few thousand or even the top tens of thousands of positions in the party hierarchy.

There is no question that firsthand accounts capture the brutal mechanics of party rule better than the sterile pages of the *People's Daily*. But insider accounts deserve the same analytical scrutiny that we ought to afford all work on Chinese politics. Otherwise, we risk making far-reaching claims based on a few anecdotal sources, which may overstate the importance of snippets of exposure to the very small number of people who call the shots in Beijing. We should at least compare these accounts with the evidence provided by the formal political system: promotions, purges, propaganda, and policies, for example. Opacity may make it unavoidable to, in Batke and Melton's words, 'use what little we do know' to make grand assumptions and 'sweeping judgments'.[20] But we must be vigilant about using as *much* of 'what little we do know' to inform our thinking.[21]

Speaking out against the party carries costs. Neither Shum nor Cai can ever return to China. Shum's son with Duan may never see his mother again. Cai lost her pension and she fears for her daughter and grandson, who still live in China. Dissenters to Xi's rule who did not leave, such as legal scholar Xu Zhangrun 许章润 and property tycoon Ren Zhiqiang 任志强, have suffered professional ruin and imprisonment, respectively. We owe them and others an enormous debt of gratitude for courageously sharing their stories with the world. We can only hope, for the sake of greater openness and freedom of expression in China, that the future breaks down the walls around the party's 'hall of the monologue' 一言堂.[22]

GHOSTS OF MAO AND DENG

Ben Hillman

AT THE COMMUNIST Party of China (CPC) Congress in October 2022, Xi Jinping 习近平 was confirmed for a third term as the party's general secretary. The party had already passed a historic resolution the year before — only the third in its 100-year history — establishing Xi as the 'core of the central committee and of the whole party' and Xi Jinping Thought on Socialism with Chinese Characteristics for the New Era as the party's guiding ideology. The conspicuous absence of potential successors on the new Politburo Standing Committee suggests that Xi will remain the strongman ruler of the People's Republic of China (PRC) for at least another five years beyond his current term (2022–2027) and possibly for life. Since coming to power in 2012, Xi has systematically sidelined potential rivals, promoted loyalists, and taken charge of all key decision-making processes at the top of Chinese politics. His lieutenants have cultivated his personality cult, projecting the image of Xi as commander-in-chief of the New Era in which he will lead the party's historical mission to restore China's civilisational greatness and proper place in the world.

Given Xi's seemingly unassailable position at the apex of CPC power, students of Chinese politics have naturally been interested in his life and leanings. Much less attention has been given to the system that has enabled Xi to concentrate power in his own hands. How did Xi sidestep the protocols of powersharing and consensus decision-making that the post–Mao Zedong leadership — determined not to suffer a repeat of Mao's calamitous final years in power — intended to shape Chinese politics into the future? How did the party, with its supposedly established norms — such as those limiting its top leaders to two five-year terms and ensuring its members represented diverse ideas and interests — fail to constrain Xi from amassing such power? Leninist systems tend to produce strongman rule by virtue of their pyramid structure and because Leninist parties sit above the law. But the CPC was supposed to have solved this problem.

Paramount Leader Deng Xiaoping

The received wisdom, both in and beyond China, is that Deng Xiaoping 邓小平, China's paramount leader in the 1980s and early 1990s, promoted a collective leadership model and new powersharing conventions that provided the political stability underpinning China's meteoric rise. But conventional narratives arguably overstate the extent to which elite politics changed under Deng and successive CPC leaders.[1] After Mao's death, Deng manoeuvred his way to power by drawing on a network of alliances and his formidable authority as a revolutionary elder. Although Mao's successor as party chairman, Hua Guofeng 华国锋, remained in that role until 1981, Deng and his allies effectively sidelined him, and then abolished that position as well as those of vice-chairmen, at the Twelfth CPC Congress in 1982, after Hua's brief stint as vice-chairman. The party would henceforth be formally led by a general secretary. Deng emerged as paramount leader, acquiring and consolidating this power without ever becoming the formal leader of the CPC (he was vice-chairman from 1977 to 1982 and retained his equivalent position on the Politburo Standing Committee until the Thirteenth Congress in 1987), although he did chair the Central

Wang Jiaxiang, Mao Zedong, and Deng Xiaoping
Source: Wikimedia Commons

Military Commission, enabling him as commander-in-chief to keep a tight rein on the military, whose leaders deeply respected him for his military accomplishments.

If Deng practised a collective style of leadership, recent research by Joseph Torigian as well as a forthcoming book by Fred Teiwes and Warren Sun suggest his approach reflected the unique demands of the time (the need to unite the leadership after a period of intense and bitter division) and Deng's own proclivities rather than institutional change.[2] Biographers and party historians contend that Deng was more interested in the strategic picture than policy details, so he was content to delegate major responsibilities to others.[3] Deng arguably could have asserted more personal control over political and policy decisions if he had wanted, but he preferred others to thrash things out. Nevertheless, when he decided to intervene in a decision, people obeyed him, even when he held no formal position other than chairman of the Chinese Bridge Association. Deng made the fateful decision to send the army into Tiananmen Square in 1989. And it was Deng who mobilised the party to reignite economic reforms in the 1990s, without consulting General

Secretary Jiang Zemin, by touring southern China and making public statements about the country's future in 1992. At the time, many senior party leaders were arguing that the reforms had endangered socialism, but even they fell into line after Deng made his views known.

So, while Deng was collectivist when he needed to be, he remained the strongman of his era. He oversaw leadership appointments, including the appointment of Hu Yaobang 胡耀邦 as general secretary of the party in February 1980, and his successor, Zhao Ziyang 赵紫阳, in 1987. Deng orchestrated the removal of both general secretaries after their apparent reluctance to squash student protests in 1987 and 1989, respectively. Deng also greenlit Jiang Zemin's ascension to the position of CPC general secretary in 1989. In 1992, Deng handpicked Hu Jintao for appointment to the Politburo and anointed him as Jiang's successor-in-waiting. Deng did not oversee these leadership appointments by operating in accordance with newly established rules and party norms. He was able to anoint new generations of leaders because, like Mao before him, his personal revolutionary authority was beyond question.

The End of the Revolutionary Elders

By the time Hu Jintao 胡锦涛 — the last of Deng's appointees — stepped down in 2012, Deng and all the revolutionary elders were dead, and Jiang Zemin was in his late eighties. There was no person or mechanism that could prevent Xi Jinping's accumulation of power, which he began almost immediately, deftly using an anticorruption campaign to weaken potential networks of opposition within the party and instilling fear in others. Himself a 'princeling' son of Red nobility (his father, Xi Zhongxun, was a first-generation revolutionary and party leader), Xi was able to stuff the Politburo with allies at the Nineteenth Party Congress in 2017. At the congress in 2022, Xi secured a third term as CPC general secretary and eliminated the last vestiges of potential opposition from the party's highest levels. The humiliating exit from the 2022 congress of Xi's predecessor, Hu Jintao — officially due to health reasons — incited much discussion in China and among outside analysts. Some saw it as an expression of Xi's now total grip on power. More broadly, it symbolised a curtain-close on the Dengist era in which the revolutionary party elders could influence leadership appointments, and thus maintain a modicum of powersharing.

In preparation for Xi's third-term coronation in October 2022, the CPC passed a historic resolution — only the third in its history (Mao oversaw the first resolution in 1945 and Deng the second in 1981).[4] The official purpose of the resolution was to articulate (and update or revise where necessary) the official narrative of the party's historical experience and major achievements, as well as to locate new policy and governance directions in a grand narrative that begins with the party's founding in 1921 and ends (in the future) with the rejuvenation of the Chinese nation and civilisation. A more practical purpose of the resolution was to cement Xi's control of the party by emphasising the importance of his leadership in steering China through the next chapter of its development, just as previous resolutions cemented Mao's and Deng's domination of the party. Despite covering all periods of party history, two-thirds of the text of the resolution was devoted to discussing the party's achievements during Xi's then nine years in power; Xi was mentioned more times than Mao or Deng.[5]

The resolution presents Xi as the leadership 'core' for the New Era and affirms Xi Jinping Thought on Socialism with Chinese Characteristics for a New Era as the party's guiding ideology. According to the resolution, in the New Era, Xi will lead the party towards the centennial goals outlined at the start of his tenure: China became a moderately prosperous society by 2021, which was the one hundredth anniversary of the founding of the CPC; and will become a rich and powerful nation by 2049, which is the one hundredth anniversary of the founding of the PRC. The historic resolution contends that only Xi Jinping can steer the nation to its destiny, navigating an external environment characterised by 'acute national security challenges, as evidenced by unprecedented external pressure, intertwined traditional and non-traditional security threats, and frequent "black swan" and "grey rhino" events'.

The resolution purposefully explains why Xi's era must be considered a new one, without mentioning what most distinguishes it from the previous era — the return to strongman rule — even if Xi is a different strongman to Mao and Deng (Xi's power stems from his ability to dominate party institutions and processes and not from revolutionary prestige). The resolution does, however, emphasise the need to 'uphold the Party core' (Xi), 'the Central Committee's centralised, unified leadership' (under Xi), and 'adhere to democratic centralism'. Herein lies the secret to Xi's power. Written into the party constitution since its founding, 'democratic centralism' permits differences of opinion within party ranks while a subject is still under discussion, but once a decision is made, all party members must fall into line and resolutely implement the decision whether they agree with it or not. Xi has been able to harness this fundamental organisational principle to make himself the ultimate arbiter in a way none of his predecessors since Deng has been able.

Although Deng recognised the need to restrain one-man rule, he failed both to institutionalise the checks and balances that would prevent the return of an all-powerful party boss and to de-Maoify the party. Deng rejected a personality cult for himself, but he did not repudiate Mao's. The party's second historic resolution, of 1981, which Deng oversaw, condemned the excesses of the Cultural Revolution, for example, but largely exonerated the Great Helmsman himself, blaming the chaos and destruction on the Gang of Four. Mao's mistakes were 'the errors of a great proletarian revolutionary'. That resolution stated that Mao's 'contributions to the Chinese revolution far outweigh his mistakes' and affirmed that Mao Zedong Thought would continue to be the party's guiding ideology.

Under Deng, the party thus continued to embrace Mao as the lead protagonist in its grand historical narrative. As a figure of reverence, Mao's portrait still towers over Tiananmen Square, just as it hangs on many living room walls across the country — most notably, in rural areas. In Mao's final decade, that of the Cultural Revolution, his Little Red Book took on a mythical — even magical — status, as official media reported that the mere recitation of it could bring about miracles, including the ability to undergo surgery without anaesthetic. (Later, in the Reform period, there was a time when taxi drivers adopted Mao as a kind of god of traffic safety, dangling charms with his portrait from their rearview mirrors.)

After the Twentieth Party Congress in October 2022, Xi took members of the newly appointed Politburo Standing Committee — the seven most powerful people in China — to Yan'an, which is a site of great symbolism for the CPC. It was there that Mao established himself as the undisputed leader of the party and the party adopted Mao Zedong Thought as its guiding ideology. Xi's choice of pilgrimage communicated the message that he was the unrivalled party leader of his generation. Airbrushed portraits of Xi Jinping increasingly portray a similar aura to those of the ubiquitous portraits of Mao at the peak of his personality cult — one of godly benevolence. Xi's personality cult has not reached the giddy heights of Mao's (and likely never will; Mao, after all, was a founding member of the party and led the party to victory in civil war, establishing the PRC). However, Xi does appear to seek to *zhanguang* 沾光, or borrow, some of Mao's 'shine' as national saviour.

Xi's strongman rule is arguably a continuation of the Leninist tradition in Chinese politics — a natural tendency that was tempered for some years by the outsized influence of the revolutionary elders — most notably, Deng Xiaoping. It is time to revisit commonly held assumptions about the extent of institutionalisation of Chinese politics in the post-Mao period. Deng reined in the excesses of Mao's calamitous final years in power and promoted powersharing in accordance with the perceived needs of the times and his personal proclivities. But Deng did not institutionalise leadership succession or powersharing. Once Deng's handpicked leaders had departed the scene, the ambiguous 'rules' and expectations passed down from his era were insufficient to constrain an ambitious politician armed with the powers of high office.

CHAPTER 1 —
ECONOMY AND
SUPPLY CHAINS

THE CHINESE ECONOMY: BURSTING BUBBLES, TERMINAL TROUBLES?

Jane Golley

It is an understatement to say that 2022 was not a great year for the Chinese economy — and the world has taken note. With gross domestic product (GDP) growth projections 'slashed' by the World Bank in June,[1] and again in September,[2] to 2.8 percent, there is no doubt the Chinese government will fail to reach its target of 5.5 percent growth. It set that target at the beginning of the year, before Xi Jinping's strict zero-COVID policy locked down city after city, precipitating what *The Guardian* called 'an unprecedented and widening mortgage boycott', resulting in a 'total collapse in confidence',[3] and creating supply chain 'chaos'[4] that reverberated around the world. Domestically, youth unemployment reached a record high of 20 percent in August, feeding into a 'jobs crisis',[5] 'deepening gloom'[6] underpinned a fall in consumer confidence, and the People's Republic of China (PRC) continued what *Foreign Affairs* described as its 'doomed fight against demographic decline'.[7] Geopolitical tensions and a struggling global economy added trouble to the mix. The United States imposed sweeping export controls that a *CNN* headline contended could 'throttle China's [high-tech] ambitions and escalate the tech war'.[8] Others worried that 'debt traps' related to Chinese investment were 'pushing vulnerable countries into crisis'.[9] If all these headlines could be taken at face value, perhaps the *Financial Times* was right to declare in its own late-October headline that 'China's economy will not overtake the US economy until 2060, if ever'.[10]

But is China really on track for the 'collapse' that Gordon Chang famously first predicted in his 2001 book, *The Coming Collapse of China* — one he still thought was imminent in 2022?[11] Or is Tom Orlik, author of the 2020 book *China: The Bubble That Never Pops*, more likely to be correct, writing in October in *Bloomberg* that although the 'China bubble is losing air', it is 'not going to pop' because of the nation's 'unparalleled record of surmounting crises'?[12]

The question of whether China can keep rising looms large in the reporting and analysis published in *Foreign Affairs*. It is a theme to which they return time and again, presenting competing narratives, with no obvious bias.[13] In October 2021, an article by Michael Beckley and Hal Brands was titled 'The end of China's rise: Beijing is running out of time to remake the world'.[14] The authors begin by asserting that, despite China 'moving

Bursting bubbles: Economists have speculated whether China is heading towards an economic collapse
Source: Drew Beamer, Unsplash

aggressively to forge a Sinocentric Asia and replace Washington atop the global hierarchy', there is little for the West to worry about because 'China's government is concealing a serious economic slowdown and sliding back into brittle totalitarianism. The country is suffering severe resource scarcity and faces the worst peacetime demographic collapse in history.' China is, in short, 'running out of people' and the 'economic consequences will be dire'. This, combined with the government's 'force-feeding [of] capital through the economy since 2008', leads Beckley and Brands to argue that 'China is tracing an arc that often ends in tragedy: a dizzying rise followed by the spectre of a hard fall'.

A second article, by Jude Blanchette in November 2021, conjures a very different picture, titled, 'Xi's confidence game: Beijing's actions show determination, not insecurity'.[15] Blanchette challenges the 'collapsing China syndrome' head-on, arguing that, while the 'doomsayers' are not entirely wrong in identifying the factors that constrain China's growth, they fail to weigh these against Beijing's potential and real strengths.

Perhaps Blanchette's most contentious point is that Beijing's biggest strength is its 'effective authoritarianism': its ability to mobilise and channel resources with 'remarkable speed'. The efforts to minimise the economic impacts of COVID-19 in 2020 is one example. While acknowledging this 'disregards the rights and freedoms of Chinese citizens', he contends that the Communist Party of China (CPC) 'in 2021 has been stronger, more capable, and in command of more resources than at any other time in its 100-year history'.

China's population is shrinking and its birth rate reached a historic low in 2022
Source: Xiangkun ZHU, Unsplash

This chapter reflects on some of the topics that obsessed the English-language press reports on China in 2022, alongside others that perhaps should have received more attention, to identify the key challenges affecting that nation's economic health. Assessing these challenges based on evidence and fact — rather than fear and fiction — is essential for understanding where the Chinese economy is headed and what might prevent it from getting there.

'Running Out of People'?

For decades, I travelled around China asking people what they thought was the country's biggest challenge. Time and again they would say, 'Too many people'. In the 1950s and 1960s, Mao Zedong had pushed the narrative that 'many people would make China strong'. This 'population optimism' fed into China's population boom during that time (from just under 544 million people in 1949, when the People's Republic was founded, to 929 million in 1976 when Mao died).[16] Chinese demographers had already started to think this was a serious problem, but the fate of economist Ma Yinchu 马寅初, who warned in 1957 of the dangers of overpopulation and was attacked as trying to 'discredit socialism', served as a cautionary tale for those who would say so out loud.

Deng Xiaoping, who oversaw Ma's political 'rehabilitation', including a formal apology to him from the CPC in 1979, adhered to a different narrative. He was 'population pessimistic', believing that reducing China's population growth was key to increasing per capita income. He launched the One-Child Policy in the early 1980s, aiming to bring population growth to zero and quadruple per capita income by the year 2000. He did not quite reach zero population growth, but per capita income did quadruple by 1996.

While a decline in fertility was not the only driving factor, it was a significant one. According to Cai Fang 蔡昉, former director of the Population Institute at the Chinese Academy of Social Sciences, about one-quarter of the increase in China's per capita income during its 'growth miracle' years from 1978 to 2010 can be explained by declining fertility.[17] There is a simple logic behind this demographic dividend: a reduction in fertility leads to a reduction in youth dependency and a surge in the working-age population, and because there are now relatively more workers and fewer dependents in the population, output or income per capita increases.

Fast forward to the introduction of the Two-Child Policy in 2016 and the Three-Child Policy, which was written into law in 2021. Cai strongly advocated for this policy relaxation and I, too, on non-economic terms, support it. But in purely economic terms, if reducing fertility was so important for raising per capita income, how could increasing fertility also be a good thing? Would it be catastrophic if — as looks likely to be the case — China is headed for a 'low-fertility trap' as, despite the freedom to have more, many Chinese couples now choose to have only one child?

I argue it would not be. China's working-age population is projected to decline by 18 percent between 2020 and 2050. If labour force participation rates do not change, its workforce will also decline by the same amount. Yet, considering labour's contribution to aggregate output (currently about 60 percent), in terms of the impact on average annual GDP growth, that amounts to a reduction of just 0.35 percentage points per annum through to 2050.

Having more babies now will not change these figures much, because those babies will not join the workforce for about twenty years. Investments in education are one obvious way to boost productivity in the long run. But other policy changes could produce a faster boost to GDP growth and per capita income gains. One is raising the retirement age. Back in 2015, there was talk of new policies that would gradually raise the age from sixty for men and fifty and fifty-five for white-collar and blue-collar women, respectively.[18] These changes were touted to begin in 2022 and, true to its planning word, the State Council in 2022 announced a gradual extension of the retirement age to be achieved by 2025 — although the details of how high it will go are scant, apart from noting that it will vary according to age groups.[19] Equalising the retirement age for women — the gender with universally higher life expectancies — with their male peers could readily extend China's workforce with the stroke of a pen. (Political leaders are ostensibly expected to retire at sixty-eight, but the rules do not seem to apply to Xi Jinping, who is sixty-nine and about to begin his third five-year term in office.)

Another policy to offset population ageing would be to increase labour force participation rates, especially among women. The record on this is even less positive, with just 62 percent of women over the age of fifteen engaged in the labour force in 2021. While high by developing-country standards, this is a three-decade low for China, and on a declining trend, having fallen steadily from 73 percent in 1990.[20] With China's global gender gap ranking at 102 in 2022[21] — a sharp decline since its peak rank of five in 2008 — and the number of women on the previously twenty-five-person (now twenty-four-man) Politburo Standing Committee falling from just one to zero, there is little reason to think Xi will act to boost the number of women workers more generally. Indeed, given the high youth jobless rate, due to a record number of university graduates seeking limited jobs in an economy beset by COVID uncertainties, Xi may continue to undermine the female workforce, focusing instead on raising participation among young men.[22] Either way, underemployment and unemployment among youth and women counter the argument that China is 'running out of people'. They do, however, reveal other challenges for China's long-term growth prospects.

Returning to Mao and Deng, both were at least partially right. High fertility rates in the Mao era did help China become powerful because, in power terms, size matters. Lower fertility then made Chinese people richer. It is true that China's population is ageing more rapidly than that of other countries at comparable levels of development, and that comes with problems. But fertility decline also leaves its citizens much better off, on average at least. As China heads into a period of population decline — beginning in 2022 — this point is worth bearing in mind, while also reflecting on the social security and other challenges that an ageing population and declining workforce will bring.

'Common Prosperity': Rhetoric or Reality?

In 1985, in pursuit of his goal of quadrupling per capita GDP, Deng famously said that some regions and people could become prosperous before others and that would help others gradually achieve common prosperity. He insisted that there must ultimately be 'no polarisation of rich and poor' because 'that's what socialism means'. Those waiting patiently for some of China's immense wealth to trickle their way have been doing so for four decades. In 2021, disposable income per capita in rural households was just 40 percent of their urban counterparts — an improvement from 32 percent a decade earlier, but still a substantial income gap.[23] By 2022, China's 539 billionaires were collectively worth nearly US$2 trillion, while the World Inequality Lab reported that the top 10 percent of its population earned fourteen times more than the bottom 50 percent.[24] Despite official claims that absolute poverty was completely eradicated in 2020 (measured as US$2.30 per person per day),[25] studies have since revealed a new pandemic-induced poverty wave, taking the poorest Chinese people further backwards.[26] Could Xi Jinping's latest solution finally give those people reason to hope? Since 2021, Common Prosperity 共同富裕, has become a signature policy goal in

Xi's Socialism with Chinese Characteristics for a New Era. Yuen Yuen Ang has written in *Foreign Affairs* that 'common prosperity' is not just rhetoric but also 'a set of instructions for government officials who are tasked with implementing Xi's vision'.[27] This vision 'is not a call for egalitarianism': it is rather a commitment to 'encouraging wealth creation through diligence and innovation'. Among other things, it involves 'proactively leveraging the important role of the state-owned economy in advancing common prosperity' and calling on those who 'got rich first to voluntarily share their wealth'.

Yet, for all the billionaires rushing to prove that they were listening by donating money to various charities, philanthropy cannot solve rural–urban inequality — or the gender, regional, and other forms of inequality that remain so prevalent in China today, which stem from gross underinvestment in health and education in the countryside. In their 2020 book *Invisible China: How the Urban–Rural Divide Threatens China's Rise*, Scott Rozelle and Natalie Hell wrote that to address these inequalities, which relate to 'structural issues within China's political system', China must first reform the *hukou* system (of residence permits), which has 'maintained and reinforced inequality through law'.[28] Second, it must recentralise the fiscal system so that poor areas are able to fund better education and health outcomes, and, third, it must shift the focus from short to long-term growth, to prepare for the future. Should the Chinese government carry out these three reforms, Rozelle and Hell contend, the country can escape the 'middle-income trap' (when countries develop to a certain point but then growth plateaus) and deliver sustainable, inclusive growth for decades to come. If it does not, in the worst-case scenario, the impact on China's long-term growth prospects would be 'catastrophic'.

China's track record offers little cause for optimism. For example, reform of the *hukou* system has been under way for several decades now, and has stepped up in recent years, especially in small and medium-sized cities. Yet, by October 2022, just one 'megacity', Zhengzhou, the capital of Henan province, with a population of twelve million, had plans in place to abolish all restrictions.[29] Abolishing *hukou* is simply not on the agenda for most megacities. For example, in June, Shanghai announced a relaxation of its regulations: its coveted *hukou* would now be granted to 'non-locals who've graduated from the world's top 50 universities and work in the city'.[30] This smacks of a fragmented and elitist authoritarianism — as opposed to Blanchette's 'effective' kind — in which wealthier provinces and cities implement policies that counteract Beijing's equalising ambitions, ensuring that wealth continues to trickle up, not down. The impacts on China's long-term growth prospects could be profound.

Chains of Debt

China's overseas and internal debt 'crises' were an ever-present topic in Western media throughout 2022. The former is invariably linked to accusations of 'debt-trap diplomacy' — a phrase ubiquitous in Western discourse about the Chinese government's Belt and Road Initiative (BRI) and other global investments. Deborah Brautigam, a scholar of China–Africa relations, has described how within twelve months of the first appearance of the phrase 'debt-trap diplomacy' in 2017, nearly two million search results could be found on Google. The concept, she says, somehow began 'to solidify into a deep historical truth'. Yet, Brautigam draws on a database of more than 1,000 Chinese loans to Africa to argue that she 'has not seen any examples where … the Chinese deliberately entangled another country in debt, and then used that debt to extract unfair or strategic advantages'. Other scholars support this finding, including in the oft-cited case of Sri Lanka, as in Lee Jones and Shahar Hameiri's report on *Debunking the myth of China's 'debt-trap diplomacy'* in which they, like Brautigam, conclude that the debt-trap narrative is 'simply incorrect'.[31]

This is not to say that the Chinese government is innocently and only pursuing 'win-win' development in its global economic engagements, including through the BRI. Of course, it is pursuing power and influence as well. And some of its multinational companies — state-owned and otherwise — behave badly in the process. Again, this is indicative of a less than entirely effective authoritarianism: not all domestic actors behave in accordance with the wishes of the centre. It is also true that countries across the globe have taken on substantial Chinese (and other foreign) loans that could cause them — and their Chinese lenders — problems in the future. The lack of transparency in many BRI projects could make those problems more significant than anticipated. The full facts in this particularly complex zone, where geopolitics, economics, and grand strategies intertwine, is impossible to ascertain. But we should at least rule out the fictions.

This is harder to do when talking about China's internal debt challenges, including in the real estate sector. According to one narrative, the Evergrande crisis that began in August 2020 (when it was revealed that the country's second-largest property developer was more than US$300 billion in debt) has now spilled over to the industry to the point where there is 'a total collapse in confidence, and only [more] government intervention can save the day'.[32] A *Financial Times* report in October characterised China's 'property crash' as a 'slow-motion financial crisis'.[33]

In the same month, writing in *Bloomberg*, Tom Orlik pointed out that '[f]or more than a decade, analysts have warned that excesses in borrowing and building have pushed China's property sector onto an unsustainable trajectory'. Yet, when policymakers 'get ahead of the problem by cutting off sources of financing to overleveraged developers', those same analysts are the ones who cry out for more intervention, not less. Orlik sees it differently, describing the history of China's real estate sector as a

> series of exuberant booms and near-disastrous busts. Every time it appears the end is nigh, policymakers have tweaked the dials on down-payment requirements, mortgage rates, and financing for developers to get things back on track. They're doing so again, though this time their goal isn't engineering another boom, but moderating the pace of decline.[34]

Crises are, by definition, unpredictable events and economists are notorious for incorrectly predicting them. Simply put, the risks are high and rising, and there is contention about how well the Chinese government can mitigate them.

Conclusion

Tom Orlik has used the term 'Sinophrenia' to describe a 'condition of modern commentary that combines the belief that China will imminently collapse with the belief that it is taking over the world'.[35] The article by Beckley and Brands falls into this category. In contrast, Jude Blanchette's article might seem 'Sinophoric', although placed in the broader context of his writings, this would be inaccurate. He previously described how President Xi's gamble on consolidating power in his own hands has set him on a 'current course [that] threatens to undo the great progress China has made over the past four decades'.[36] In October 2022, he observed that 'authoritarian systems and authoritarian leaders always appear solid on the outside — until suddenly, they don't'.[37]

No-one doubts that the lockdowns in response to Xi's zero-COVID policy made 2022 a very rough year for China's economy (and its people). With the Russia–Ukraine war, rising tensions in the Taiwan Strait, and the ever-escalating rivalry between the United States and China, the geopolitical headwinds are growing stronger. Add to these the economic headwinds identified here and it is certainly possible to construct a narrative of crisis or collapse. But it is also possible that the Chinese government will demonstrate more flexibility than it has in recent times, adopting effective policies that not only stave off crisis, but also set the country on the path to long-run, sustainable, and inclusive growth.

The Untold Story of Chinese

Banking and Why It Matters

ADAM Y. LIU

Coal Supply Chains: No Bright

Outlook for Australia

JORRIT GOSENS

THE UNTOLD STORY OF CHINESE BANKING AND WHY IT MATTERS

Adam Y. Liu

IN MID-2022, thousands of angry depositors stormed the Henan office of the central bank of the People's Republic of China (PRC). The cause was a classic bank-run trigger: people were unable to retrieve their deposits from some of the lesser-known village and township banks 村镇银行 that rarely feature in discussions of China's financial system. Many of the depositors/ protesters were from outside Henan province; a substantial number had travelled thousands of kilometres from Guangdong province to join the rally. Clearly, the banks in humble Henan province had managed to attract depositors nationwide. Who were these village and township banks? How did they manage to draw deposits from so far afield? And why were they underregulated to the point of generating unrest? What happened in Henan was hardly unique. Indeed, it could be the beginning of a much bigger challenge with which China's new economic management team will have to grapple carefully but resolutely into the future. The root cause of the Henan crisis lies in the kind of market that the Communist Party of China (CPC) has cultivated in the world's largest banking system (the assets of which are equal to 40 percent of global gross domestic product), particularly since the mid-1990s. I call it a 'state-owned market system'. This market has a Leninist foundation, its organisation mirrors that of the party-state, and the incentives for market competition go far beyond economic profits. It is a system in which market and administrative financial allocations coexist, party discipline and market discipline both matter, and profits and politics reign in uneasy tandem.

The Grand Bargain

Most China watchers know that the country's banking system is firmly controlled by the party-state. Yet, state control has not precluded market diversification and competition. The stereotypical view of Chinese banking, based on the early reform years, sees a system dominated by the Big Four banks: the Industrial and Commercial Bank of China, the China Construction Bank, the Bank of China, and the Agricultural Bank of China. This picture is obsolete and analytically misleading. While the Big Four once controlled almost all banking assets in China, their asset share has now dwindled to less than 25 percent — a dramatic transformation.

What happened, though, was hardly a liberalisation of the sector. Private and foreign banks still play a negligible role in the Chinese system. Instead, underlying the shrinking market share of the Big Four is the proliferation of banks owned or controlled by lower-level governments, which I term 'local state banks' (for example, the Shanghai Bank, Beijing Bank, and Baoshang Bank). Since the mid-1990s, these banks have proliferated exponentially, numbering more than 2,000 by the mid 2010s. While the Big Four remain the largest players in the system, in many localities, they have lost their market dominance to the local state banks.[1]

The rise of the local state banks was never simply a story of market reform, i.e., it was never about supporting underfunded private firms and small businessowners in the first place. In fact, it was the outcome of a 'grand bargain', a political quid pro quo.[2] Throughout the 1980s and early 1990s, a decentralised fiscal system incentivised China's local governments to pursue economic development. Unlike the Mao Zedong era, when all revenue had to be handed over to the central

While the Big Four banks once controlled almost all banking assets in China, their asset share has now dwindled to less than 25 percent
Source: Japanexperterna.se, Flickr

government, local governments could keep the remainder after sharing with the central government a prescribed amount of taxes. However, by the early 1990s, localities were amassing almost 80 percent of the country's total revenue. Beijing worried that this high degree of fiscal decentralisation could sow the seeds of political disintegration, as had occurred in the former Yugoslavia. So, the central government decided to take a large chunk of revenue away from the localities — that is, to recentralise. From 1993 to 1994, the central government's share of revenue increased dramatically,

from about 20 to 55 percent. However, Beijing did not achieve this through blunt administrative fiat. To keep localities happy and ensure they remained incentivised to pursue local development, the centre compensated them. It helped localities meet their responsibilities after recentralisation through fiscal transfers and tax returns and permitted them to organise local government financing vehicles (LGFVs) to borrow and sell land to real estate developers.

Less well known is the most crucial component of Beijing's offer: allowing local governments to enter banking. Beijing even promised to assist by transferring some central financial assets to help kickstart local banks. Vice-premier Zhu Rongji repeatedly highlighted the possibility of allowing localities to organise their own banks when negotiating the details of recentralisation with the localities.

Herein lies the fiscal–financial nexus of China's banking market transformation. It explains why most of China's local state banks appeared immediately after the 1994 fiscal recentralisation reform. Before 1998, local governments could veto the personnel appointments of the Big Four banks' local branch managers; premier Zhu brought this power to an end. Later, when Beijing sought to sever local government ties with the Big Four's local branches, it gave the local state banks even more privileges, such as the authority to build branches outside their own cities and provinces.

Political Competition and Market Expansion

Localities ran with Beijing's offer. But immediately on entering the banking business, they faced an existential crisis: how to compete with local Big Four branches,

which already had a sweeping presence across the country by the mid-1990s. Despite this, the local state banks took off quickly. There were several factors behind their success, the most critical being local government support.

Local governments injected fiscal revenue into the new banks in the early years to get them going. They then coordinated with local state-owned enterprises and other government departments or work units to make enterprise deposits and set up payroll systems with the new banks. They also pressured wealthy local private businesses to borrow in advance, even when the firms had no need for funding, to beef up the banks' balance sheets. And they pushed local religious organisations — 'patriotic' churches and temples — to deposit their donations in the new banks.[3]

One reason local governments lend a strong helping hand is that they wish to have their cake and eat it, too. This is a rational choice for all local governments in China, as they need financial resources to outcompete their peers. This is also the whole point of the central–local grand bargain: allowing localities sufficient financial wherewithal to grow and compete.

With strong local government support, the new banks aggressively expanded their turf and engaged in various market campaigns to grow their presence — for example, sending employees to residential compounds to sell bank products and services. Most importantly, they have been covertly raising deposit rates above central ceilings, such as handing out cash rewards proportional to the size of the customers' deposits and keeping these transactions on separate books.[4]

The local state banks have also borrowed from central policies to further expand their market reach. For example, during the administration of Hu Jintao and Wen Jiabao, a top central priority was rural development, with Beijing encouraging the formation of more rural financial institutions. Numerous local state banks (most of which were based in cities) seized the opportunity and applied for licences to set up village and township banks. The trick was that many localities in fact ended up situating these so-called village and township banks in urban areas to attract more customers; in recent years, they have also capitalised on fintech and collaborated with internet firms to reach potential customers nationwide. In some cases, the centre has lost track of what these banks are doing, as happened in Henan province, because village and township banks are usually not connected directly to the Central Clearing and Settlement System but only via the local state banks that created them.

The aim of local governments is not to monopolise local financial resources but to aggrandise them. For one thing, in their localities, they do not have the capacity to squeeze out the Big Four, which ordinary Chinese still view as the most stable financial institutions. More importantly, because local officials are like roving bandits who are transferred between localities every few years, they do not even bother trying to monopolise, because their successors can free-ride on their efforts.

That is why local governments have in fact played a crucial role in diversifying the local banking markets, by proactively inviting even more banks to enter their jurisdictions. They benefit from this open-door policy in two ways. First, new entrants must usually sign deals with local governments that require them to make loans to designated local enterprises within a short period. Second, by reducing the Big Four's local market share, new entrants help boost 'local financial development', which is included in upper-level governments' evaluation criteria for local officials.

The rise of the local state banks unleashed ferocious competition in China's state-owned banking market, with the result that the Big Four are no longer dominant. Setting aside Tibet, for every Chinese province, 60–70 percent of banking assets and bank branches today are controlled by the local state banks. The city of Hangzhou, for example, had 671 bank branches and credit unions in 1990, but by 2015, this number had reached almost 5,000, only 38 percent of which belonged to the Big Four.[5]

So What?

What has the rise of local state banks meant for the Chinese economy? In short, it has created a state-owned banking market in which a variety of state agents are engaged in market competition, and the dynamism and dynamics of the markets change as the state's priorities shift. When the constraints of state control and command were loosened, banks in China competed as any commercial banks would, albeit within the bounds of the party-state. That said, things could change quickly now that Beijing decided to tighten its regulatory and policy grip.

In 2014, Nicolas Lardy's suggestively titled book *Markets Over Mao* debunked the myth that China's banking system continued to discriminate against private borrowers. In fact, thanks to the proliferation of smaller regional banks, Lardy argues, the banking system has become highly competitive, and that, in turn, has helped non-state borrowers.[6] Elsewhere, I have provided more systematic empirical evidence consistent with Lardy's conjecture.[7] But not all private borrowers are born equal or treated equally. It remains the case that politically connected firms have better access to bank loans and credit.

The most crucial outcome of intense bank competition has been an overconcentration of lending in the real estate sector, particularly by local state banks. When the economy was still booming, it made sense for small, young banks to ride the rising housing tide — even embracing real estate firms as major shareholders to strengthen their balance sheets. It was the fastest way for the banks to expand. The downside of this expansion strategy, however, is now all too clear: the banks and real estate firms could sink together.[8] This is exactly what happened to the Shengjing Bank and the Evergrande real estate company, which was once the bank's biggest shareholder. As the real estate giant tottered, the bank also faltered and went through a radical restructuring to pre-empt a local banking crisis. More such events can be expected in the coming years.

Local governments encouraged this enmeshment between local state banks and real estate firms: they needed a booming housing sector to extract land rents, and they needed local state banks to grow so they could rely on them when fiscal problems arose, as happened during the 2008–2009 Global Financial Crisis. We know that China muddled through that disaster by pumping money into the economy. Far less

known is that the local state banks together, through their LGFVs, provided even more funding to local governments than did the Big Four.

The Regulatory Dilemma

So where were the regulators? Why did they not check the wild expansion of local state banks, especially their excessively cosy relationship with the real estate sector? The answer hearkens back to the central–local grand bargain. As well as its concrete policy concessions, Beijing made clear it would not meddle with how localities raised and spent money. So, after the required taxes were submitted to the centre, all money-related matters could basically remain local 'secrets'.[9] And Beijing honoured its word.

This explains why, before Xi Jinping assumed power, China's banking regulators essentially focused on the Big Four and left the local state banks untouched. The pre-Xi era was one of 'great development', in the words of one regulator I interviewed. No-one really cared or dared to keep the local state banks in check. One municipal branch of the Banking Regulatory Commission tried in vain to remove a local state bank president in a north-eastern province in the early 2000s, but the city government fought successfully to protect him.[10] Notably, local party secretaries and government bosses have proven much more powerful than the regulators.

After the stock market crash on 15 June 2015, President Xi did make a serious effort to ramp up regulatory pressure on the securities and banking markets. The number of punishments and warnings that central regulators issued to banks increased fifteenfold between 2012 and 2020, reaching 5,290 in the first year of the global pandemic. Yet, as growth decelerated, China–US relations worsened, and the self-destructive dynamic zero-COVID policy continued, Beijing backed down, and the number of bank punishments shrank dramatically to below 3,000 in 2021.

The Future

What will happen to Chinese banking? This is a crucial question for the world to ponder, because it matters not just to China's economy but also to the world's. Let us assume the CPC will remain in power. Now that Xi has relaxed his zero-COVID policy, and once the economy bounces back, we will see the return of significant regulatory pressure on the banks. There will be less intense competition among banks than before Xi took power. As the state strikes back, banks will again make more loans aligned with government policies, as they did in the early years of reform. The private sector will suffer as a result.

In the post-Xi era, presumably sometime after 2032, we might see the revival of a more dynamic state-owned banking market, but we should not expect any massive entry of private or foreign banks, as that would be inimical to party rule. Nor should we expect large waves of central or local state bank failures. Problematic banks will continue to be merged with others or acquired by the central government, as has always been the case. In this state-owned market made by the party, there will be no creative destruction, only creative reorganisation.

COAL SUPPLY CHAINS: NO BRIGHT OUTLOOK FOR AUSTRALIA

Jorrit Gosens

IN SEPTEMBER 2020, President Xi Jinping announced a commitment by the People's Republic of China (PRC) to achieve net-zero carbon emissions by 2060, with an intermediate target of peaking carbon emissions by 2030. This is a considerable challenge given that China is still the biggest user of coal globally, by some margin.

In 2019, China was responsible for about 55 percent of the total global consumption of thermal coal (used primarily for electricity generation) and about 60 percent of global consumption of coking coal (used in steelmaking). The bulk of this is supplied by domestic mines; imports made up 7.2 percent of thermal coal consumption and 13 percent of coking coal consumption in 2019.[1] Despite this relatively large dependency on domestic suppliers, China has faced difficulties in sourcing secure and affordable supplies of coal for its power and steel plants over the past few years. Prices for thermal coal in seaborne markets spiked to more than US$400 per tonne in early May 2022[2] — the highest price in at least fifty years[3] and about five or six times as expensive as usual. Prices for coking coal similarly jumped, to about US$600 per tonne, or four times usual prices. This came at a time when Chinese power and steel plants were already scrambling to find alternative suppliers after the unofficial import ban on Australian coal in late 2020, which was instigated by the Australian government's insistence on an investigation into the origins of the COVID-19 pandemic.[4] The country supplied about 20 percent of China's thermal coal imports and 40 percent of coking coal imports in 2019.

There were also disruptions in electricity supply in different parts of China in both 2021 and 2022, leading to power rationing, and affecting both industrial production and residential consumption.[5]

In mid-2022, *Bloomberg's* sources claimed that China was considering lifting its ban on Australian coal imports: the compounding energy crises had Beijing so desperate, rumour had it, it was willing to look past its political strife with Canberra for the sake of renewed access to Australian coal.[6] That storyline, however, does not match the underlying causes of the energy crises, nor recent developments in Chinese energy markets.

Volatile spot prices for seaborne coal have affected all coal-importing countries and have been due mostly to supply issues.[7] Consumption levels of coal, both globally and in China, have returned with unexpected rapidity to levels seen before the COVID-19 crisis, while supply has not kept up. This is due in part to COVID-induced mine closures and transport disruption — again, both globally and in China. Just as Australian exporters soon found new buyers for their coal after the Chinese import ban,[8] Chinese buyers quickly managed to find new suppliers. For thermal coal, China turned to Indonesia — a supplier of relatively cheap coal that was already fulfilling much of China's needs (see Figure 1). China replaced Australian high-quality coking coal with imports from the United States and Canada, at high cost, although Beijing has since been working to reduce dependence on these suppliers. Supplies from Russia have increased, too, though those are of different, lower-quality types of coking coal that would not compete with Australian hard coking coal. In short: Beijing's insistence on cutting Australian imports had some upward effect

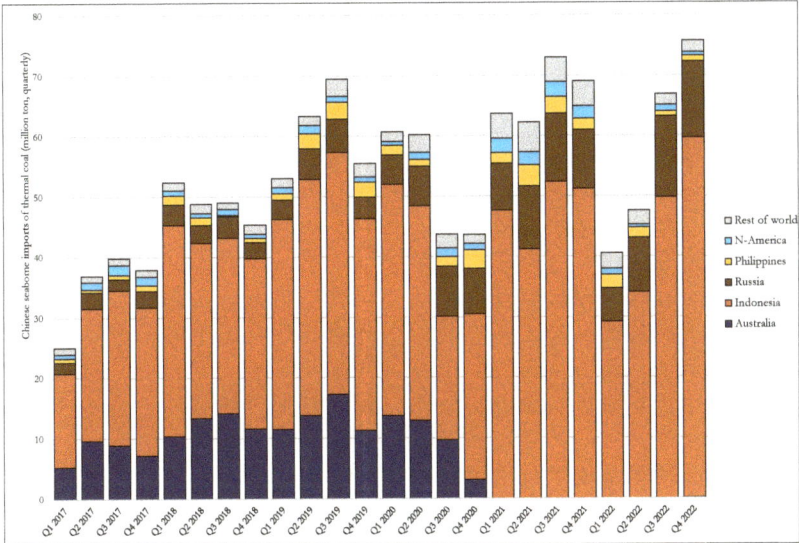

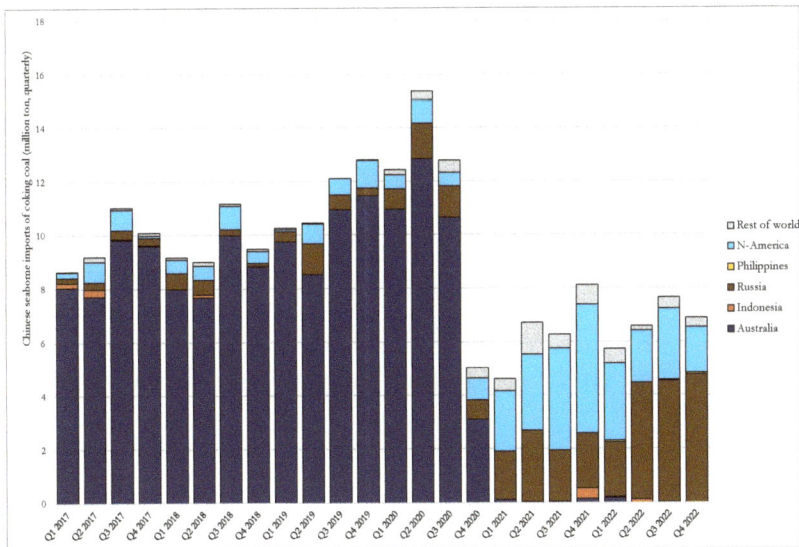

Figure 1: Chinese seaborne imports of thermal coal (top) and coking coal (bottom) (million tonnes, quarterly)

Source: Data from Kpler (graph created by author)

Note: This does not include overland imports from Mongolia or Russia.[9]

on the prices that its domestic consumers had to pay, but the bulk of those price increases were due to causes that have raised prices for all importers in global coal markets.

The power shortages in the summer of 2021 were largely tied to the high prices in international coal markets, as well as reduced domestic production due to both COVID-induced mine closures and heavy rainfall flooding mines in key coal-producing areas.[10] This led to power shortages due to an ongoing but incomplete liberalisation of energy markets in China.[11] Coal prices are allowed to fluctuate according to market dynamics, although the National Development and Reform Commission — the market and pricing regulator — can intervene, mainly with regards to levels of coal production or imports,[12] when prices fall or rise beyond a specified range.[13]

Power prices, on the other hand, are more strictly regulated: market dynamics may cause fluctuations of no more than 20 percent above or below provincial-level benchmark prices.[14] This is already more generous than the limit of 10 percent above benchmark prices in place until October 2021. That change

was enacted after coal-fired power plants — faced with rising fuel costs but limited ability to recoup these through higher electricity prices — stopped producing power to prevent operating at a loss, in some cases claiming a need for maintenance. Decarbonisation policy also contributed to the power shortages, as local cadres sought to adhere to emission targets, even if that meant shuttering factories or denying power to big consumers.[15]

The summer of 2022 saw further power shortages, this time during the longest and hottest heatwave in recorded history. This led to increased power demand from air-conditioning use throughout China, at the same time as the south-western provinces in particular experienced shortfalls in electricity generation.[16] In these provinces, power production largely relies on hydropower, which was severely hampered by the drought that saw even the water flow of the Yangtze River — the world's third-largest river, an important source of drinking water, a vital shipping conduit, and a crucial source of hydroelectricity — drop to 50 percent below a five-year average.[17] Supplies of Australian coal would have done little to relieve either power crisis. While the crisis in 2021 was related to the high cost of imported coal globally, the crisis in the summer of 2022 would not have been solved with more Australian coal. Domestic production of the fuel was already back at record levels, but the power networks in the south-west needed water, not coal, to operate.

Wider developments in China's coal markets have further reduced the need for imported coal in general. First, while Chinese COVID-19 stimulus measures have typically spurred carbon-intensive economic activity, the growth of coal-fired power consumption appears to be plateauing. Throughout the first six months of 2022, coal-fired power consumption was down 3.9 percent, or roughly forty-five megatonnes.[18] Since then, the strong heatwave over summer saw drastically reduced hydropower, which created additional, though temporary, demand for coal-fired power. For the full year, coal-fired power production was up 0.9 percent — equivalent to an increase of roughly twenty megatonnes.

The future looks brighter, as provincial governments have announced plans for renewables that, when added together, would result in 1,200 gigawatts of solar and wind generation installed by 2025 — a level targeted by the national government for 2030.[19] China has always been a big market for solar photovoltaics, with fifty-five gigawatts of installations in 2021 alone — equal to about one-third of the global total.[20] Over the first eight months of 2022, Chinese investment in solar photovoltaics was up by a whopping 323.8 percent on the previous year.[21] Nuclear energy will also contribute to decarbonising power generation, but much more marginally than renewables, with an official target of seventy gigawatts by 2025 — up from fifty-five gigawatts by the end of 2022.[22] Steel output also appears finally to have peaked, down 2.1 percent from the previous year,[23] which is equivalent to an annual reduction in coking coal consumption of fifteen megatonnes. Continuing concern about the health of the real estate sector — one of the biggest consumers of steel — will certainly weaken the outlook for future steel demand. To put those numbers in perspective, over the period 2018 to 2020, China's average annual imports of thermal coal were about 225 megatonnes and imports of coking coal were about seventy-five megatonnes.

Chinese plans for improved energy security further reduce the need for coal imports. Domestic production of coal was up by 9 percent over 2022, or an astonishing 371 megatonnes of additional coal output[24] — well more than total Chinese imports in a typical year.

Combined with expected reductions in consumption, this will lead to massively increased stockpiles or drastically reduced imports, and probably both. On top of this, in late 2019, China opened the Haoji Railway,[25] which can carry 200 megatonnes of coal from China's key coalmining centre of Ordos in Inner Mongolia to its central provinces — the ones most badly hit by the 2021 power shortages. This cuts the delivery costs of coal and lessens the need for imports.[26] Another new railway links China's steelmaking heartland in Hebei with the Tavan Tolgoi mine complex in neighbouring Mongolia, which supplies high-quality and cheaply mined coking coal.[27] Again, this will lessen reliance on seaborne coal imports.[28]

In summary, China is reducing and will continue to reduce its consumption of coal. It will source the coal that it does consume increasingly from domestic mines, as well as from Mongolia, which has few other markets to which to sell given its geography, and from Russia, which is constrained in its exports by the international sanctions due to its invasion of Ukraine.

Recent indications that China is ready to drop the import ban[29] will not be because it is desperate for Australian coal, but because it no longer needs it.

二

CHAPTER 2 —
CLIMATE PROBLEM,
TECH SOLUTIONS

SUPERCHARGING CHINA: CARS, BATTERIES, AND LITHIUM

Barry van Wyk

With no internal combustion engine and no burning of fossil fuels, electric vehicles (EVs) — running solely on batteries — are coming in their billions to electrify mobility. By 2035, at least half of all global passenger vehicle sales will be of EVs, and the proportion will keep increasing.[1] The roadmap for the global energy sector to reach carbon neutrality developed by the International Energy Agency (IEA) requires the number of EVs to increase from eleven million in 2020 to 350 million in 2030 and almost two billion by 2050.[2] In the global race to build batteries and battery-powered cars and to access the vital lithium, cobalt, and nickel that go into them, the People's Republic of China (PRC) is winning hands-down.

A Potent Mix

The most expensive component of an EV is its battery. Up to 99 percent of all batteries currently installed in EVs and hybrids (which have an internal combustion engine as well as a battery) are lithium-ion. Lithium-ion batteries contain base metals such as aluminium, copper, and iron as well as expensive precious metals — notably, lithium, cobalt, nickel, and manganese.

To produce electricity, lithium-ion batteries move lithium ions from the anode to the cathode electrodes via the electrolyte layer, which contains a microporous separator. Graphite — the only natural form of carbon apart from diamonds — is used to conduct heat and electricity in the anode and is the only material that can be used for this purpose.[3] Lithium is the battery's active material and key component, but most of the precious metals are contained in the cathode, which is therefore the most expensive part of the battery. The cathodes contain an ever-increasing share of nickel,[4] which facilitates energy density and longer battery life; cobalt, which prevents the cathodes from easily overheating or igniting; and manganese, which decreases the risk of combustibility.

Given the complexity of the battery and the various components, it is difficult to establish exactly how much of these precious metals go into each battery. One estimate[5] puts the proportion of precious metals at about eight kilograms of lithium,[6] thirty-five kilograms of nickel, twenty kilograms of manganese, fourteen kilograms of cobalt, and as much as seventy to 100 kilograms of graphite.[7] Other estimates differ.[8]

Extracting these metals poses a variety of environmental and human rights challenges. For one thing, the mining required is highly energy-intensive. Large lithium mines feature big lithium 'ponds' of varying hues (depending on the concentration of lithium carbonate), which have been described as 'surreal landscapes where batteries are born',[9] and have begun to appear in the 'lithium triangle' of Chile, Bolivia, and Argentina.[10] High-pressure acid-leach nickel plants in Indonesia — the leading producer of this metal—have a high carbon footprint, among other environmental concerns.[11] These mining operations cause soil degradation and environmental damage and use vast amounts of water — for example, in the 'lithium triangle', every tonne of lithium requires the use of about 2.2 million litres of water[12] as the mineral is found dissolved in salt flats and must be separated via evaporation.[13] In fact, harmful environmental effects are nearly ubiquitous in the lithium supply chain.

Two-thirds of the global supply of cobalt are mined in the Democratic Republic of the Congo (DRC), where concerns have been raised about human rights abuses and labour issues,[14] involving not only Chinese companies, but also many from the West. In May 2022, for example, the Swiss mining company Glencore, one of the world's largest traders of cobalt, reached a settlement with the US Department of Justice in which the company pleaded guilty to decades of bribery, corruption, and market manipulation in seven South American and African countries,[15] including the DRC, where Glencore has a long record of human rights abuses.[16] And such abuses are not confined to the DRC: there have been violations of the rights of indigenous communities by Chinese and Western companies in Latin America[17] and workplace safety issues occur also in China[18] and Australia.[19]

Battery and EV Kings

CHINA STORY YEARBOOK | Supercharging China:
CHAINS | Cars, Batteries, and Lithium
Barry van Wyk

In 2021, almost seven million EVs were sold worldwide,[20] and a full 51 percent of these were sold in China. Germany (10.2 percent) and the United States (9.3 percent) were a long way behind. According to data from China's Ministry of Public Security,[21] as of the end of September 2022, there were 412 million vehicles in China, including 315 million cars, and 499 million drivers. Of those vehicles, 11.49 million, or 3.65 percent, were EVs, of which 3.71 million were newly registered in 2022. The EVs included 9.26 million pure electric vehicles — a proportion of 80 percent. In 2022, 6.49 million new-energy vehicles, mostly EVs, were sold in China — a year-on-year increase of 96 percent from the 3.31 million sold in 2021.[22]

EV sales in China are riding a wave of supportive government policies and incentives, including cash subsidies and purchase tax exemptions. EVs are also a key component of China's 'double carbon' objectives[23] — first proclaimed by Xi Jinping at the UN General Assembly in September 2020 — to reach peak carbon use by 2030 and carbon neutrality by 2060. In September 2022, the Ministry of Finance announced that EVs purchased throughout 2023 would remain exempt from vehicle purchase taxes — the third time the policy was extended since it was first implemented in 2014.[24]

The year 2022 recorded a steady drumbeat of achievements in the meteoric rise of BYD (Build Your Dreams) Auto 比亚迪, a company from Guangdong province that was founded in 1995 as a battery manufacturer. In the first half of the year, BYD became the world's leading EV company, with sales of 640,748 units — a fourfold increase on the previous year — and 76,748 units more than Tesla, which is its closest rival. In just one year, it increased its global market share from 5.9 percent to 15.4 percent.[25] In April, BYD announced that it had ceased building combustion engine vehicles and would focus exclusively on EVs.[26] In May, BYD's monthly EV sales in China breached 100,000 units for the first time. In June, the company's market capitalisation exceeded one trillion yuan (almost US$150 billion), which was larger than Volkswagen Group and third on the list of auto giants behind Tesla and Toyota.[27] In October, BYD sold a record 217,800 EVs in China —

EVs sales in China are riding a wave of supportive government policies
Source: Chuttersnap, Unsplash

the eighth consecutive month of record sales.[28] This represented a year-on-year increase of 168.78 percent and 16,541 units more than in September. According to the China Passenger Car Association, 680,000 EVs were sold in China in October, which would give BYD a market share of 32 percent. From January to October, BYD sold 1.19 million passenger vehicles — a year-on-year increase of more than 160 percent — surpassing Tesla's 909,000 units.[29]

The profits are rolling in for BYD. In the third quarter of 2022, it announced a net profit of 5.72 billion yuan (US$788 million) — an increase of 350.3 percent year-on-year. Its global market offensive is in full swing as well. In September, it entered the European market with the Han sedan, the SUV Tang, and compact SUV Yuan Plus.[30] Through 2022, BYD entered markets in Australia (in February), New Zealand and Japan (July), Cambodia and Israel (August), Thailand (September), and India (October).[31] In October, the company signed an agreement with the European rental car company Sixt to purchase 100,000 BYD EVs over the next six years.[32] BYD also announced it was ordering eight cargo ships, at a total cost of five billion yuan (US$689 million), to transport its vehicles to overseas markets.[33]

Yet, an even more meteoric and relentless rise is that achieved by China's largest battery manufacturer, Contemporary Amperex Technology Limited (CATL) 宁德时代, which was founded in 2011 in Fujian province. In 2021, the average capacity of a single EV battery was about fifty-five kilowatt hours (kWh). By the end of June 2022, the cumulative installed capacity of batteries in China was 110.1 gigawatt hours (GWh) (each gigawatt hour is equal to one million kilowatt hours).[34] This represented almost a doubling of cumulative installed battery capacity from the previous year; CATL accounted for nearly 48 percent of this total. Globally, by the end of the third quarter of 2022, cumulative battery capacity had reached 341.3 GWh, with CATL supplying 35.1 percent of that.[35] (BYD ranked third, with a market share of 12.8 percent; it, too, saw tremendous growth in this area, with a year-on-year increase of 177 percent.) Profits at CATL are soaring. In the third quarter of 2022, CATL announced total revenue of 97.37 billion yuan (US$13.32 billion) — a year-on-year increase of 232 percent — and a net profit of 9.42 billion yuan (US$1.3 billion), which was an increase of 188 percent.[36]

In June 2022, just when CATL joined the 'trillion yuan' market capitalisation club,[37] the company launched its third-generation Qilin 麒麟 EV battery,[38] named after a mythical Chinese beast sometimes likened to a unicorn. The Qilin has a record volume utilisation rate (the percentage of a battery used for driving) of more than 72 percent, and an EV with this battery can drive 1,000 kilometres without having to recharge. When it does need to be recharged, it can reach 80 percent capacity in ten minutes, outperforming Tesla's batteries, thanks to CATL's large surface-cooling technology. Yet, for CATL's founder and chairperson, Robin Zeng (Zeng Yuqun 曾毓群), the Qilin is just the first step. He has promised more advanced batteries to come,[39] including ones based on 'condensed matter', which, as he said at the Qilin's launch in June, 'no-one has heard about'. Zeng, who completed a PhD in condensed matter physics at the Chinese Academy of Sciences from 2002 to 2006, did not elaborate further, but it is likely that condensed-matter batteries will make use of graphene technology. Graphene is a material consisting of a one-atom-thick layer of carbon that has virtually unlimited industrial potential, including as a conductor of heat and electricity.

All Chains Lead to China

For BYD, CATL, and all EV and battery companies around the world, access to lithium and other precious metals is the key to success. But the Chinese companies have one big advantage: China controls crucial links in the supply chains.

Each of the four key metals used to produce batteries, plus the metal-like graphite, requires different conditions for production.[40] Lithium is extracted from brine in high-elevation areas in South America or from hard rock, mostly in Australia. In 2021, China produced 14,000 metric tonnes of

The Greenbushes lithium mine in Western Australia
Source: Calistemon, Flickr

lithium, making it the world's third-largest producer after Australia (55,000 metric tonnes) and Chile (26,000 metric tonnes).[41] In 2021, at least 65 percent of China's lithium needs were met by imports.[42]

Nickel is extracted from two types of deposits: sulphide (mostly in Russia, Canada, and Australia) and laterite (mostly in Indonesia and the Philippines). In 2021, Indonesia was the world's largest producer with one million metric tonnes, while China was the seventh largest, with 120,000 metric tonnes.[43]

Cobalt is a by-product of copper or nickel mining. About 70 percent of cobalt comes from the DRC, where Chinese companies are estimated to control 60 percent of cobalt mining and 80 percent of cobalt refining.[44] In 2021, Chinese companies owned or partially owned fifteen of the nineteen cobalt mines in the DRC.[45]

Manganese and graphite are easier to obtain. Manganese, which is the most widely distributed of all the metals used in batteries, can be extracted at relatively low cost. As for graphite — the relatively common crystalline form of carbon — it can be mined or produced synthetically, and China controls about 80 percent of global graphite mining.[46]

Since 2021, high demand for lithium-ion batteries has led to a spike in the prices of lithium, nickel, and cobalt, which have been exacerbated by supply chain pressures such as COVID-19, Russia's invasion of Ukraine, and limited production capacity. From January 2021 to May 2022, lithium prices increased sevenfold and cobalt prices doubled, while nickel prices almost doubled.[47] To increase their access to lithium, nickel, and cobalt reserves, Chinese companies have undertaken a range of direct investments, equity deals, and supply or sales agreements with mining companies in Africa, South America, Indonesia, Australia, and Canada.[48] In January 2022, BYD, for example, was granted a contract by the Chilean Ministry of Mining to extract 80,000 tonnes of metallic lithium for US$61 million,[49] although the deal was suspended by a court in Santiago two days later after an appeal by the local governor and a group of indigenous communities on the grounds that the bidding process violated the principles of environmental protection and economic development.[50] In May, however, BYD had reportedly identified six lithium mines for acquisition in Africa that would yield one million tonnes of lithium carbonate — enough to guarantee the company's production for a full decade.[51]

Downstream of mining, China dominates production at every stage of the battery supply chain, from the fabrication of the positive and negative electrodes to the manufacturing of the cells and their assembly into modules and then battery packs.[52] About 75 percent of the global production of battery cells occurs in China, as does 70 percent of production of specialised cathodes, and 85 percent of anode materials. China also produces 66 percent of separators and 62 percent of electrolytes.[53]

The Epic Rush for Lithium

In June 2021, CATL opened the world's largest battery plant, in Yibin, Sichuan province, with a total investment of sixty-four billion yuan (US$9 billion).[54] The plant has capacity to produce thirty gigawatt hours annually. By the end of September 2022, a Chinese newspaper had counted twenty-six new projects to expand battery production in China in that year,[55] involving all the largest battery producers, and a cumulative investment of 290 billion yuan (US$40.7 billion).

Collectively, they would account for a total production capacity of 820 gigawatt hours annually. According to China's Ministry of Industry and Information Technology, national lithium-ion battery production in the first half of 2022 exceeded 280 gigawatt hours, which was a year-on-year increase of 150 percent.[56] CATL's total electric battery production capacity alone was set to reach 440 gigawatt hours by the end of 2022, and the company expected to enter the one terawatt hour (TWh) era by 2025. By 2030, global battery production capacity is expected to exceed three terawatt hours, of which China will account for about 45 percent.[57]

This headlong expansion of battery production has driven up the price of lithium relentlessly. As more exploration has taken place, estimated global lithium reserves increased from 3.4 million metric tonnes in 2001 to 21 million metric tonnes in 2020.[58] In May 2022, a majority stake in a lithium mine in Sichuan province sold for two billion yuan (US$298.6 million) on the auction platform of online retailer JD.com 京东, which was 596 times the opening price.[59] By September 2022, the price of lithium carbonate was hovering around 500,000 yuan (US$72,200) per tonne, compared with only 40,000 yuan (US$5,700) a year earlier.[60] On 28 October, the price was 559,000 yuan (US$76,700) per tonne.[61] By the end of February 2023, however, the price of lithium carbonate had again fallen below the 400,000 yuan (US$57,500) per tonne mark, a drop of 21.6% from the beginning of the year. According to Robin Zeng of CATL, current global reserves of lithium can produce 160 terawatt hours of lithium batteries, so there is no shortage,[63] but there is pressure on supply until investment in exploration and mining can catch up. According to the International Energy Agency (IEA), lithium shortages could occur by 2025 — before an expansion in mining can be fully implemented.[64] Because of the complicated processes involved, lithium mining has a very long lead time. According to an IEA report, lithium mines can take an average of 16.5 years to develop 'from discovery to operation'.[65]

With the sharp increase in the price of lithium since 2021, the largest profits in China are currently going to the upstream mining companies rather than the battery or EV manufacturers. In the second quarter of 2022, for example, companies extracting lithium from brine achieved a gross profit margin of more than 90 percent, while the gross profit margin of battery manufacturers was less than 15 percent and as low as 10 percent.[66] In the first three quarters of 2022, the net profits of nine Chinese-listed lithium mining companies more than doubled.[67] These included market leaders Tianqi Lithium 天齐锂业 with 15.98 billion yuan (US$2.19 billion) and Ganfeng Lithium 赣锋锂业 with 14.79 billion yuan (US$2.02 billion).

Tianqi Lithium holds a controlling stake in Chile's largest lithium producer, Sociedad Química y Minera de Chile.[68] Ganfeng Lithium — which supplies lithium to Tesla as well as BMW, Volkswagen, and others[69] — obtains most of its lithium from the Mount Marion mine in Australia (which holds the world's second-largest reserves of high-grade lithium concentrate), in which it holds a 50 percent share.[70]

With the highest profits concentrated in upstream mining, China's lithium battery industry in 2022 was marked by a trend of vertical integration, in which electric battery companies invested in raw materials and raw material companies produced batteries. In April 2022, BYD, for example, made an investment in a lithium mining and battery factory project in Yichun, Sichuan province, of 28.5 billion yuan (US$4.1 billion).[71] In July, mining company Ganfeng Lithium started construction of a 5.4 billion yuan (US$758.6 million) battery production base in Chongqing.[72] Much of the focus of new lithium mining projects in China is in Sichuan, which contains 6.1 percent of global and 57 percent of China's lithium ore reserves. By 2025, Sichuan could have a total lithium mining capacity of five million tonnes.[73]

Alternatives: Can Anything Replace Lithium?

Lithium-ion batteries currently constitute as much as 99 percent of all batteries used in transportation. A more sustainable type of lithium battery, the solid-state battery, is expected to be used in EVs from 2025. Solid-state batteries use solid ceramic material instead of liquid electrolytes, making the batteries lighter, faster to charge, and cheaper. They will reduce the carbon footprint of an EV battery by 24 percent. Although these batteries use up to 35 percent more lithium than current lithium-ion batteries, they use far less graphite and cobalt.[74]

Alternative types of batteries that do not operate with lithium or the other precious metals have been under development for decades, but none of these has reached the stage of mass production. This, however, is about to change. In October 2022, CATL announced that it would start mass producing sodium-ion batteries in 2023,[75] and it is not alone. In September

2022, there were 36 companies listed on China's main stock markets involved in the development of sodium-ion batteries, some of which will start to mass produce cathode and electrode materials for sodium-ion batteries in 2023.[76] Sodium-ion batteries are 20–30 percent cheaper than lithium-ion batteries because they do not require lithium, cobalt, nickel, or manganese. The energy density of sodium-ion batteries is inferior to lithium-ion batteries, however, so they are so far mostly used in small vehicles operating over short distances, such as two-wheeled scooters.[77]

Toyota, Hyundai, and BMW have released cars with hydrogen fuel cell batteries that convert hydrogen into electricity using a hydrogen tank. In May 2022, Great Wall Motors 长城汽车 announced plans to launch a new hydrogen fuel cell brand. Hydrogen-powered vehicles produce waste emissions of water instead of carbon dioxide. These batteries are, however, still very expensive. The technology depends on a highly complex production chain, and hydrogen refuelling stations are much more costly to construct than regular EV recharging stations.[78] Nevertheless, the hydrogen energy industry in China has strong government backing and the fuel cell vehicle industry is being pushed forward in five national fuel cell vehicle demonstration clusters. The number of fuel cell vehicles is still small: from August 2021 to August 2022, a total of 2,590 number plates were issued for fuel cell vehicles in the five demonstration clusters.[79]

Another emerging battery technology is redox flow batteries that use the malleable metal vanadium. Vanadium batteries are much safer than lithium-ion batteries, have a long lifecycle, and are almost completely recyclable; China has 39 percent of global vanadium reserves. So far, such batteries have only been used for large-scale power storage for electricity grids as current versions have relatively low energy density.[80] Still other options that are currently in the exploratory research stage include batteries using seawater, iron, magnesium, hemp, and silicon.[81] For now, however, lithium is king, and China is the centre of the EV world.

China's 'Green Steel':

Unchaining from Australia

HONGZHANG XU

CHINA'S 'GREEN STEEL': UNCHAINING FROM AUSTRALIA

Hongzhang Xu

IN JUNE 2022, the Chinese Ministry of Ecology and Environment and sixteen other government departments jointly released their *National Climate Change Adaptation Strategy 2035*.[1] The document outlined plans for the People's Republic of China (PRC) to become a 'climate-resilient society' by 2035. It emphasised the need for adaptation and mitigation — namely, reducing emissions through new technologies and renewable energy.

Coming less than two years after President Xi Jinping announced the PRC's 2030–2060 targets, the strategy reaffirms China's determination to achieve its decarbonisation goals:

a peak in carbon dioxide emissions before 2030 and achieving carbon neutrality before 2060.[2]

The iron and steel industry is the second-largest carbon emitter in China and accounts for about 17 percent of its total emissions.[3] 'Green steel', made from a carbon-free reductant such as hydrogen (produced using renewable energy resources) instead of carbon monoxide (from coal), is being hailed by scientists and policymakers as a global solution for reducing carbon emissions.[4] China's push towards greener steel production, even though this cannot happen overnight and requires costly changes within the industry, will have a profound impact on Australia's export industry.

Decarbonising the Steel Industry

Adopting low-emission technologies is just one of the three main approaches the PRC has adopted to accelerate the decarbonisation of its steel industry.

Less production means fewer emissions. In the early 2010s, China addressed the issue of overproduction by closing steel mills that failed to meet pollutant emission and energy consumption standards. In 2018, the Ministry of Industry and Information Technology (MIIT) set up 'capacity replacement' rules under which a new steel mill can only be built if its capacity is less than 80 percent of the one it is replacing.[5] Essentially, new steel mills are required to produce less.

Since the 2030–2060 targets were announced in September 2020, the steel sector has moved further to reduce steel output.[6] In 2021, China's crude steel output was 1.03 billion tonnes — a 3 percent drop from the previous year.[7] It was the first decrease in six years.

Steel output during the first five months of 2022 dropped a further 3.81 million tonnes, or 8.7 percent year-on-year.[8]

China also plans to use more scrap steel as feedstock, instead of iron ore, to achieve a circular economy[9] for environmental and political purposes. This will help China to decarbonise its steel sector and reduce reliance on iron ore imports from Australia.[10] Scrap steel comes from various sources including offcuts from the steel industry itself as well as obsolete materials, such as railway tracks, ships, cars, and steel cans. The proportion of China's crude steel production from scrap steel is still relatively low, lagging far behind other big steel producers, like the European Union and the United States, where steel produced from scrap accounts for half of all production.[11] However, things are changing quickly. In 2020, China used 220.3 million tonnes of scrap to produce 20.7 percent of its crude steel, replacing 410 million tonnes of iron ore.[12] The lifting of China's ban on imports of scrap steel in January 2021 is a clear sign of an increased domestic demand for recyclable steel.[13] Experts have projected an increase of about 500 million tonnes in China's domestic scrap steel resources in the next three decades, with the majority coming from end-of-life steel-containing products.[14]

Hydrogen-Based Steelmaking Comes Slowly and With a Big Price Tag

There are two ways hydrogen can be used in steelmaking: as an auxiliary reducing agent injected into a blast furnace (technically referred to as H_2-BF) or as the sole reducing agent in a process known as direct reduction of iron (H_2-DRI).[15] Although the former shows promise, the cooling effect of hydrogen limits injection rates (the volume of hydrogen being injected per minute). This method reduces emissions by only about 15 percent.[16] The second method, on the other hand, requires high-quality iron ore with an iron content of 67 percent or more. High-grade ores are in short supply and can be very costly to produce.[17]

In January 2022, the MIIT, the National Development and Reform Commission, and the Ministry of Ecology and Environment jointly published the *Guiding Opinion on Promoting High-Quality Development of the Iron and Steel Industry*,[18] which stipulates that the steel industry should invest 1.5 percent of its profits in developing green technologies, including the use of hydrogen in production. This is the first time hydrogen-based steelmaking has been formally included in national policy.

Although major state-owned steelmakers like Baowu Steel (the world's top steel producer since 2020) and Ansteel Group have started trialling hydrogen-based steel production, this does not mean China is already entering a new era of carbon-free steelmaking. A shift towards hydrogen entails total reconstruction of the steel industry and its value chain, from producing goods to delivering products.[19]

More than 92 percent of Chinese steel is still produced using blast furnace–basic oxygen furnaces (BF-BOFs) with coking coal acting as both a heating source and a reductant.[20] The average age of China's BF-BOF mills is just over eight years, with most built or rebuilt to meet the high standards on air pollutants emissions set in the early 2010s.[21] Upgrading or rebuilding steel mills is not only

China is the world's largest importer of iron ore
Source: Eugene, Adobe Stock

wasteful but also financially risky as new technologies are still under development.

So, for now, reducing steel output remains the primary approach to reducing emissions[22] and is projected to account for 45 percent of China's steel industry decarbonisation by 2060.[23] The use of scrap will reduce emissions by another 39 percent; hydrogen's contribution will be less than 10 percent.[24]

End of the Road for Australian Iron Ore?

China is the world's largest importer of iron ore. It imports about one billion tonnes of iron ore annually,[25]

constituting 82.3 percent of its iron ore consumption. Australian iron ore accounts for about 67 percent of the total imports.[26]

Australia is, however, close to losing its place as China's number one supplier, for several reasons. First, China has been looking for new suppliers of high-grade iron ore. It has previously turned to Brazilian producers[27] and more recently to Guinea to wean itself off reliance on Australia.[28] Second, China is unhappy with Australia's domination of the pricing of iron ore. To counter this, Beijing plans to set up a centrally controlled group that will act on behalf of all Chinese companies to get lower prices through bulk purchases.[29] Last but not least, China's move to decarbonise its steel sector will reduce demand for Australia's iron ore as well as other raw materials such as coking coal. Recent research projects Australian coal exports will fall by 20 percent by 2025.[30]

Australia has abundant natural resources, but it is not sustainable for its economy and environment to depend on metallurgical coal and iron ore exports to China. Australian policymakers and investors must consider a more sustainable use of Australia's resources, such as shifting to domestic manufacturing of 'green' steel, which, aided by Australia's abundant solar and wind resources, will be of significant value to Australia's future exports.[31]

聚焦

FOCUS: WOMEN

IN CHAINS

WHAT HAVE WE LEARNED FROM 'THE WOMAN IN CHAINS'?

Joel Wing-Lun

DURING THE CHILLY days before the Lunar New Year of 2022, a video began circulating on Chinese social media of a woman standing alone in an outdoor shed wearing a thin pink sweater.[1] She is shackled to the wall by a chain around her neck. The man behind the camera asks if she is cold, but it is unclear whether she can understand. The woman, whom authorities referred to first as Ms Yang, and later as Xiao Huamei 小花梅 ('Little Plum Blossom'), was revealed to be the wife of a Mr Dong from Feng county, Jiangsu province. Although the birth-control policies in the People's Republic of China (PRC) have only recently been relaxed to allow three children per couple, Ms Yang had given birth to eight children, seven of whom were sons.

The video is shocking and deeply disturbing. On the Chinese internet, it stirred an outpouring of anger, which overcame China's internet restrictions and united liberals, feminists, and nationalists in outrage. The woman became known as 'the mother of eight children' 八孩母亲 or 'the woman in chains' 铁链女. According to *The New York Times*, Weibo posts about the woman garnered more than 10 billion views, 'rivaling those about the Beijing Winter Olympics'.[2]

Part of this outrage was directed at the government response. Within two weeks, local governments issued four contradictory statements. On 28 January, a day after the video went viral, officials in Feng county claimed that Ms Yang was legally married to Mr Dong and was restrained because of mental illness.[3] Two days later, they claimed Mr Dong's late father had found Ms Yang begging on the street and local officials had found her competent to consent to marry the younger Mr Dong.[4]

Then, on 2 February, the Xuzhou City government — which has jurisdiction over Feng county — announced that Little Plum Blossom had travelled east with a Ms Sang from her hometown in Yunnan province in south-western China, ostensibly to seek treatment for her mental illness, when she went missing.[5] Finally, on 10 February, Xuzhou authorities reported that Mr Dong, Ms Sang, and Ms Sang's husband, a Mr Shi, had been arrested and charged with trafficking a woman, *guaimai funü zui* 拐卖妇女罪, and that the Feng county government was providing support to Ms Yang and her children.[6]

Journalists and internet sleuths have continued to challenge the authorities' claims. Journalists who visited Little Plum Blossom's supposed hometown in Yunnan have cast doubt on her identity. Two women who travelled to Feng county to conduct their own inquiries were arrested. The authorities' initial failure to detect the trafficked woman and her captivity as well as their lack of appropriate action when the story broke damaged their credibility among sceptical internet users.

In response to the public uproar, seventeen local officials lost their jobs. The provincial government investigated and, on 29 March, the deputy director of the Xuzhou Public Security Bureau was arrested. Also in March, Premier Li Keqiang urged stricter enforcement of trafficking laws and announced measures to reunite trafficked women and children with their natal families.[7]

The case of Little Plum Blossom has reverberated throughout China in a way that previous trafficking cases have not. But the contours of her story, as far they can be known, are familiar from a long history of women being sold into marriage,

What have we learned from 'the Woman in Chains' 铁链女?
Source: Nikhil, Flickr

and from the fact that thousands of women and children are still bought and sold each year despite human trafficking being punishable by up to ten years in prison or even the death penalty. The trade in women and children is fuelled by poverty, inequality, and, despite decades of government efforts to persuade people that daughters are just as valuable as sons, the ongoing pressure, especially in rural communities, to produce a male heir to continue the family line. The One-Child Policy introduced at the beginning of the 1980s led to skewed sex ratios that have also contributed to trafficking as families seek desperately to obtain wives for their sons. The Feng county case shows that at least some local officials must have been looking the other way.

Yet, the case also shows that, in certain contexts, the line between 'legitimate' marriage and the purchase of a woman or girl can be blurry at best. If history is any guide, ending the sale of women and children would require rethinking what forms of marriage and family are acceptable on both a local and a national scale.

Qing China

Trade in women and children was not, and is not, limited to China. As late as the nineteenth century, selling one's wife — not to mention slavery — was accepted practice in England, North America, and Australia. Human trafficking continues across the globe today. However, the historical sale of women and children in China had characteristics shaped by neo-Confucian ideology and skewed sex ratios. The common understanding in late imperial China was that sons supported their parents and performed vital ancestral rites. Daughters married out and provided labour for their husband's family. A strong preference for sons led to widespread female infanticide, which was conceived of as a kind of 'postnatal abortion'.[8] This differed even from Tokugawa Japan (1603–1867), where infanticide was common but parents aimed to keep a balance of sons and daughters. Research by James Lee and Wang Feng shows that in some populations in Qing (1644–1911) China, in some years, up to 40 percent of female births ended in infanticide.[9]

Sons may have been prized over daughters, but every parent hoped their son would marry and produce male heirs as well. Fewer girls reaching maturity in a community meant fewer wives available for the community's sons. The marriage market was real, and men's marriage prospects were determined by their class and status. A wealthy man might take a wife and a concubine (multiplying their chance of producing sons), whereas a poor man might have no marriage prospects at all. Unmarried men were known disparagingly as 'bare sticks', *guanggun* 光棍. Sexually frustrated and unable to fulfill their ritual obligations to their family and their ancestors, these men were considered a threat to social order. As the empire expanded, single men migrated to the frontiers as either soldiers or settlers. Many married local women, who might have consented, been coerced, or sold outright.

Women's experience of marriage differed dramatically depending on status and class, including, for example, if they were a primary wife or a secondary wife or concubine. However, for women, marriage was almost universal.

Women in imperial China were bought and sold, and most of these sales occurred within the framework of marriage. Marriage was typically conceived of as a transaction, a contract not between the bride and groom but between their respective families.[10] The groom's family would pay a bride price, and the bride's family would provide her with a dowry. The bride price was usually larger than the dowry and was considered compensation for the bride's family having raised her. That said, there could be considerable variation in marriage practices even within a single community. My own research in Guizhou, in what was then the Qing's south-western frontier, indicates that some young women chose their own marriage partners and received a say in how their dowries were spent. Other girls were married off as children to even younger boys, and were raised by, and in turn toiled for, their husband's family.

One important factor affecting a woman's experience of marriage was how far from her husband's home was her natal village. If close, a woman's birth family might provide her with regular material and emotional support and intercede on her behalf in disputes with her husband and his family. In some communities, including those I have studied in Guizhou, married women might spend weeks or months visiting their natal home. In contrast, if a woman married or was sold far from home, she would be separated from her kin and left with no-one to turn to if she was treated badly.

In late imperial China, only a few wealthier women received an education, so it can be difficult to recover the voices of poor women who were bought and sold. Yet, records show the difficult choices some women faced to keep themselves and their families alive. In a legal case from 1749 analysed by Matthew Sommer, the indebted husband of a woman surnamed Zhang sold her loom and asked her 'to sleep with his creditor'.[11] When she refused, he sold their daughter. Zhang ultimately killed her husband, aided by her mother and sister, in what Sommer calls 'an extreme but telling example of a woman's natal family standing up for her'.

Ning Lao Taitai 宁老太太, an elderly woman from Shandong interviewed extensively by American social worker Ida Pruitt in the 1930s, recounted how, in the late nineteenth century, her opium-addicted husband sold her younger daughter, twice. The first time, she retrieved her child after challenging the buyer on the legality of the sale. The second time, after tracking down the child, she was convinced by the buyer, the childless second wife of a wealthy official, that her daughter would have a better life with them.

The poor woman conceded, 'I knew that her words were true, so I went away.'[12]

The Republican Era and the Mao Years

The turn of the twentieth century saw a change in elite attitudes to the place of women in the state and society. Reformers like Liang Qichao 梁啟超 (1873–1929) and feminist writers like He-Yin Zhen 何殷震 (1884–1920?), Bing Xin 冰心 (1900–1999), and Ding Ling 丁玲 (1904–1986) critiqued the patriarchal order and advocated for women's education and independence. A small cohort of women and girls were educated in modern schools, albeit with the expectation on the part of male reformers that

they would make better wives and mothers in the service of the modern nation.

Intellectuals were concerned about the plight of rural women and what it said about the nation they were trying to build. Shen Congwen 沈从文 (1902–1988) wrote of the child bride Xiaoxiao 萧萧, married at age eleven to her two-year-old husband.[13] Coerced into sex by an older farmhand, she is threatened with drowning or resale when her pregnancy is discovered. Her life is saved when she gives birth to a son whom the family agrees to raise. Cui'er 翠儿, a protagonist in a story by Bing Xin, is less fortunate: she is no older than fourteen when her mother-in-law beats her to death.[14]

Agitation by elites led to government legislation. In 1910, a year before the fall of the dynasty, the Qing attempted to outlaw slavery and human trafficking. As Mara Yue Du observes, the Republican civil code of 1929–1930 reconfigured marriage from a contract between the parents of the betrothed to one between the bride and the groom, implying that their consent would be required.[15] However, the sale of women and children continued throughout the Republican era.

Woman and child wearing a tiger hat, circa 1920
Source: Sidney D. Gamble Photographs Collection

As Johanna Ransmeier writes, urbanisation and commercialisation, wartime conditions, and long-distance transportation created new opportunities for traffickers and matchmakers to exploit vulnerable people.[16]

Mao Zedong claimed that women's liberation was vital to the revolution he would go on to lead. In his 1927 *Report on an Investigation of the Peasant Movement in Hunan*, Mao described rural women as oppressed by the state, the lineage, religious authority, and their husbands.[17] Women fought with the communists against the nationalists and the Japanese, though as David Goodman writes, communist leaders prioritised 'economic mobilisation' over 'raising women's political consciousness'.[18] After the PRC was established in 1949, the *Marriage Law* of 1950 forbade forced marriages and interference in selecting a partner by third parties, including parents.[19] It prohibited polygamy and child marriage and allowed a woman to sue her husband for divorce. Yet, as Gail Hershatter has shown, women seeking a divorce faced intense pressure, and sometimes violence, from their families and even local officials, making divorce a difficult, even dangerous, choice.[20]

Less attention has been paid to trafficking under Mao, but as writer He Qinglian observes, the economic calamity and famine that followed the Great Leap Forward (1958–1962) were ideal conditions for human traffickers.[21] She suggests that the sale of women was an accepted strategy for survival in poor rural communities. She also recalls a young boy from her block who was kidnapped off the street (boys could be 'adopted' as heirs by childless couples). National census data suggest that female infanticide declined under Mao, but girls were more likely to die of neglect than boys during the famine of 1959–1961.[22] While reliable statistics are hard to come by, human trafficking may have been more difficult under Mao given the tight social and ideological controls.

Reform and Opening

The reforms of the 1980s gave the trade in women and children a new lease on life. The social and economic reforms implemented under Deng Xiaoping allowed for more physical and economic mobility while contributing to widening inequality. At the same time, strict birth-control policies limited most couples to a single child, though many families, especially in rural areas, found ways around them. These policies made it harder to ensure a son and male heir, which remained an imperative for many families despite efforts to promote daughters as equally valuable. By the late 1980s, sex-selective abortion and the abandonment of female infants contributed to more than 110 male births being reported for every 100 registered female births.[23]

As in earlier periods, poverty, skewed sex ratios, and the continued importance of male heirs fuelled the trade in women and children. A pioneering account of human trafficking from 1989 identifies Xuzhou, the regional transportation hub in northern Jiangsu that includes Feng county, as the epicentre of a burgeoning trade in women across provincial lines. It claims that between 1986 and 1989, 48,100 women were purchased in Xuzhou alone.[24] Xuzhou Train Station was a key nexus in the trade, and forty local taxi drivers helped traffic 101 women and girls as young as thirteen.

Women and children were typically trafficked from poorer 'peripheral' provinces to 'core' provinces in the north and east. The authors of the 1989 report alleged that in one village in Xuzhou, two-thirds of young wives had been purchased from the south-western provinces of Yunnan, Sichuan, and Guizhou. More recent studies show this pattern continuing in the twenty-first century. Tiantian Zheng calculates that more than 90,000 women and children were sold in China between 2000 and 2013, with more than 90 percent coming from poor provinces in south-western and central China.²⁵ Others came from neighbouring countries including Vietnam, Myanmar, and North Korea. During my fieldwork in Guizhou in 2018 and 2019, women recalled children being snatched from the side of the road. Far from home and, in the case of children, sometimes unregistered under the household registration system, *hukou* 戶口, women and children could find it difficult to run away. Young children might not even know the names or address of their parents.

Accounts of human trafficking suggest a degree of social acceptance, particularly in communities where sales of women and children are more common. They also show something of the slippery slope between legal marriages and illegal trafficking. A male villager quoted in the 1989 report asks: 'What is the difference between buying [a wife] from a matchmaker [*meiren* 媒人] or from a trafficker [*fanzi* 贩子]? I really don't get why buying a woman from a matchmaker is legal, but buying a woman from a trafficker is illegal.'²⁶ While the villager saw these transactions as comparable, a trafficker selling women across provincial lines could make ten times as much as an ordinary matchmaker, usually a woman, would receive in Yunnan.

The line between trafficking and legal marriage has not always been clear to the trafficked women either. And although they were initially sold to their husbands, many of them eventually chose to stay. A woman interviewed by researchers in the early 2000s was acutely conscious that she had been trafficked.²⁷ In 1990, when she was seventeen years old, she was tricked on to a train in Kunming, Yunnan, then held by a trafficker in Xuzhou. He locked her in a room, where prospective buyers, *maizhu* 买主, came to inspect her. Her eventual buyer — her husband — also kept her locked up. When she refused food and drink, he threatened to sell her on to an older man in his seventies or eighties. She said that in the early years, she ran away several times, but stopped running away when her child, born in 1991, was older.

Another woman's account was more ambivalent. In 1987, aged twenty-one, she agreed to travel from Yunnan to Shandong to marry a man she had never met.

His family gave her parents a few hundred yuan and paid her travel expenses. She felt cheated when she discovered that her husband was not as well off as the broker claimed, but he treated her well, buying her rice because she was unused to the wheat eaten in northern China. She described her feelings nearly two decades later: 'He [her husband] treated me well, it's only that I was homesick ... They [her husband's family] said: "What do you mean, you're homesick? Your parents are both dead."' [28]

She continued: 'If I went home I would feel out of place. No matter how good my home is, it would still feel out of place. I will stay at this [her husband's] home. Even if it's no good, I have to make do.'

A New Era?

Despite the attention brought to the issue by the case of Little Plum Blossom, it is unlikely that public outrage or even legislation will end the sale of women and children in China. For one thing, it is questionable whether there is the political will to do so, given the leadership's general disinterest in addressing most kinds of discrimination faced by women.

In recent years, the government has put in place regressive policies promoting traditional gender roles, including a new divorce law making it harder for women to leave their husbands. [29] As has been widely reported, for the first time in decades, the new twenty-four-member Communist Party of China (CPC) Politburo includes no women (see Focus, 'The Communist Party of China: Where Are the Women?', pp.147–153). Easing birth-control policies could balance sex ratios over time, reducing demand for trafficked brides. Authorities have proposed increasing criminal penalties for buyers of women and children — currently no more than three years in prison — to equal those of the traffickers themselves. But politics and policy are only part of the problem.

One of the most gut-wrenching moments of the video from Feng county comes in its opening seconds. The videographer is led to the shed by one of the woman's young sons. He has no sense that there is anything wrong and explains that he brings his mother food every day. In an earlier video, filmed by the Feng county government to promote the success of its targeted poverty alleviation program, Mr Dong proudly shows off his seven sons without any hint that he is aware of committing a crime.[30] The local government's blindness towards the woman who gave birth to these children suggests that her sale and detention were acceptable in the local community.

Demographic and material constraints mean that not every man will be able to marry and produce a male heir. Ending the sale of women and children would require, among other things, rethinking marriage and the family so that 'success' is not measured by the number of sons. The stigmatisation of unmarried men and women and of childless couples would have to end and forced marriages and human trafficking become socially unacceptable as well as illegal. The case of Little Plum Blossom has drawn a wave of attention to the plight of trafficked women. The government has signalled a crackdown, but can it address the root causes, particularly poverty, inequality, and patriarchy?

VIOLENCE AGAINST WOMEN: CAN THE LAW HELP?

Pan Wang

THE FURORE surrounding the chilling internet video of 'Xiaohuamei' 小花梅 or 'Little Plum Blossom', the chained woman in Jiangsu, had barely died down when a restaurant surveillance camera captured more disturbing vision of violent and misogynistic behaviour that stunned the world and once again put gender relations in the People's Republic of China (PRC) under the spotlight.[1]

It is 2.40am on 10 June 2022. Three young women are dining in a barbecue restaurant in Tangshan, Hebei province, when a middle-aged man — a stranger — approaches one of the women and puts his hand on her back. The woman, who is dressed in white, pushes his arm away and raises her voice at him, questioning his intention, and telling him to leave her alone. The man slaps the woman in the face. While she stands up to fight back, one of her friends (dressed in black) breaks a beer bottle on the man's head. The woman in black is pulled away immediately and beaten by the man and two of his companions. Meanwhile, several other men drag the woman in white outside by the hair; the harasser kicks her repeatedly and smashes a beer bottle on her head. The video ends with the woman lying on the ground, covered in blood, and it is unclear what has happened to her friends off-camera.

As with 'the woman in chains', this incident triggered a nationwide uproar on social media, with more than 4.8 billion views of the leaked surveillance footage within a few days of it appearing on Sina Weibo.[2] It resonated with many other gender-based acts of violence caught on camera, including the high-profile domestic violence case of Kim Lee, an American, who shared photos of her bruises online in 2013 after being brutally beaten by Li Yang, her Chinese husband and creator of the famous English learning method Crazy English.[3] Then there was footage of a woman being attacked by a man in a Beijing hotel in 2016, with no bystanders or staff stepping in to stop the assault;[4] the livestreamed murder of Tibetan vlogger Lhamo 拉姆, who was set on fire by her ex-husband in 2020 as her horrified followers watched;[5] and a husband frenetically beating his wife right next to their toddler at home in Xi'an, Shaanxi province, in 2022.[6]

Wave after wave, these stories spilled into the public consciousness. Each time they triggered momentary outrage, which then subsided until the next wave rose. Violence against women has been widespread in China but hidden from sight; however, it seems to have become more prominent in recent years, triggered by heightened misogyny that has come about as a backlash against rising feminism. What does it tell us about gender relations, the rule of law, and social morality in China today?

Gender Relations

In 1949, women in the PRC gained constitutional rights equal to those of men as well as increased mobility and higher than ever social and economic status. They were aided by the banning of arranged marriages and concubinage and, in the mid-1950s, by Mao Zedong's dictum that 'women hold up half the sky' (he was commenting on a report that when a village decided to allocate women the same number of 'work points' as men, productivity tripled). However, this did not result in a fundamental change in gender relations. China remains a modern patriarchal society in which most of the power is held by men at all levels of the social and political hierarchy, from the party-state down to the

Wave after wave, stories of gender-based acts of violence spilled into the public consciousness in 2022
Source: Mika Baumeister, Unsplash

village level. And women still live with various forms of gender inequality, from disparity in wages and educational opportunities, workplace discrimination, and unfair distribution of domestic labour, to rampant sexual harassment, and domestic violence. Tech-savvy feminists have been calling out these issues on social media for years — exemplified by the 'Bloody Brides against Domestic Violence' campaign in 2012, in which young women wore red-spattered wedding gowns in public to draw attention to the problem; the #MeToo movement, which began in 2018; and the #SeeingFemaleWorkers campaign on Weibo in 2020 that called for the recognition of women's contribution during the COVID-19 pandemic.[7]

Despite official crackdowns on feminist protests, including the detention of the Feminist Five in 2015 for planning to protest sexual harassment on public transport, feminism has grown stronger in China in recent years, as exemplified by the growing feminist discourse (and its discontents), emerging feminist activities, and rising accusations against and condemnation of sexual offenders. This has been accompanied by a patriarchal, misogynistic backlash, causing a 'gender war' in cyberspace, where misogynistic sentiment fuels the use of sexist labels such as 'feminist whores' 女权娘 (Chinese feminists who criticise Chinese men harshly but behave warmly towards Western men),[8] 'green tea bitch' 绿茶娘 (an ambitious woman who pretends innocence), and sayings likening women older than thirty to tofu dregs 女人三十豆腐渣.[9] Intertwined with rising nationalistic sentiments, misogynistic labelling was also applied to former US House Speaker Nancy Pelosi during her high-profile visit to Taiwan in early August 2022: misogynistic nationalists mocked her as an 'old witch' 老巫婆, 'old devil' 佩老妖, and an 'unhinged hag' 神经病老太婆 on different online platforms.[10]

Looking back at the Tangshan restaurant attack, even as the majority of netizens were condemning the gang of abusive men, some were blaming the women for going out too late at night or for reacting too strongly to the harassers, with some even calling the attack 'a fight between street rogues'.[11] Authorities censored discussion of the attack, suspending 900 accounts on Chinese social media site Weibo for breaches of the rules against attacking national policies and stirring 'gender confrontation', and the messaging app WeChat removed several articles on this topic.[12] In the contemporary Chinese patriarchal environment — one that exists within an increasingly commercialised society — there is an emerging Sino-'manosphere' (described by Xiaoting Han and Chenjun Yin as 'a fragmented group of digital communities promoting misogynist discourses').[13] It is similar to the misogyny in Western societies that Laura Bates describes in her book *Men Who Hate Women*.[14] This also echoes some feminists' view that sexism functions to maintain the patriarchy and misogyny serves as its 'police force'.[15] From this perspective, wherever women are subjected to the degrading view that they are sexual commodities and inherently inferior to men, misogynistic men may resort to violence when confronted with women strongly defending their rights or 'breaking the gender rules'.

The Chinese government under Xi Jinping is campaigning for boys to toughen up and be more 'masculine'. It also promotes traditional feminine virtues and encourages women to have several (ideally, three) children. While the last has to do with the need to address China's demographic imbalance and ageing population, taken as a whole, these campaigns are about consolidating national identity, social stability, and familial harmony — at the same time as reinforcing patriarchal norms and structures. In this context, misogynistic violence could grow new roots.

Rule of Law

Violence against women takes various forms, including sex trafficking, domestic/intimate partner violence, and sexual harassment and assault — all of which can cause physical, mental, and emotional harm.[16] Soon after the PRC was founded, the Communist Party of China (CPC) implemented a *Marriage Law* (1950) that abolished arranged marriages, the extraction of money or gifts in connection with marriage, and the buying and selling of wives. However, these practices have never completely stopped. Trafficking of women (and children) still happens today in poor and remote areas of China despite a decline in reported trafficking cases, from 14,458 people in 2000 to 1,135 in 2021.[17] With marriage matchmaking and bride prices resurgent, many rural dwellers still do not distinguish between a legitimate marriage and the purchase of a woman.[18] The gender imbalance created by unknown incidents of female infanticide and sex-selective abortion in the years of the One-Child Policy has made many — particularly rural men — desperate. Statistics on the 'missing' girls resulting from sex-selective abortion vary; some sources indicate it is more than 40 million, while others suggest it is likely to be fewer because this figure includes unregistered births of girls.

Under Chinese criminal law, traffickers can be sentenced to five to ten years in prison or death, depending on the seriousness of the crime.[19] However, those who purchase women face maximum imprisonment of three years, and some can evade criminal liability if they do not obstruct the women from returning home if they wish.[20] Three years is less than what the criminal code prescribes for buying a panda (ten years in prison) or two rare birds (five years).[21] It is a good sign that China has launched a nationwide crackdown on human trafficking since the 'Xiaohuamei' incident, but, more must be done. At the very least, China's lawmakers must consider increasing the penalty for human trafficking, including for the buyers.

In 2001, the Chinese government first introduced the term 'domestic violence' 家庭暴力 into its revised *Marriage Law* and made it a valid reason for divorce (previous laws only prohibited mistreatment 虐待 and abandonment 遗弃 rather than domestic violence. The revised law, however, does not cover marital rape).[22] In 2016, China also introduced its first, belated *Anti–Domestic Violence Law*. This increased public awareness of domestic violence, as evidenced by a growing number of calls to police and anti-domestic-violence hotlines, as well as post-sharing about domestic violence on social media.[23] However, in practice, domestic violence tends to be downplayed by local police as 'a family affair' 家事. They are often unwilling to intervene, in part because the law

does not provide details about punishments for such violence.[24] Domestic violence remains rampant: according to the All-China Women's Federation, one woman experiences domestic violence every 7.4 seconds in China.[25] During the COVID-19 pandemic, this problem was amplified not only in China, but also worldwide, when lockdowns trapped women at home with abusive partners.[26]

China has implemented different regulatory frameworks to deal with sexual harassment and assault, including the kinds of gendered violence detailed above. These include the *Law on the Protection of Women's Rights and Interests* (2005), the *Public Security Penalties Law* (2012), the *Criminal Law* (2020), and the *Civil Code* (2020). However, these have not done as much as might be hoped to stem the tide of sexual harassment, assault, and gendered violence; there have been few wins among #MeToo cases, and many Chinese women do not report harassment or assault for fear of victim-shaming and for other reasons. There have also been cases in which the victims were punished and worse off after revealing their plight.[27]

It is reassuring that, after the Tangshan restaurant attack, the deputy chief of the Tangshan police bureau was removed from office for the delay in arresting the women's attackers and that the state launched a 100-day 'Thunderstorm' 雷霆风暴 campaign to 'crack down on illegal behaviours to eliminate security problems'.[28] It is also a relief that the Chinese authorities charged twenty-eight people with eleven different crimes two months after the incident. On 29 August, Chinese state broadcaster *CCTV* also released an eleven-minute segment featuring police officers' description of the attack and a brief account from one of the victims.[29]

However, to date, many questions remain unanswered about the shocking display of violence in Tangshan — for example, why was there no news conference on this incident? Why do the censors appear to be cracking down on internet discussion of the incident? Why is there no detailed information about the victims' injuries (with doctors claiming they had 'second-degree light injuries' and that their conditions were improving) and no direct word from any of the victims or their families? While there is a crackdown on gangs, there is no detailed information about the gangs' 'protective umbrella' (corrupt officials) despite the public loudly demanding answers on these issues.

Social Morality

'Cry out at the sight of injustice, give a hand when others are in need' 路见不平一声吼 该出手时就出手 are lyrics from *The Song of the Heroes* 好汉歌, the very popular theme song of the 1990s TV series *The Water Margin* 水浒传, which was adapted from one of China's four classic novels. This spirit, however, is fading in present-day China. In the security footage from Tangshan, it is disheartening to see that no other men stepped in to stop the violence, leaving the three women diners to defend themselves. In the middle of the fight, one woman bystander tried to intervene but was immediately dragged back by her partner. Others watched and filmed the attack: Were they scared about being beaten or being charged with civil liability if they hurt someone (as has happened in the past)? Did they even care about what was happening to the victims?

In recent decades, people have grown increasingly unwilling to help strangers in distress for fear of extortion, as indicated by online surveys run by Chinese state media including the *People's Daily* and Sina Weibo.[30] There have been several cases of individuals who helped elderly people who had fallen in public spaces but were sued by them as a result, leading to tremendous financial loss.[31] Chinese media have compared these cases with Aesop's fable *The Farmer and the Viper*, in which a kind-hearted farmer is killed by a viper after placing it inside his coat to keep it warm on a freezing day. There have been other incidents that have led to much agonised self-reflection, including that in which a two-year-old, Wang Yue 王悦 (known as Xiao Yueyue 小悦悦), was run over by two vehicles on 13 October 2011, with eighteen passers-by failing to help the little girl, who lay critically injured and bleeding for more than seven minutes before a woman (a rubbish collector) stopped to help. Wang died of severe brain damage within a week.[32] One witness confessed that she did not help because she was afraid of being prosecuted by the girl's family, who might have accused her of causing the child's injuries.[33]

At the time, the media was reporting rising numbers of staged accidents ('porcelain bumping' 碰瓷). These cases, together with reports of abuses of power, official corruption, toxic additives in food, and officials' and celebrities' extramarital affairs, run against the moral frameworks and 'positive energy' the state intends to build.[34] They have triggered widespread concern and debate about the decline of social ethics and morality in contemporary Chinese society. This widely shared perception of a moral crisis has also inspired soul-searching within society.[35] Gendered violence could be unavoidable in patriarchal societies. Whether a 'moral awakening' will result in positive changes will take time to see, as it requires the long-term efforts of both the state and the society working together to address gender inequality.

In a nutshell, violence against women in China reveals numerous issues: systemic inequality between men and women, rising misogyny, loopholes in the criminal justice system, gang violence connected to official corruption, and a general deterioration in the moral sphere. For China to build a genuinely harmonious, violence-free, and gender-equal society, profound reforms in education, law, policing, and social ethics must be made.

THE COMMUNIST PARTY OF CHINA: WHERE ARE THE WOMEN?

Junyi Cai

AT THE TWENTIETH National Congress of the Communist Party of China (CPC), not a single woman was elected to the Politburo. Women's participation in Chinese elite politics has stalled as men continue to dominate political power. The systemic underrepresentation of women in elite politics in the People's Republic of China (PRC) clashes with the party's propaganda about increasing 'the proportion of female cadres in the leading groups of state organs, ministries and commissions'.[1] Is there still hope for fair representation of women in the political arena?

Women in Elite Politics

Historically, only thirty-two women have ever held top positions in the state and the party at the national level 正/副国级, commonly referred to as 'party and state leaders' 党和国家领导人. Among them, only six women have ever been full members of the Politburo: Ye Qun 叶群 (1969–1971), Jiang Qing 江青 (1969–1976), Deng Yingchao 邓颖超 (1978–1985), Wu Yi 吴仪 (2002–2006), Liu Yandong 刘延东 (2007–2017), and Sun Chunlan 孙春兰 (2012–2022). Two women, Wu Guixian 吴桂贤 (1973–1977) and Chen Muhua 陈慕华 (1977–1987), were alternate members 候补委员.

Unlike her predecessors, Wu Yi was the first female leader to make it to the top political circle in post-reform China, and the first to do it without being married to a party or state leader. The three post-reform female members of the Politburo have also served as vice-premiers of the PRC's State Council at different times: Wu Yi (2003–2007) was in charge of foreign commerce, trade, and health affairs, and Liu Yandong (2013–2018) and Sun Chunlan (2018 to present) were overseeing the broad portfolios of health affairs, education, and sports. There has never been a woman on the Politburo Standing Committee (PSC), which is the most powerful governing body of the CPC and has seven members today.

Although there is nothing new about the underrepresentation of women in elite politics, 2022 marked the first time since 2002 that women were completely absent from the Politburo, which has twenty-four members. In the leadup to the Twentieth Party Congress, Chen Yiqin 谌贻琴, the only woman provincial party secretary in China; Shen Yueyue 沈跃跃, president of the All-China Women's Federation (ACWF); and Yu Hongqiu

喻红秋, deputy secretary of the Central Commission for Discipline Inspection of the CPC, were all spoken of as likely to be promoted to the Politburo. None was, and only Chen made it on to the CPC's Central Committee, becoming one of only eleven women among the 205 full members, who make up 5.36 percent of the membership. The only small improvement was in the proportion of female representation in the overall congress: of 2,296 delegates, 27 percent (621) were women, compared with the Nineteenth Party Congress, which had about 24 percent women delegates.

The lack of explicit institutional quotas means there are no guarantees or protection of women's representation in CPC politics. There have been no regulations or policies specifically aimed at promoting women cadres at the national level. In the latest Program for the Development of Chinese Women — a five-year plan for women's development in major aspects, including economic participation, health, education, participation in decision-making processes, and social welfare — strategies for political participation are vague and general. For example, 'a certain

Wu Yi meets governors of Hainan
Source: Philip McMaster, Flickr

percentage' rather than a specific goal is required for proportional representation.

Greater emphasis is given to promoting women at the local level. The most recent published research on female provincial leaders shows that thirty-one women were selected among 276 governors and deputy governors, or 11.2 percent, in 2018. Among the 2016–2017 cohort, there were thirty-four (9.1 percent) women among 375 members of provincial CPC standing committees.[2] According to the *Opinions on Further Improving the Work of Training and Selecting Female Cadres and Recruiting Female Party Members*, issued by the CPC in 2001, party committees, governments, people's congresses, and people's political consultative conferences at provincial and prefectural levels should each have 'more than one female cadre in its leadership'.[3] While the proportion is still low, the gender quota in local governance at least is explicitly regulated in official documents. Research shows that women's representation in provincial leadership is not just tokenism; these female leaders have similar qualifications to their male counterparts.[4] Although greater participation by women in elite politics does not necessarily mean that women's interests are being represented, it is a starting point.

Current scholarship suggests that Chinese political leaders, in both party and state systems, are selected and promoted based on the criteria of age, education, years of membership in the CPC, and relevant career trajectory.[5] While political allegiance continues to be the dominant factor, educational background and work experience have each played an important role in the progress of post–Mao Zedong elites in China. However, women are disadvantaged in all these aspects. They have fewer options to advance in politics because even official posts reflect a gendered division of labour, with women typically overseeing 'soft' areas such as health care and education while men manage such things as industry and development.[6] This deprives women of the relevant social networks required to achieve higher public positions.[7]

Representing Women's Interests within the State

If women have limited access to the core of state power, how likely is it that the party-state will formulate women-friendly laws and policies? Who represents women's interests within the Chinese state? Theoretically, the National People's Congress (NPC) is the highest organ of state power and has the authority to enact laws, amend the constitution, and elect members to the central state organs; and the State Council, chaired by the premier, functions as the highest administrative body. Women hold less than half of all seats in the NPC: there are 742 female deputies in the Thirteenth NPC, accounting for only 24.9 percent of the total of 2,980 seats. There are only nineteen women among the 175 members of the current Standing Committee of the NPC; of the Standing Committee's fourteen vice-chairpersons, only one is a woman. Given that the process of lawmaking in China is a 'multistage and multi-arena' process involving not only the NPC and its Standing Committee, but also the CPC and the executive branch of the state,[8] women's substantive representation in the process is severely constrained.

National organisations for women seem to be the party-state's primary forums for demonstrating its commitment to women's political participation while separating women from the mainstream political domain. There are two official women's organisations in China: the National Working Committee on Children and Women (NWCCW) 国务院妇女儿童工作委员会, which is a government bureaucracy, and the All-China Women's Federation 中华全国妇女联合会, a CPC-led 'mass organisation'.

The NWCCW, established in 1990, was the first and remains the only state-level government organ dedicated to the rights of women and children in China. Current director, Sun Chunlan, who is also the vice-premier of the State Council, has held the post since 2018. One of the committee's three deputy directors, Huang Xiaowei 黄晓薇, has also been the vice-president of the ACWF since 2018; the other two deputy directors are high-ranking male bureaucrats. The committee oversees China's National Program for Women's Development and National Program for Children's Development.

However, the efficacy of the NWCCW in advancing the position of women is questionable. It is not a policymaking institution, nor does it participate in the processes of policymaking by consultation

or other visible means. Other than the programs it oversees, it is hard to find any substantial contribution that it has been able to make to women's advancement. The absence of documentation of the NWCCW's work could be the result of its relationship with the ACWF, which supervises and guides its work — a 'mass organisation' in charge of a government organ.

The ACWF

The ACWF, established by the CPC in 1948, has played an important role in pushing forward laws that advance women's causes, including equality. The ACWF does not have any policymaking or legislative power, but it has the capacity to influence policymaking and legislative processes. An overlap in personnel also improves the likelihood of the ACWF's policy advocacy reaching policymakers: the presidents and vice-presidents of federations at all levels simultaneously belong to the standing committees of the people's congress at the same level. The ability of its representatives to directly submit bills and proposals to the NPC is convenient for the ACWF, but only to advocate for policies: it does not in any way guarantee that the federation's proposals will be approved. Lobbying from both local federations and the ACWF is essential to persuade policymakers to support their proposals. The ACWF has directly participated in the drafting and revising of national policies and laws including the *Marriage Law*, the *Law on the Protection of Women's Rights and Interests*, and the *Anti–Domestic Violence Law*. Because of its privileged relationship to the party, the ACWF does the work of a national women's governmental organ without being one. As a government official once pointed out, 'We have no specific governmental department [for women's advancement] in our country, but the Women's Federation takes this responsibility and functions as a national institution for the improvement of women's status.'[9]

Established during the party's revolutionary emergence, the ACWF has over the years prioritised party-directed assessments, inspections, activities, and projects. The ACWF's work predominantly serves the party-state's broader interests and ideological goals. When advancing women's rights has aligned with bigger plans, the ACWF has been able to leverage party and state support; when it has not, women's interests have been subordinated to the needs of the party-state.

Following Xi Jinping's emphasis on 'the unique role of women in the family', family-centred discourses have become the focus of ACWF's recent work, including its Family Happiness and Wellbeing Project 家家幸福安康工程 and the recently adopted *Family Education Promotion Law* 家庭教育促进法, both of which reinforce the domestic role of women, traditional constructions of masculinity and femininity, and rigid gender roles within a patriarchal family structure.

The Party-State's Gender Ideology under Xi

The sidelining of women in the PRC's political sphere reflects the retrogressive gender agenda under Xi Jinping. Xi has particularly highlighted his idea of *jia guo tianxia* 家国天下, which considers families 'an essential foundation' for national development and social harmony. In the name of promoting Chinese traditional culture, the party-state today draws on the conservative content of Confucianism — such as social harmony, respect for authority, obedience to one's superiors, devotion to the state, and protection of the family — to regulate people's behaviour, and women's behaviour in particular. In his speech to the new leadership of the ACWF in 2018, Xi pointed out that the federation 'needs to help women strike a balance between family and work to become women of the new era who can take up social responsibilities while contributing to their families'. The party invokes Confucian values in the domestic sphere in a way that associates traditional ideas about marriage and family, including women's domestic obligations and subservience to men, with the preservation of social stability.

The party-state has accordingly become more interventionist in matters of family and marriage. In 2020, the ACWF and the Ministry of Public Affairs jointly issued *The Instructions on Strengthening Educational Work on Coaching in Marriage and Family* 关于加强新时代婚姻家庭辅导教育工作的指导意见. The document asserts the importance of 'publicising and carrying forward the excellent traditional Chinese marriage and family culture' and the necessity of 'establishing pre-marital education and consultation' to reduce conflicts within the family.

The party-state's paternalistic agenda includes the now compulsory thirty-day 'cooling off' window for couples who want to divorce, the newly adopted *Family Education Promotion Law*, and the Three-Child Policy. The emphasis on 'women's unique role in promoting family virtues' exacerbates the essentialism of women's domestic role and, along with pressure on young women to marry and ideally have three children, further disadvantages women when it comes to working in the political sphere.

Conclusion

In a nutshell, it is unlikely there will be a significant improvement in women's status in Chinese politics in the coming years, in terms of both descriptive representation and substantial representation. Under President Xi, in 2022, a general deterioration in women's access to political power was clearly observed in tandem with the promotion of the 'traditional family virtues of the Chinese nation'.

154
155

三

CHAPTER 3
— ERASING
IDENTITIES

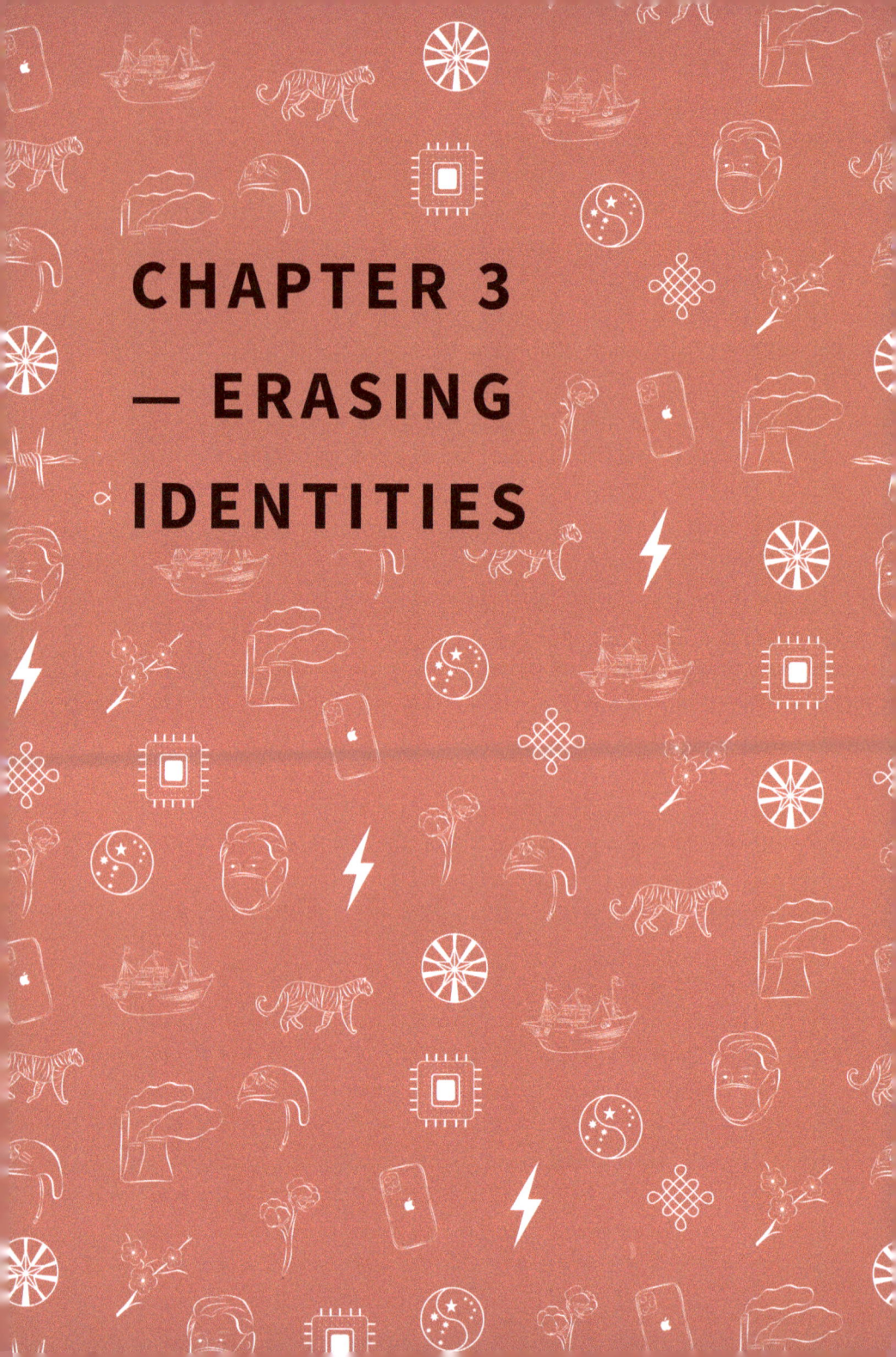

(IDENTITY) POLITICS IN COMMAND: XI JINPING IN XINJIANG

James A. Millward

Xi Jinping, the paramount leader of the People's Republic of China (PRC), toured eastern Xinjiang on a four-day 'investigative tour' 考察调研 in mid-July — his first visit to the Uyghur region since 2014. On the surface, the trip and its public messaging do not appear to differ much from those of previous general secretaries of the Communist Party of China (CPC) during their visits to Xinjiang. Flanked by Xinjiang Uyghur Autonomous Region party secretary Ma Xingrui 马兴瑞, Xinjiang governor Erkin Tuniyaz, and other officials, Xi took in cultural, economic, and tourist sights, stopped off at a village, reviewed the military, and sat as a guest in a Uyghur home. He engaged in 'informal chats' with common folk, like the Bingtuan (aka Xinjiang Production and Construction Corps or XPCC, 新疆生产建设兵团) farmer who just happened to be working in a cotton field when Xi showed up. Xi spoke of Xinjiang's fantastic development, stability, progress, and prosperity, and of its core position on the Silk Road Economic Belt. And he repeated the mantra that 'since ancient times, Xinjiang has been an inseparable part of our country'.

In that way, then, the official *Xinhua* images and reporting of Xi's remarks at various venues project an air of normalcy.[1] But the situation is not normal. Starting in 2017, central CPC policy directives led, at the height of the campaign in 2019, to the extralegal internment in camps of one to two million people based on dubious allegations of 'extremism',[2] and another half-million wrongfully imprisoned after processing through the judicial system.[3] In this mass roundup, a huge swathe of the academic, cultural, and political elites of Uyghur society were 'disappeared'. Meanwhile, Xinjiang cities have been excruciatingly securitised through high and low-tech means. Thousands of Uyghurs, Kazakhs, and other non-Han Xinjiang people abroad have been threatened and forced to seek asylum in democratic countries.[4] The United States, Canada, the European Union, the United Kingdom, and other states and international organisations have issued denunciations and findings of genocide and have slapped economic sanctions and import bans on Xinjiang individuals and entities. These entities include the Bingtuan, which is a massive state–corporate conglomerate, principal implementer of colonial policies, and serves as the third arm of control in Xinjiang (after the party and regional government). President Xi's Xinjiang policies, while not the only reason for the precipitous decline in Sino-US and Sino-European relations during Xi's tenure, are a leading contributor to that crisis and to plummeting international esteem for China generally.

The projection of a business-as-usual atmosphere stands out for what is not said. Xi's visit to Xinjiang University would have been poignant, for example, for those who know that its former president, Tashpolat Tiyip, is reported to have been sentenced to death as a 'two-faced official' (a political label meaning, in effect, insufficiently loyal non-Han cadre), or that the internationally renowned Professor Rahile Dawut was taken by state authorities in late 2017 with no news of her whereabouts since. The sense of strained normality is all the more salient when one considers what is missing from *Xinhua*'s account of Xi's remarks: in contrast with other official statements regarding Xinjiang over the past five years, in July, Xi did not mention terrorism, extremism, or separatism, or refer to the so-called vocational training centres (internment camps) that were the central feature of his policies.[5] Nor did he mention the labour transfer program that has displaced hundreds of thousands of Uyghurs, especially from the predominantly Uyghur south, from camps or villages into forced labour in factories in Xinjiang or across the PRC. Though implemented in the name of 'poverty alleviation', this proletarianisation of rural Uyghurs is breaking up families, keeping them from more lucrative entrepreneurial opportunities, and removing them from lands where they have lived for centuries.

The closest Xi came to acknowledging the elephant in the room — at least in the official account of the trip — was during a visit to the Eighth Division of the Bingtuan, in Shihezi, in northern Xinjiang. There, in praising the Bingtuan's contributions to stability through 'garrisoning the frontier' (Xi uses both the modern 安边固疆 and the historical 戍边), Xi was dog-whistling: due to its problematic past and costly overheads, the Bingtuan was disbanded after the Cultural Revolution, only to be re-established in 1981 due to the PRC's fear of Islamic movements. Everyone involved with the Bingtuan knows that despite its heroic self-image, it does not defend the PRC's border (the People's Liberation Army does that). Rather, protecting the 'frontier' means hedging against domestic unrest from Xinjiang's non-Han indigenous peoples.

The Bingtuan was formed when the victorious CPC settled 80,000 Kuomintang 国民党 soldiers in Xinjiang in 1949. It acquires and occupies land, promotes Han in-migration by offering land, and runs prisons and internment camps, including many of those built in the past few years. Bingtuan state farms and factories grow, purchase, and process much of Xinjiang's cotton, which makes up 80 percent of China's total cotton production. Because of its close involvement in repression and forced labour, the Bingtuan is now subject to international sanctions — throwing the global fibre, textile, and garment trade into confusion as fashion brands are forced to rethink their supply options.[6] Xi's call for the Bingtuan to 'adapt to new conditions and demands' 兵团要适应新形势新要求[7] is perhaps a reference to this recent global attention and the ban on imports of Bingtuan products to the United States.[8] Overall, however, by reiterating praise and support for the Bingtuan and its unspecified but well-known role in bolstering colonial occupation, Xi doubled down on his policy trajectory of the past several years.

Not Just Folk: Shifting Definitions of *Minzu*

The rhetorical messages of Xi's 2022 Xinjiang trip differ from those of past leaders in another way — one as significant as it is subtle. To appreciate the shift requires understanding some history of how the CPC has talked about non-Han peoples in the PRC. (While amounting to less than 10 percent of the total population, China's non-Han groups collectively, as a country, would be the ninth or tenth most populous in the world — about the size of Russia. So, they are not numerically insignificant.) Since the 1950s, the PRC has officially recognised fifty-five 'minority' groups in addition to Han Chinese.[9] All these groups, including the Han, are labelled *minzu* 民族, which is a neologism coined in Japan in the late nineteenth century to mean 'folk' or 'nation'. The PRC first used *minzu* to translate the Russian *natsional'nost'* and mimicked the Soviet parlance to define China's demographic and cultural diversity in terms of 'nationality' and the PRC as a multinational nation-state. Since the 1990s, however, official Chinese rhetoric has shed the Soviet model to discuss diversity in terms more like those used in Europe

Zhonghua is a complex, shifting signifier
Source: tian yake, Flickr

and the United States. For example, what had been translated as the State Nationalities Affairs Commission 中华人民共和国国家民族事务委员会 changed its official English name to the State Ethnic Affairs Commission, while retaining the original terminology in Chinese, and still applying *minzu* even to ancient groups whom many Western historians and anthropologists would call neither a nation nor an ethnic group. Because this mutability of the term is doing a lot of ideological heavy lifting, I leave it in Chinese, as *minzu*, below.

Similarly, the ideologically central keyword *Zhonghua* 中华 is a complex, shifting signifier. Its first use as a general transhistorical term for 'Chinese' in a national sense is credited to Liang Qichao 梁启超, who sought a Chinese-language equivalent to Western words for 'Chinese'. Liang meant *Zhonghua* roughly in the sense we use the word 'Han' today, but in early twentieth-century discourse about the territorial and demographic makeup of the Chinese nation, politicians in the Republic of China (1912–1949), while promoting their territorial claims over Tibet, Mongolia, and Xinjiang, extended *Zhonghua* to include peoples from these other parts of the former Qing empire (who, like Chinese in the PRC, declared independence from China on the fall of the Qing or in subsequent decades). Both Sun Yat-sen 孙中山 and Chiang Kai-shek 蒋介石 pushed strained racial or historical arguments that Uyghurs, Tibetans, Mongols, and Manchus were all originally Chinese but had diverged from their Chinese roots over time. The PRC initially dropped such pan–*Zhonghua*-ist assertions and, after acquiring Tibet and Xinjiang, accommodated its imperial diversity through the fifty-six–*minzu* system. But in 1989, sociologist Fei Xiaotong 费孝通 wrote an influential article that re-established the idea of *Zhonghua* as a kind of super-*minzu*.[10] Fei's formula, called the 'many origins/one entity pattern of the *Zhonghua* nation' 中华民族多元一体格局, retained distinct identities for the fifty-five non-Han *minzu*,[11] but superimposed a *Zhonghua minzu* on top of them as the culmination of modern nation-building and national self-awareness processes: *Zhonghua* was a *national* identity that emerged after the Opium Wars.[12]

Zhonghua Rules

Minzu, then, became a fundamental building-block of the PRC's identity and governance. Since 1949, the PRC's public presentation of its 'minority *minzu*' 少数民族 — that is, those other than Han — has always showcased their cultures, albeit usually only their superficial, non-religious, and unthreatening aspects, and famously through kitschy-costumed song-and-dance performance. Han, as audience and monochrome counterpoint to these displays, were implicitly the more advanced Self, juxtaposed against the colourful *minzu* Other.[13]

True to form, when visiting the Xinjiang Regional Museum in July, Xi Jinping watched costumed performers of the *Manas*, the Kyrgyz oral epic about the heroic deeds of medieval khans. But more than his predecessors, who might be said to have been simply ticking an obligatory box by observing such *minzu* cultural displays, Xi and those helping craft his ideology are now mobilising culture and identity in Xinjiang for a specific strategic purpose — one intrinsic to Xi's broader ideological program of 'Chinese civilisation' (using *Zhonghua*, the cultural term, not *Zhongguo*, the political one). Xi's penchant for ancient Chinese phrases, affection for Confucian sentiments, and sunnier assessment of pre-nineteenth-century China (its 'feudalism' 封建 notwithstanding) have been widely noted in the context of his Chinese Dream 中国梦 slogan. Xi's ideology rolls up Xinjiang's peoples into this Chinese Dream and not, as in the past, merely as less-developed, junior siblings of the Han. A 1981 central CPC Xinjiang work group launched the catchphrase 'Han are inseparable from minority *minzu*, and minority *minzu* are inseparable from the Han' 汉族离不开少数民族，少数民族离不开汉族. Party general secretary Jiang Zemin later added that the minority nationalities were also inseparable from one another 各少数民族之间也相互离不开, resulting in the Three Inseparables 三个离不开 formula.[14]

Xi Jinping on a billboard in Xinjiang
Source: Carsten ten Brink, Flickr

In contrast with the former paternalistic apposition of Han to the less-developed 'minorities', Xi's published remarks from the Xinjiang trip — dense as they are with ideological rhetoric — do not use the character for 'Han', 汉, once. Xi does not discuss the relationship of *Hanzu* 汉族 to non-Han 'minority *minzu*' at all. Instead, we get '*Zhonghua*' twenty-eight times. The central tension in the Uyghur 'Autonomous Region' arises from heteronomous control by the Han-dominated party-state, which is promoting Han colonial settlement, offering Han special access to jobs unavailable to Uyghurs and other local peoples, letting Han pass freely through checkpoints while subjecting non-Han to mobile phone scans and physical searches, criminalising Islamic practices but not Han customs, progressively illegalising Uyghur language in favour of Mandarin — and on and on. Though they would not describe it in these terms, anyone in Xinjiang knows Uyghurs and other non-Han groups are treated very differently from the Han, just as whites and blacks all knew the score in the Jim Crow American South. But, despite the stark colonial divide between Han and non-Han, or rather, because of it, Xi's ideology attempts to erase the opposition between Han and 'minority *minzu*', in favour of big-tent inclusivity under the newly emphasised rubric of *Zhonghua*.

This core ideological message resonates in Xi's remarks at the Xinjiang Regional Museum in Ürümqi, and in his speech to cadres from the Xinjiang party, government, and the Bingtuan. After inspecting an exhibition of 'Xinjiang historical artefacts' and viewing the *Manas* performance, Xi proclaimed:

Zhonghua civilisation is broad and deep, with ancient origins and a long history, and formed from the confluence of the hundred rivers of each *minzu*'s excellent culture.[15] We must strengthen research into the history of the *Zhonghua minzu* community, and the many origins/one entity pattern of the *Zhonghua minzu*.

中华文明博大精深、源远流长，是由各民族优秀文化百川汇流而成．要加强中华民族共同体历史、中华民族多元一体格局的研究．

And:

Each *minzu* of Xinjiang is an important member of the great family of the *Zhonghua minzu*, with whom its bloodlines are linked and destiny is shared.

新疆各民族是中华民族大家庭血脉相连、命运与共的重要成员．

When instructing the cadres, Xi emphasised culture and history, deploying the new array of party-line catchphrases and stressing the notion of a common *Zhonghua* identity:

We must firmly forge consciousness of the *Zhonghua minzu* community, promote the communication, exchange and intermingling of all *minzu*. *Zhonghua* civilisation is the site of the root vein of the culture of every Xinjiang *minzu*. We must educate and lead the many cadres and broad masses to correctly understand Xinjiang history, especially the history of each *minzu*'s development. We must cultivate a *Zhonghua minzu* historical outlook, firmly forge a China heart and Chinese soul. We must, in particular, thoroughly promote the 'foundation building' project for the youth, and construct a shared spiritual garden of the *Zhonghua minzu*.

要铸牢中华民族共同体意识，促进各民族交往交流交融. 中华文明是新疆各民族文化的根脉所在. 要教育引导广大干部群众正确认识新疆历史特别是民族发展史, 树牢中华民族历史观, 铸牢中国心、中华魂, 特别是要深入推进青少年'筑基'工程, 构筑中华民族共有精神家园.[16]

Cadres would have immediately understood what Xi was referring to by 'correctly understand Xinjiang's history' and the 'cultivation of a *Zhonghua minzu* historical outlook'. In 2016, at the onset of the current period of extreme repression, a group of Uyghur writers, editors, and publishers was arrested and convicted of separatism[17] for the crime of publishing a set of (state-approved) Uyghur-language and culture textbooks[18] that Xi's regime decided gave too much autonomous stature to Uyghur history and culture.[19] A new 'summary' 纪要 of historical points, determined by the Central Work Coordination Small Group on Xinjiang, was circulated within the party from 2017.[20] Like other recent pronouncements on ethnic diversity in Chinese history, the summary dates the 'unification' of tribes and confederations with the proto-Han (Huaxia 华夏) as early as the Qin (221–206 BCE) and Han (202 BCE – 202 CE) empires, then skips rapidly ahead to the twentieth century.[21] If, as the new approach argues, *Zhonghua*-ness began so early, subsequent developments, such as the 1,000 years between the eighth and eighteenth centuries when no China-based state occupied or had influence in the region now called Xinjiang, do not matter. Xi can then assert that all peoples in today's PRC have been part of the *Zhonghua* collective for millennia. This logic, which is central to Xi's historical strategy, depends on the generic, ahistorical sense of *Zhonghua*. But, unlike Fei Xiaotong's use of the word, it does not treat the emergence of *Zhonghua* identity as a modern phenomenon, instead, rolling it back to the very beginnings of the Chinese-language historical record.

This *Zhonghua*-centric historical catechism undergirds Xi's central ideological program for non-Han peoples — namely, the Five Identifications 五个认同: identification with the great homeland 伟大祖国, with the *Zhonghua minzu* 中华民族, with *Zhonghua* culture 中华文化, with the CPC 中国共产党, and with Socialism with Chinese Characteristics 中国特色社会主义.[22] Focusing on affiliative identity — specifically Chineseness — in this way, without reference to economic base or class status, is not particularly Marxist, and even departs from Stalin's definition of a nation (with its common-language criterion), on which the early PRC attempted to base its *minzu* policies.[23] But that is just what Xi ordered at the Second Central Work Forum on Xinjiang in 2014 when he raised the issue of ethnic and religious identity above economic diagnoses of the Xinjiang problem; previously, development had been treated as both a fundamental cause of and the ultimate solution to unrest.[24] This new focus on the psychological (or 'spiritual') rather than the 'material' led to the massive effort to re-engineer the identity of millions of non-Han *minzu* in Xinjiang by subjecting them to psychological and physical maltreatment in prison camps. (Many journalistic accounts group all the non-Han *minzu* of Xinjiang, including the Uyghurs, under the term 'Muslim minorities'. Many members of these groups are Muslim, or culturally Muslim, but those who are not practising are also persecuted. They are persecuted for ethnonational, not religious, reasons, though religious extremism is used as the excuse. Secular Uyghur elites were the first to go. The state has also put Mongol *minzu* in Xinjiang under pressure, though they are not Muslim.)

In July 2022, Xi called on Xinjiang officials to stay the course, explaining that cultural identity is the deepest layer of identity, and enjoined them to:

> Correct historical and cultural recognition and highlight the special characteristics of *Zhonghua* culture and the visual image of the *Zhonghua* peoples. We must, in a multifaceted and wholistic way, construct and promulgate the commonality of *Zhonghua* culture, and [construct and promulgate] a discursive system and effective media for conveying the historical fact of pan-*minzu* communication, exchange and intermingling from Xinjiang to central China.

> 文化认同是最深层次的认同. 要端正历史文化认知, 突出中华文化特征和中华民族视觉形象. 要多角度全方位构建展现中华文化共同性、新疆同内地各民族交往交流交融历史事实的话语体系和有效载体.[25]

The vocabulary here is remarkable: Xi is explicitly calling for a discourse to be constructed and for a particular visual image of *Zhonghua*-ness to be promoted — an image that includes Xinjiang's non-Han people as part of the

Zhonghua minzu community since ancient times. In short, Xi repeats the CPC claim — now a few years old — that Uyghurs (and other non-Han Xinjiang natives) have always been *Zhonghua* people. Note that the term used is not *Zhongguo ren* 中国人, citizens of the political state of China; such a claim would be still more demonstrably untrue, since for 1,000 years before 1759 no state based in geographical China had control over what is now Xinjiang. But by means of the vaguer cultural identifier *Zhonghua*, it is easier (if still inaccurate) to claim perduring connection and even identity of Central Asians with Sinitic peoples. Following a 2019 White Paper, Ürümqi's mayor and deputy party chief Yasheng Sidike published an op-ed in the *Ürümqi Evening Post* in which he went so far as to assert that Uyghurs were not related to the Turks of the Turkic Khaghanate but were 'part of the Chinese nation'.[26]

That claim is not supported by history, linguistics, or genetics. After the breakup of the Turkic Khaghanate in the mid-eighth century, the medieval Uyghur tribal confederation controlled what is now Mongolia. One hundred years later, they migrated to Gansu and the eastern part of what is now Xinjiang. Modern Uyghur language developed from old Turkic, as attested by eighth-century inscriptions found in Mongolia, and more recently, from the Central Asian Turkic literary language of Chaghatai, and was enriched by many Persian loanwords. Most modern Uyghur vocabulary, such as words for 'automobile' (*mashina*) and 'communism' (*kommunizm*), was borrowed from Russian, rather than Chinese — the legacy of tsarist and Soviet influence in Xinjiang in the nineteenth and early twentieth centuries. The Uyghur population is genetically diverse, reflecting movements of peoples and cultural exchanges from across Eurasia since before the Bronze Age.

Xi's revision of Xinjiang history is not just for internal consumption. Foreign hearts and minds are not to be neglected either. Xi ordered officials to:

> Launch multilevel, omnidirectional, three-dimensional propaganda about Xinjiang directed abroad, perfect the work of 'inviting in' [bringing selected groups on Xinjiang propaganda tours], and tell the Chinese Xinjiang story well.

要多层次、全方位、立体式开展涉疆对外宣传，完善'请进来'工作，讲好中国新疆故事.[27]

In sum, while Xi's July Xinjiang tour in some ways resembled those of his predecessors, the ideological focus of the remarks he made there was on a new message — one promoting a historical narrative of primordial *Zhonghua*-ness in which Uyghurs, Kyrgyz, Kazakhs, and other indigenes of Xinjiang were a component from the beginning. This is an aggressively inclusive narrative that minimises non-Han ethnic identity not through exclusion, but by engulfing it within a larger invented category. Xi's *Zhonghua*-ism has, in effect, weaponised the imagined community for colonial purposes, complete with shared history, shared land, and shared blood flowing through 'root veins'.

Hats Off

Finally, the photos. The set of images accompanying reports on Xi's Xinjiang trip, again, look like those documenting previous leaders' trips there (or elsewhere in the PRC).[28] General secretary of the CPC, president, and Central Military Committee chairman Xi is pictured front and centre, or otherwise distinguished from others in the scene by an item of clothing or, in the cotton fields of Shihezi, by a pair of sporty Ray-Ban–style sunglasses (not like Joe Biden's Aviators, more like Tom Cruise's black rectangular Wayfarers in *Risky Business*). Xi is often the tallest man in the shot, especially when amid crowds of Uyghurs, over whom he towers; in a tableau photographed in the Tianshan neighbourhood of Ürümqi, Uyghur women and children were posed in the front, near Xi, while Uyghur men stood in the background, allowing Xi to rise head and shoulders above the applauding people.

But one, formerly *de rigueur* image is missing from this gallery. In the past, when in Xinjiang or interacting with Xinjiang people, Chinese leaders always posed wearing a *minzu* hat, such as the Uyghur doppa (*huamao* 花帽 in Chinese).[29] Xi's predecessors Mao Zedong, Deng Xiaoping, Jiang Zemin, and Hu Jintao each put one on; Xi himself did so in 2014, but not in 2022 —

though the group photo with the Kyrgyz *Manas* troupe offered an obvious opportunity. I could have missed a photo elsewhere, but no party-secretary-in-a-*minzu*-hat picture is among the nineteen much reposted images in the *Xinhua* report of Xi's 2022 Xinjiang visit.[30] Why?

Each *minzu* in Xinjiang has its own distinctive headgear. (There is no official Han hat; no image of a *Zhonghua* hat comes to mind.) The Chinese imperative to represent non-Han peoples in 'native costume' perpetuates the stereotype of *minzu* as eternally quaint, ethnic, traditional dancing monkeys, as opposed to people who wear a business suit to work or a stylish dress for a night out.[31] But the hats do symbolise each group's unique culture and, by donning the cap, a leader recognises that *minzu*'s individuality. Considering Xi's call on cadres to construct the 'visual image of the *Zhonghua* people', I wonder whether, as Xi phases out the 'Han plus fifty-five minority *minzu*' plural language of discrete groups in favour of the unitary 'great *Zhonghua* national family', he intentionally declined to wear the hat, to avoid even that minimal nod to distinctive identity outside the *Zhonghua* corral?

Dispossession and Defiance

in Hong Kong

LOUISA LIM and LINDA JAIVIN

DISPOSSESSION AND DEFIANCE IN HONG KONG

Louisa Lim and Linda Jaivin

L OUISA LIM, a journalist, academic, and the co-host of *The Little Red Podcast*, is the author of *Indelible City: Dispossession and Defiance in Hong Kong* (Riverhead Books, 2022). She answers ten questions from *China Story Yearbook* co-editor Linda Jaivin.

Q1. The 'King of Kowloon' is a man who, convinced that the British stole Kowloon from his family, devoted his life to graffitiing his genealogical claims to the territory across Hong Kong. He is a central figure in Indelible City. Why is this marginal yet iconic figure — poor, not well-educated, possibly mad — the perfect symbol for Hong Kong (so often seen as wealthy, sophisticated, and cosmopolitan)?

I've been really interested in the 'King of Kowloon' because he is so fungible and flexible as a symbolic and almost prismatic figure. Early on, people mainly talked about the fact that he was working-class, marginalised, an outsider. There was very little discussion of his claim over the land, the idea of sovereignty. That came up later as the situation changed in Hong Kong. People labelled him the first localist. At the same time, he was also becoming a brand that represented Hong Kong — a shorthand for

Hong Kong. He was commoditised by actual brands, big and small, from the high-end fashion designer William Tang, all the way down to Goods of Desire, who reproduced his calligraphy on underwear and bags. Later he was seen as an artist even though he never saw or called himself that. It was how he could be viewed in different ways across time that attracted me. The legislator Ted Hui, now in exile in Australia, described the King of Kowloon as 'a prophet'. Other people called him a shaman. The changes in how people viewed him attracted me as a writer, as well as the idea of a mystery, a story that you could really unpack and explore; I've always been interested in stories that are hard to tell.

Q2. You liken Hong Kong to a 'shimmering chimera that was constantly changing shape depending on the angle of viewing'. How has its shape changed in your view?

No place is static, but I think Hong Kong has really changed, and in so many ways. Its shape has changed physically over the years since I grew up there. The harbour has grown smaller and smaller, and whole areas of the sea have been reclaimed, to make the airport of Chek Lap Kok, for example. So, the physical shape of Hong Kong has changed, but also its height, as skyscrapers have become ever higher. There have been other changes as well: it's a place in motion. But what we see now is an attempt by the Hong Kong government and China to pin down Hong Kong, to cement one version of it and one version of its history — the official narrative. How Hongkongers have seen themselves and Hong Kong has also changed over the years. Early on it was much more of a sojourners' place, where people went on the way to somewhere else. It was only in the Sixties and Seventies that that began to shift; it became not just a destination or place of transit but a home. Now how the people view Hong Kong is changing yet again. For many Hongkongers, those changes are turning their home into something quite unrecognisable.

Q3. You write that the history of Eurasians in Hong Kong — a community of which you were part — is one of 'disappearance'. On the one hand, they were often, as you say, 'excluded from the clan lineage records that anchored Chinese identity'. On the other, they 'erased themselves from sight'. How did this happen, and what does the future look like for Eurasian and other non-Chinese Hong Kong people under an increasingly nationalist regime?

It's a feature of the history of Eurasians that they have not just been excluded from versions of history, even family histories, but that they have excluded and erased themselves. In the nineteenth century, the very category of Eurasians disappeared from the historical records, as no-one was willing to identify as Eurasian, even though the number of Eurasians was increasing. To me, that idea of self-erasure is really tragic.

Back then it was almost impossible to function as someone who was both Chinese and Western. They would have to choose to be either Chinese or Western; few managed to navigate that successfully. The nationalism nowadays in Xi Jinping's China and the Communist Party's conflation of state and party — its capture of the very notion of Chineseness — is, I think, really alarming for Eurasians and non-Chinese Hong Kong people as well. It's deliberately exclusionary, and that bodes ill not just for Eurasian people but for Hong Kong's future as an international city.

Q4. In contrast to so many histories of Hong Kong that begin with the Opium Wars, you examine its ancient history and myths. An interviewee remarks that the King of Kowloon struck such a 'deep chord' in Hong Kong because 'the Cantonese mindset is characterised by a subversive and revolutionary yearning for lost dynasties'. What does this mean, and why did we not receive that memo sooner?

Hong Kong was the place to which the last heirs to the Song dynasty [960–1279 CE] fled, and that act of imperial flight left a profound mark on Hong Kong culture. The site of enthronement still exists — there's even an MTR [Mass Transit Railway] station named after it — and there's also a popular feast dish of various delicacies layered in a large bowl, *pun choi*, that supposedly dates to that time. My interviewee was also referring to Hong Kong's physical and political distance from the imperial centre of power, and how that helped shape a rebellious, subversive mindset, amplified by the use of a different language, Cantonese, from the imperial centre.

I think that memo — as you put it — hasn't been passed on because it has not been in the interests of Hong Kong's successive colonial rulers to frame Hong Kong identity in those terms. Both the British and the Chinese rulers of Hong Kong have hewn closely to the same message: that Hongkongers have always been economic actors without much interest in politics. It seems they hoped that if they repeated this fiction enough, even Hongkongers would come to believe it. We can see from the events of the past ten years how wrong that turned out to be.

Q5. What is it about Hong Kong Cantonese that is so central to Hong Kong identity — and what role has it played in protests?

Cantonese is central to Hong Kong identity, because it is the language of Hong Kong, and I use the word 'language' advisedly. Many scholars would argue that Cantonese is closer to Classical Chinese than *Putonghua*, the standard Mandarin that is spoken on the mainland. In its written form, Cantonese uses ancient participles and *fantizi* 繁體字, the traditional characters that are no longer used on the mainland. Cantonese is integral to the Hong Kong identity in many ways. One, it

is not the language of the mainland — until recently, even the Cantonese spoken across the border in Guangzhou was different from that spoken in Hong Kong. Just learning and speaking Cantonese can be an assertion of a separate identity. The nature of Cantonese is profane, it's sweary, it's a little bit subversive. It's much more flexible than Mandarin. There is this linguistic inventiveness of a level not allowed on the mainland. Protesters even created new characters. The most famous example was the creation of a character for the phrase used by a policeman against some protesters, 'freedom c**t'. The new character uses a combination of the three characters that make up freedom, 自由, and c**t, 閪 (see illustration opposite).[1] Activists made all these posters and T-shirts using this new Chinese character, 'freedom c**t', written in Roman letters as 'freedom-hi' after the Cantonese pronunciation. These new Chinese characters were unintelligible to mainlanders.

Q6. During the Occupy Central with Love and Peace Movement of 2014, which grew out of the broader Umbrella Movement, one of the protest's leaders, Benny Tai, told

The new character uses a combination of the three characters that make up freedom, 自由, and c**t, 閪
Source: Etan Liam, Flickr

you that 'Hong Kong laws provide the protection for us to have this kind of movement'. Were he and others naive or betrayed and, if so, by whom? Was it possible to foresee the crackdown to come?

I don't think it's naive to believe in the rule of law, or to believe in a government that upholds the rule of law. It might have been naive to believe that a government ultimately loyal to the Communist Party of China would uphold a common law system in its jurisdiction, but that's exactly what One Country, Two Systems pledged. When he was sentenced for his part in the Umbrella Movement, its co-founder Chan Kin-man said, 'In the verdict, the judge commented we are naive, believing that by having an Occupy Movement [*which called for universal suffrage in the selection of the chief executive — ed.*] we can attain democracy. But what is more naive than believing in One Country, Two Systems?'

Hongkongers have been betrayed by successive rulers in different ways, but this betrayal was so painful because Hongkongers had believed they would be protected by the systems both the British and Chinese promised would remain in place for fifty years after the return of sovereignty. Some

The Umbrella Movement came after a series of actions working within the constraints of the system to widen the democratic mandate in choosing a chief executive
Source: Studio Incendo, Flickr

argue that a crackdown was always inevitable, but the speed and scope of that crackdown have been brutal and shocking. I don't think anyone foresaw how quickly Hong Kong's institutions would be dismantled.

Q7. Staying with 2014 for a moment, you write that a poster of the Umbrella Movement that read 'This is NOT a revolution' 'said it all'. What is this 'all' that it said?

The message was that this was not a movement to overthrow or forcibly replace the government. The Umbrella Movement came after a series of actions working within the constraints of the system to widen

the democratic mandate in choosing a chief executive. The *Basic Law* had always promised universal suffrage but provided no timetable. Methods for widening the mandate included running polls, which more than 790,000 people took part in, to find how the population wanted to nominate candidates for chief executive. The aim was to carry out democratic deliberations on reform through popular consultations. The act of civil disobedience that was Occupy Central was originally intended to be a one-day event. The failure of the government to compromise or give any ground during the Umbrella Movement stoked the dissatisfaction that then exploded during 2019.

Q8. You write that watching the protests of 2019, you had a feeling that people in Hong Kong had been 'living in a kind of simulacrum, a political make-believe where our imaginations had been colonised for so long that we were desperate to believe whatever our rulers told us, no matter how much evidence there was to the contrary'. Is there a danger that in the future, the people of Hong Kong will simply move from one simulacrum to another, this one designed by Beijing?

There is a danger that the people of Hong Kong are moving from one reality to another, but the evidence shows that they are far less willing to buy into Beijing's political make-believe. In this case, the challenge is epistemological. It confronts Hongkongers daily, whether it be through high-ranking officials telling outright lies or legal charges against activists and politicians that are blatantly concocted for political ends. The reality that Hong Kong's rulers are building is not so much a simulacrum but something more akin to a political re-education territory, where actions and words must be policed to avoid violating ill-defined laws that can be applied retroactively. Hongkongers' reaction to this can be seen through the large numbers leaving the territory.

Q9. In 2020 you spoke to the playwright Wong Kwok-kui about a series of plays he had created several years earlier. You write: 'The very existence of the national security legislation restricted our conversation like a corset.' The national security legislation has led to the closure of independent newspapers, the arrest of protest leaders, and the disbanding of nongovernmental organisations and unions. If open conversation on Hong Kong identity is impossible, what are the implications for that identity?

The implications for Hong Kong identity are far-reaching. We are seeing a campaign against expressions of Hong Kong identity playing out across politics, society, education, and all other arenas. One of the most concerning is the campaign of intimidation to silence academics who study Hong Kong identity itself. The same pattern recurs: it begins with attacks by the pro-Beijing state-run newspapers attempting to discredit their work, and often ends with those academics having to leave their jobs and sometimes to flee Hong Kong. Among the targets of this purge are the eminent sociologist Ching-Kwan Lee, the political scientist Brian Fong, and cultural studies scholars Law Wing-sang and Hui Po-keung. These attacks have the long-term aim of rewriting Hong Kong's history to conform to the Communist Party's official narrative. In 2019, one of my sources told me that they feared that the phrase *heunggongyan* 香港人 or 'Hongkonger' would itself one day be illegal. At the time, I thought they were overreacting. Today I fear that day is approaching.

Q10. By August 2021, Hong Kong was no longer what it used to be — culturally and intellectually vibrant and a haven for political and other nonconformists in the Chinese world. What, then, is 'indelible' about the 'Indelible City'?

Hong Kong is such a layered place, as literally shown by the city's walls with their layers of political graffiti. Layers may be covered over, but they often also resurface in unexpected ways and at unexpected times. Even if the outward manifestations of protest are covered up, those expressions of discontent have been written on to the brains of Hongkongers over the years in a way that cannot be reformatted. I like the contrast this title makes with my last book, *The People's Republic of Amnesia*, which refers to the way that the Communist Party managed to excise memories of the killings of 1989 and silence discussion, even by those who were witnesses. That same playbook will not work with Hongkongers. Figures show that 140,000 people left the territory in the first three months of 2020 alone. Hongkongers would rather leave their hometown forever than sacrifice their freedom of thought.

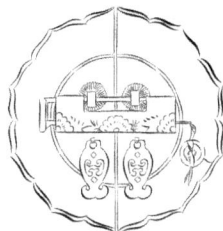

四

CHAPTER 4 — VIVE LA RÉSISTANCE

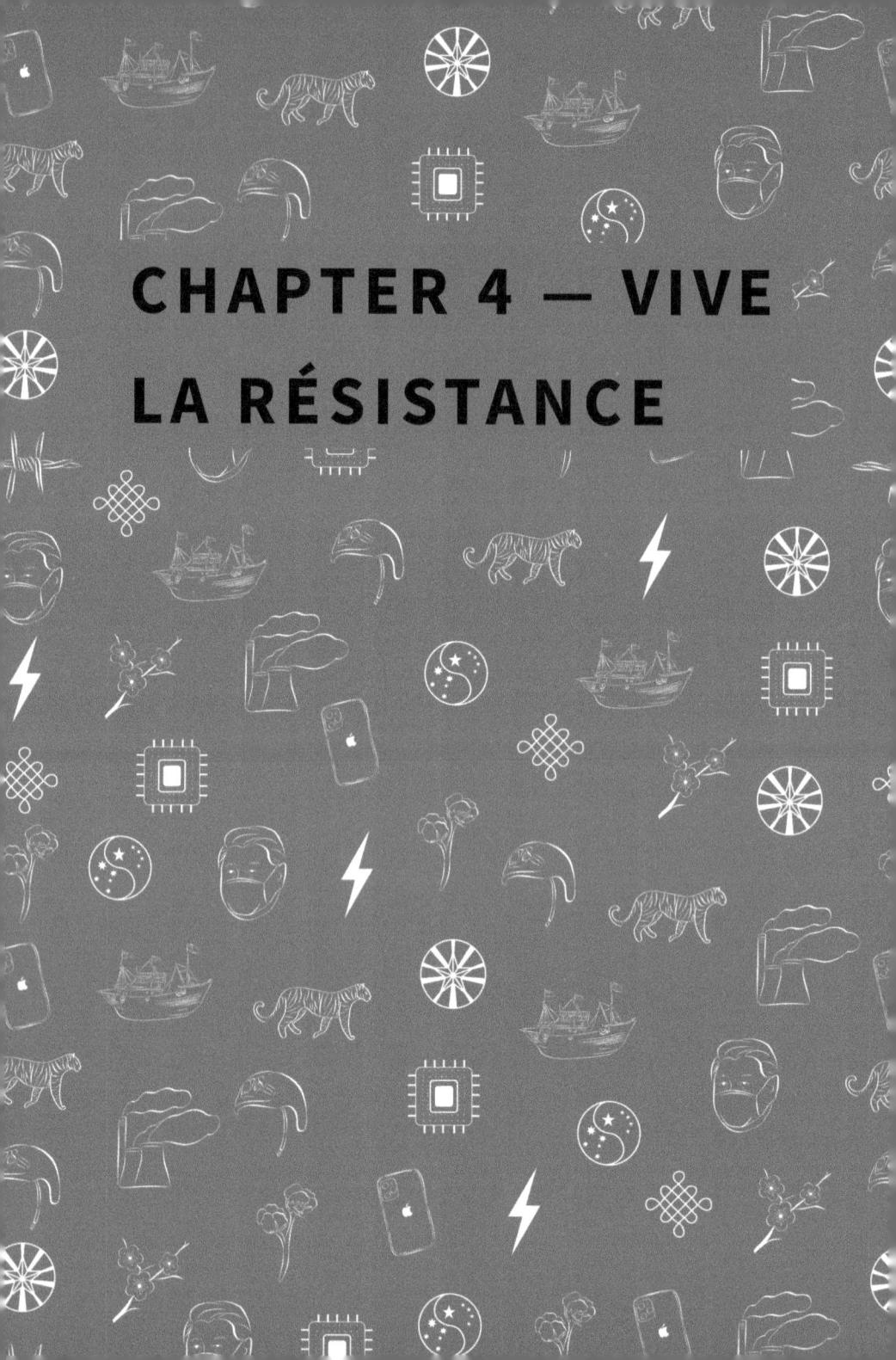

A YEAR OF PROTESTS, CEREMONIES, AND SURPRISES

Jeffrey Wasserstrom and
William Yang

Two things stand out to us when thinking about public protests in today's People's Republic of China (PRC). First, although it is easy for outsiders to view the PRC as having become a place so tightly controlled, surveilled, and censored that there is no room for dissent, this has never been the case — as the mass exodus of factory workers and burst of urban demonstrations that began in the second half of November 2022 reminded the world so powerfully. Even in an era when expressing dissenting opinions about key policies is hugely risky, people keep finding ways to give them voice. There is a common thread linking the protests of 2022 to the Wuhan lockdown protests of 2020: anger over official coverups and frustration with intense limitations on basic rights and freedoms and surveillance over the activities of even those who had not been directly exposed to the COVID-19 virus.

Second, even though it is also easy to imagine that the Communist Party of China (CPC) is so firmly established and has such an extensive media system that it no longer needs to mount displays aimed at impressing the populace and reinforcing themes in daily propaganda, this also is not the case. Every year without fail, there are both protests and CPC-staged ceremonies. Just as protests are intended to raise awareness of issues and rally public sentiment for change, the official spectacles are designed to propagate the notion of CPC greatness and rally people behind the party, extol the current leadership, and celebrate figures playing central roles in policies and campaigns. Following the initial citywide lockdown in Wuhan, for example, the authorities organised exhibitions across China to celebrate the efforts of frontline medical staff, framing them as the 'unsung heroes' in a glorious CPC-led fight against the pandemic.[1]

The year 2022 did not diverge from this enduring pattern. In autumn alone, before the November unrest at Foxconn and the vigils for victims of the fire in Xinjiang whose deaths protesters blamed on strict COVID-19 lockdown measures, there were marches everywhere from Lhasa in the far west to Guangzhou in the south-east and a daring solo act of defiance in Beijing, in which a lone man risked his life and liberty to hang banners from a bridge. There were also many notable state rituals in 2022 — the most significant being those that accompanied the Twentieth Party Congress, in October, sandwiched between the Beijing protest and those in Tibet and Guangzhou.

Three Kinds of Years

Not all years are created equal when it comes to the mix of popular protests and the elite ceremonies that are designed in part to deflect expressions of discontent. While each year witnesses both, some are remembered for just one kind: 1989 was a year of protests, for example, despite lavish state ceremonies, including the fortieth anniversary of the founding of the PRC on 1 October. In contrast, although 2015 saw many separate strikes by workers in different regions, expressions of outrage at the arrest of five feminist activists, and a protest in Tianjin by locals demanding compensation for a warehouse explosion, it was above all a year of official ceremonies. The highest-profile public event was the massive military parade in the capital that gave Xi Jinping a chance to stand beside visiting world leaders while commemorating the seventieth anniversary of the end of World War II.

Most years are mixed. Take 2008: yes, it saw the glittering opening ceremony of the Beijing Olympic Games. But there was also upheaval in Tibet, as well as expressions of anger over the high number of child deaths in the Sichuan earthquake — deaths attributed to the collapse of shoddily constructed schools, which in turn was seen as the result of corruption.

When future historians look back on 2022, as which sort of year will it be remembered? We find this an intriguing question to contemplate for two reasons. The first is that 2022 was preceded by three years that can be seen as falling on distinctly different places on the spectrum.

A good argument can be made for 2019 as a mixed year. It was clearly a year of protest for one important part of the PRC, Hong Kong, with dramatic demonstrations and street clashes that rocked the city from June until the end of the year and beyond. Yet, there were few significant protests in any other part of the PRC, and Beijing conducted grandiose rituals to mark the seventieth anniversary of the country's founding.

An equally good argument can be made for treating 2020 as a year of protest, even though only one big march took place in Hong Kong that year, on New Year's Day. The government's handling of the COVID-19 pandemic, from the belated release of information to the punishment of whistleblowers, inspired significant expressions of discontent in Wuhan, where the outbreak was first identified, and beyond. Residents in locked-down Wuhan shouted their anger from their windows on several occasions, though most public agitation tended to take online forms. The protests did not swell into a nationwide mass movement. Yet, at times, there was so much anger being expressed online that some commentators, noting that many people trapped in their homes by lockdown were binge-watching the television series *Chernobyl*, wondered whether the CPC was facing a similar crisis of faith as that depicted in the Soviet Union.

In contrast, 2021 was a year of official ceremonies. There were some protests, including new ones triggered by lockdowns, but a grudging acceptance of the zero-COVID approach to the pandemic appeared to be taking hold. The idea that COVID-19 might have a Chernobyl-like delegitimising impact on the CPC faded, just as the advent of the internet and the expanding middle class had prompted mistaken predictions that a complete restructuring of the political system would soon take place. The protests of the year were overshadowed by the many ceremonies held to celebrate the CPC's centenary, highlighted by the commemoration of the 100th anniversary of the CPC's founding and the revelation of the third historic resolution that cemented Xi Jinping's unchallengeable status in the party's history.

The First Three Quarters of 2022: Ceremonies and Protests

The second reason for asking 'what sort of year was 2022' relates to predictions. PRC politics takes surprising turns that can confound even the most expert analysts. At the start of 2022, China seemed to be headed into a second consecutive year of spectacles. In February, Beijing held a grand ceremony to kick off the Winter Olympic Games, with China's paramount leader Xi putting forward a 'united front' with Russian president Vladimir Putin. The population seemed generally reconciled to lockdowns as official media continued to emphasise the failures of alternative approaches to the pandemic, citing the high death tolls in the United States and the United Kingdom.

There were some displays of discontent triggered by frustration with new lockdowns, including in cities like Xi'an,[2] where thirteen million residents were forced into a sudden lockdown, and communities such as Wuhan that were undergoing second or third periods of mass quarantine.[3] But these were isolated rumblings of discontent spread over January, February, and March. As for ceremonies, it was a near certainty that a big once-every-five-years party congress would occur during the second half of the year with plenty of pomp and circumstance.

In April, however, much outrage was expressed online over the Shanghai lockdown, which was an especially harsh one and seemed extraordinary in part because of the city's reputation as an unusually freewheeling place.[4] Befitting the urban centre's cosmopolitan history, expressions of discontent mixed locally specific and international elements. A version of a sketch about breakfast by popular American comedy duo Key & Peele circulated online, dubbed into Shanghainese, and changed into a critique of the difficulty of securing food during the lockdown.[5] Another online post that resonated with many described T.S. Eliot's famous line about April being the 'cruellest month' taking on new meaning in locked-down Shanghai. Various testimonies about the difficulties of life under lockdown emerged, including a collection of recordings from distressed citizens across the city that was turned into an audio montage called 'Voices of April',[6] which went viral briefly before being censored; several also aired on the podcast *Stochastic Volatility* 随机波动.

Then, in May, there was a small protest, with online and in-person elements, at Peking University (or Beida 北大) — an institution with a special place in the history of Chinese social movements going back to the 1919 May Fourth Movement, but one that has rarely seen protests of any kind since

1989. The 2022 protests at Beida began after students discovered workers erecting a wall of metal sheeting to separate their dormitories from faculty housing, with many outraged by the university's attempt to restrict their basic freedoms while faculty members' lives remained largely unaffected. On 15 May, after news of the wall spread across social media platforms, at least 200, and possibly as many as 300, students gathered to demand the university remove the barrier.[7] Videos show some students trying to tear down the wall as others cheer them on.[8]

The Associated Press reported on 17 May that a school official sent to wind down the protests told students: 'Please put down your mobile phone, protect Peking University.' One student shouted in response: 'Is that protection? How about our rights and interests?'[9] Even though the protest forced university authorities to abandon the plan to maintain the metal divider, similar protests erupted on other college campuses in Beijing. Most were prompted by the authorities' attempts to impose strict lockdowns affecting the students' daily lives.

By September and October, despite increasing social and media controls associated with the all-important party congress, it began to seem possible that 2022 could end up as a year of protests. Strict pandemic control measures like daily PCR tests were generating a great deal of anger. The Beijing banner protest in October, which mixed criticism of zero-COVID policies with broader condemnation of President Xi, resonated widely: 'We want food, not nucleic acid tests. We want freedom, not lockdowns. We want dignity, not lies. We want reform, not Cultural Revolution. We want elections, not rulers. We want to be citizens, not slaves.' The original banners, the person responsible for them, Peng Lifa 彭立发 (who posted online as Peng Zaizhou 彭载舟), and online posts including photographs and videos all quickly disappeared, but the action has had a notable afterlife. The daring action by the lone protester — soon nicknamed the Bridge Man or New Tank Man (a reference to the man who stood before a line of tanks in Beijing the day after 1989's 4 June massacre) — inspired others. The words on the banners have appeared on campuses outside China but also, more daringly, have been scrawled inside toilet stalls on the mainland as graffiti.[10]

Peng Lifa's words appeared inside toilet stalls across China
Source: Twitter

In stark contrast to the protests, the party congress illustrated the underlying goals of spectacle. Official speeches, amendments to the party's constitution, and resolutions all stressed the key themes of stability and security. They also emphasised that the CPC alone could provide and guarantee this stability and security to the people, claiming this as one of its great accomplishments. If there are problems, these are treated as mistakes that local officials have made in carrying out directives, not as fundamental flaws to an approach that is tirelessly defended. The CPC does not share the prevailing international narrative that the Shanghai lockdown was botched.[11] This point was made blazingly clear in October when Li Qiang, the party secretary of Shanghai, who was responsible for that city's lockdown, was elevated to the number-two spot on the Politburo Standing Committee, just below Xi.

November Surprises

Then came November, and the protests spread throughout the country, sparked by lockdown-induced desperation, a workers' revolt, sympathy for the victims of a fatal fire and other incidents in which the zero-COVID policy contributed to people's deaths, and, of all things, the sight of maskless crowds at the soccer World Cup in Qatar, cheering on their teams in packed bleachers.[12]

As COVID-19 case numbers rose once again in the southern city of Guangzhou, officials quickly imposed lockdowns in several districts with a high concentration of migrant workers just as reports seemed to suggest that Beijing was about to start relaxing some of that city's pandemic control measures. Many residents in those districts were migrant workers from other provinces. Unable to go out to work or access government support, stretched economically, and harassed by the constant demands of testing, the restrictions on movement, and even the supply of food, these residents began marching in protest on 5 November. Scuffles broke out between frustrated workers and government staff, and angry citizens knocked down barriers put in place to facilitate the lockdown.

About the same time, dramatic videos began circulating showing workers — driven to desperation by the lockdown and insufficient food, medical supplies, and pay — fleeing Foxconn's megafactory in Zhengzhou. In the third week of November, violent clashes erupted between the remaining workers and security forces.

Then, in late November, a fire took at least ten lives in a residential building in Xinjiang's capital, Ürümqi. Word spread in Ürümqi and around the country that the people had been unable to escape the fire because of lockdown-related barriers, which had also prevented firefighters from extinguishing the blaze quickly enough. Although officials denied this was the case, the news pushed angry citizens to protest on the streets. They gathered in front of a government building, chanting slogans that demanded authorities end the strict lockdown that had been imposed across Xinjiang

'Grass mud horses' (alpacas) at Wulumuqi Zhonglu (Ürümqi Road), Shanghai. 'Grass mud horse' 草泥馬 is a homophone for 'f**k you!' 肏你媽[13]
Source: Chinese internet

for more than 100 days. Authorities in Ürümqi suddenly announced that the city had achieved 'social zero-COVID' and promised it would begin a staged relaxation of pandemic control measures in the coming days.

Even so, sympathy for those killed in the fire led to more protests around the country, including on Shanghai's Ürümqi Road, on the campuses of Beijing's prestigious Tsinghua University and the Communication University of China in Nanjing, as well as in major cities like Guangzhou, Wuhan, and Chengdu. As protests spread across the country, protesters began holding up pieces of blank paper to symbolise all they were forbidden to say, though some shouted for Xi Jinping and the CPC to step down — the latter a demand not even the students in 1989 had dared to voice. Many people recited the words of Peng Lifa's banner.

While the public protests reflected shared frustration with the zero-COVID strategy, there was no nationwide coordination. China's ever more sophisticated surveillance and censorship regime played an important role as authorities can disrupt the spread of information by artificial intelligence–driven searches for keywords and images. In most cases, core messages or important information were initially shared very quickly across social media, but once authorities began to censor relevant content or keywords, information related to the protests quickly disappeared from the internet. This hindered organisers' ability to grow the protests — although during the anti-lockdown protest in November 2022, many Chinese relied on Western social media platforms like Twitter for updates about protests happening across China, as that was where most protest-related videos and images were shared by overseas Chinese influencers. This nonetheless requires using a virtual private network (VPN), which has become increasingly difficult to obtain, and people were subject to phone searches by the police after protests in late November.[14]

In the meantime, government and other authorities (Foxconn, for example) responded to the protests by addressing the issues that were the immediate prompts, including lifting strict pandemic control measures while deploying surveillance tools, applying pressure on identifiable leaders and their families, and arresting several protesters to create a chilling effect. The protests tended to subside very quickly.

That marks the fundamental difference between the protests that took place in 2022 and the large-scale, student-led protests across China in 1989 demanding higher ideals like democracy and freedom. The protests throughout 2022 did show that Chinese citizens, despite facing greater risks and likely having to pay heavier prices for their actions, have not completely lost their will and instincts to protest oppression. However, the durability of these acts of dissent is certainly weaker than the student-led movement in 1989, which was more tightly connected by a collective goal and by more sophisticated and intentional planning.

At the time of writing (10 December 2022), protests continued to erupt sporadically but seem to have moved from a late November peak towards what might end as a winter lull. Even if the rest of the year is comparatively quiet, however, one conclusion to draw from recent events is that significant protests of widely varied kinds are still possible, even though President Xi has ramped up control and surveillance of society to unprecedented levels. But the clear awareness of the potential consequences of their actions and major obstacles to many forms of organising make it an open question exactly how citizens could create any sort of extended movement.

Many who participate in physical or online protests are doing it from personal instinct, rather than for a greater ideal, or the sake of the larger population. That said, although the unprecedented level of nationwide protests that have emerged since November has largely been triggered by Chinese people's discontent with lengthy periods of strict lockdowns and the threat they pose to people's livelihoods, what also stands out during the protests in different major cities is the collective grievance that Chinese citizens feel as they cite examples of deadly accidents caused by the extreme nature of the zero-COVID strategy, including the Guizhou bus accident, and the despair reflected through countless suicides amid strict lockdowns in different cities.[15] While Beijing tries to appease public anger and frustration by easing the zero-COVID strategy, the damage the policy has inflicted on society is one of the main driving forces of the remarkable scale of public protests.

All in all, 2022 was a year of surprises, sharply punctuated by the November protest surge, and the dramatic shifts in the party's COVID-19 policies in December. Although it is worth noting that in the narrative promoted by CPC spokespeople and periodicals, this change is viewed not as a rethinking of policy, but as somehow part of a single correct strategy that is gradually unfolding.

We can only imagine what 2023 will bring.

Double-Speak as LGBTQI+ Resistance

AUSMA BERNOT

DOUBLE-SPEAK AS LGBTQI+ RESISTANCE

Ausma Bernot

I MESSAGE a colourful rainbow emoji to my friend, who is an LGBTQI+ activist in the People's Republic of China (PRC), on WeChat. 🌈 'I'll be there in a minute!' she answers to let me know that she is online and available to connect to a virtual private network (VPN) and talk to me via an encrypted platform.

A clever code of rainbows and secret words that avoid online censorship is a must for talking to my LGBTQI+ activist friends in China these days. While a dictionary of this language does not exist and it is constantly changing, fluency in double-speak allows queer 酷儿 communities to communicate without directly mentioning 'politically sensitive' and increasingly banned phrases like 'gender and sexual diversity' or 'LGBTQI'. Just like when Chinese feminists replaced the censored #MeToo hashtag with the homophonous #MiTu 米兔, which was then translated as #RiceBunny, double-speak helps LGBTQI+ people avoid direct censorship online.

Queer Activism in the Field

The majority of my own LGBTQI+ activism in China occurred between 2014 and 2017 when I contributed to establishing Diversity, a formally registered LGBTQI+ student society at the Sino-foreign University of Nottingham Ningbo China. Over three years, we ran workshops within the university, created a student support group, and engaged with staff and students through awareness-raising activities, such as celebrating the International Day against Homophobia, Biphobia, and Transphobia. Although President Xi Jinping had been leader of China's party-state since 2012, many of his most restrictive policies had not yet been rolled out. Living in a second-tier city with a relatively relaxed political atmosphere, our activities were only directly targeted once, when we planned to host a national gathering with twenty attendees to support the trans community. A volunteer loosely connected to our student group told us they had been called by a police officer, who mumbled: 'What ... erm ... do you know about this event that is set to happen over the weekend?'

'I'm not a part of it, I'm not really sure what's happening,' they responded. Having inquired about the event, the police officer must have felt that his duty was complete, and he did not directly approach us.

It did, however, give us a big scare. While being invited to 'drink tea' 喝茶 — a euphemism for being asked to speak with police about something — is in some ways a badge of activist honour, the police interest prompted everyone to move their conversations to an encrypted platform and change venues. It was the sort of vaguely threatening encounter more common in first-tier cities that were political centres. Despite that isolated incident, those years were a time of flourishing community-building and awareness-raising about LGBTQI+ issues in society — a situation that began changing after Xi's ascent to party-state leadership.

Shrinking Digital Space under Xi Jinping

The current censorship landscape is dire. In July 2022, the administration at the top Tsinghua University in Beijing issued penalties to two students for placing handheld rainbow flags at an on-campus supermarket with notes encouraging passers-by to take them and celebrate #PRIDE.[1] 'Raising awareness' 社会意识 is now a key term on the censorship list. National legislation that is

A rainbow over Nanjing, China
Source: Richard Tao, Unsplash

not LGBTQI+ friendly, such as the 'sissy ban' of 2021 that prohibits effeminate presentations of men in visual media, adds insult to injury.[2] LGBTQI+ activists speculate that the goal of increased coercive control of LGBTQI+ communities and individuals through the media, universities, and legislation is to silo queer individuals.[3] If authorities discover evidence of my friends' conversations with me, a researcher in a university outside China, they will become a target of surveillance. Similarly, conversations among them about an LGBTQI+ group event or gathering are likely to draw attention from the ever-vigilant police, who monitor the digital communications of targeted groups and individuals as a matter of course.

The surveillance and censorship of LGBTQI+ activist and advocate groups are most intense in the Chinese digital space. For example, WeChat, the 'everything app' of China, is known to be a window for public security agencies to directly observe the activities of both informal LGBTQI+ groups and registered organisations.[4] These agencies even use the collected data to map organisational relationships between activists, according to my recent research. No conversation on the app can be presumed to be private — a fact about which no repressed group can afford to be unaware.

In their recent book on China's surveillance state, Josh Chin and Liza Lin unpack how surveillance on WeChat works. The authors note that WeChat's parent company, Tencent, 'has vehemently denied suggestions that it gives police unfettered access to WeChat's treasure trove of behavioural data'.[5] However, numerous 'coincidences' uncovered by Chin and Lin suggest otherwise — for instance, in 2017, Hu Jia 胡佳, a civil rights activist and advocate for HIV-positive individuals, received a phone call from a state security agent, who asked why he had bought a slingshot online using WeChat Pay the day before. Dr Li Wenliang 李文亮, the COVID-19 whistle-blower, had similarly been investigated for messages sent via WeChat to a private group of other medical practitioners to raise alarm over early signs that a highly infectious coronavirus was circulating.[6]

Other social media apps run by Chinese companies, including Weibo and Douban, are also required to monitor for 'sensitive terms' that entails censorship and cooperation with government authorities. In some cases, user accounts that are targeted by government agencies

undergo 'account bombing' — a practice whereby authorities 'bomb' 炸号, or freeze, social media accounts they consider sensitive for whatever reason. Another covert means of online censorship is 'shadow banning', by which authorities allow social media users to see their own posts while making them invisible to others.[7] While significantly less harrowing than direct police harassment, such practices can seriously hamper online discourse.

My recent research suggests that, as early as 2020, COVID-19 became an excuse to justify extensive surveillance and police monitoring beyond subjects directly related to the pandemic. As many cities went into lockdown, beginning in 2020 with Wuhan, which hit the record with 76 days, LGBTQI+ communities — like many others — shifted their activities to the digital space. At the same time, the digital space available to LGBTQI+ communities started shrinking. Moving activities online also meant they became more susceptible to monitoring. Many activists to whom I spoke reported being repeatedly telephoned and even threatened by police because of their online activity. These censorship strategies are like those that feminist activists have endured since the 2015 arrest of the 'Feminist Five' — five young women who were extralegally detained for 37 days for handing out anti–sexual harassment stickers in Beijing, Guangzhou, and Hangzhou on International Women's Day.[8] Online and offline harassment, censorship, and police intimidation have since accompanied feminist activism.

LGBTQI+ conversations on WeChat have been heavily restricted since July 2021 when hundreds of student-run LGBTQI+ public accounts on the platform were shuttered overnight and replaced with a vague message: 'In response to relevant complaints, all content has been blocked for violating the "Regulations on the Management of Internet User Official Account Information Services", and the account has been suspended.'

July 2021 was the end of relatively free online communication among LGBTQI+ communities in China, which had been able to share queer content online. From then on, each LGBTQI+ group or individual posting about LGBTQI+ issues online could expect to be targeted for police monitoring and censorship. The situation is similar on Weibo, an online microblogging platform run by Sina. While LGBTQI+ groups in different geographic locations face unequal amounts of intrusive censorship and police attention, most agree that civil society under Xi Jinping's leadership is extremely restrictive, unlike in the relatively tolerant times under previous leader Hu Jintao.

五

CHAPTER 5 — TAIWAN: TROUBLE IN THE FIRST ISLAND CHAIN

SEMICONDUCTORS, SUPPLY CHAINS, AND THE FATE OF TAIWAN

Samuel George

Innovation in science and technology has become the main battleground of the global strategic contest.[1]

— Xi Jinping, 28 May 2021

Realising the complete reunification of the Motherland is the shared longing of all Chinese sons and daughters and represents the essence of National Rejuvenation.[2]

— Xi Jinping, 13 March 2023

Introduction

At the Two Sessions in March 2023, the president of the People's Republic of China (PRC), Xi Jinping, defined complete 'reunification'[3] with Taiwan as the 'essence' of China's goal of national rejuvenation, to recover the partly imagined power, dignity, and territory enjoyed by China's last imperial dynasty at its apex. However, the 'Taiwan problem' in recent years has been complicated by an issue that dominates global headlines: the emergence of Taiwan Semiconductor Manufacturing Company Limited (TSMC) as the global leader in the manufacturing of advanced logic chips. Taiwan now sits at the centre of a global contest for hard power and systemic legitimacy.

A country's access to — or control over — TSMC's advanced semiconductor manufacturing capabilities determines its ability to acquire the critical military and economic power enabled by frontier technologies such as artificial intelligence (AI). TSMC's leading role has complicated both the Chinese and the US strategic calculus on Taiwan. On the one hand, the company's advance to global prominence has increased both China's incentive to pursue reunification and the United States' incentive to prevent it. On the other, the reliance of both countries on TSMC has historically acted as a deterrent to any conflict that would compromise their access to its critical technology. The United States' move to sever Chinese access to TSMC and reshore its own manufacturing capabilities could decrease the deterrent value of the company to both sides, further destabilising what President Xi in his report to the Twentieth Party Congress described as a 'turbulent period of transformation' 动荡变革期 in global affairs.

At a deeper level for the Communist Party of China (CPC), Taiwan's leadership in a fundamental technology also inflames deep-rooted historical wounds. China was forced to cede Taiwan in 1895 after losing a war against Japan, which had beaten China to the modernisation process and grown strong by adopting Western technology from the Industrial Revolution. Taiwan is therefore a symbol of national humiliation as well as a cautionary tale of the risks of falling behind the global technological frontier. These issues of power, technology, and history are crystallised in US–China competition over TSMC.

The Global Semiconductor Industry

Semiconductors 半导体 — also called chips 芯片 and integrated circuits 集成电路 — fall into three categories. Logic chips act as the processing centre of devices and systems; memory chips store information; and analogue chips typically convert electrical signals into another type of energy, such as sound or movement, which interacts with the real world.

The semiconductor supply chain has three main steps — design, manufacturing, and assembly — that are underpinned by intellectual property, specialised software, equipment, and chemicals. Because of its high capital costs and complexity, the semiconductor supply chain has evolved to become globally distributed and specialised in a small number of countries. These global hubs of specialisation have created mutual dependencies across national borders, but also strategic chokepoints in the supply chain. Through its world-leading corporations, the United States occupies a dominant position in several crucial segments: the industry's underlying intellectual property (IP), chip design — especially electronic design automation (EDA) software — and manufacturing equipment. Over the past ten to fifteen years, TSMC has become the world's leading contract manufacturer of advanced logic chips, serving global giants such as Apple and Qualcomm, and conveying a major geopolitical advantage to Taiwan. China, a late starter in the global technology race, has long been uncomfortable with its dependence on foreign, and especially US and Taiwanese, semiconductor technology.

Hard Power

Semiconductors, as a fundamental and enabling technology, go to the core of hard-power considerations in Beijing and Washington. They are the building blocks of the digital world and a prerequisite for any country intending to lead the technologies of the future, including AI, quantum computing, biotechnology, and next-generation weaponry. The State Council's *Outline for Advancing the Development of the Nation's Integrated Circuit Industry* 国家集成电路产业发展推进纲要, published in 2014, offers the following assessment: 'Accelerating the development of the integrated circuit industry is of major strategic significance to the transformation of the model of economic development, to safeguarding national security, and to increasing comprehensive national power.'[4]

It is advantageous for any nation to have a certain level of self-sufficiency in semiconductor technology. Defensively, it offers secure priority access to the semiconductor technology required for the economic and military applications that underpin national strength. Offensively, it provides leverage over weaker countries, whether deployed as strategic denial through trade restrictions or as offensive cyber-capabilities. It is worth noting that in the wake of the revelations of Edward Snowden in 2013, official Chinese media insinuated — despite a lack of evidence in the public domain — that US semiconductor companies were complicit in the extraterritorial data-collection activities of the US National Security Agency.[5]

Advanced logic chips — the production of which TSMC leads — are especially significant as they are crucial to AI, which the State Council's 2017 New Generation Artificial Intelligence Development Plan identified as 'a new focus of international competition' and 'a strategic technology that will lead in the future'.[6] AI supports a wide range of Chinese government objectives, such as an 'intelligent' 智能化 military, an upgraded industrial base, and 'smart' government.[7] Given the centrality of AI to the economic and military goals of Beijing, Washington, and other capitals, the stakes for access to TSMC-produced leading-edge logic chips are only rising.

The Historical Stakes for China

> In modern history, one of the root causes of China's backwardness and vulnerability to attack was its backwardness in science and technology.[8]

— Xi Jinping, 9 June 2014

For China, the presence of TSMC in Taiwan is not simply a hard-power consideration. It is inseparable from Beijing's deeper historical commitment to 'reunify' with Taiwan and a present-day incarnation of old anxieties. Central to the narrative of China's Hundred Years of Humiliation is the decisive role played by advanced technology in determining national power. Recent official accounts trace the Qing dynasty's (1644–1912 CE) most shameful defeats to its failure to grasp critical inflection points in the global development of technology.[9]

According to CPC historiography, the failure of the Qing to engage with the First Industrial Revolution that emerged in the United Kingdom in the 1760s led to China's vulnerability to attack and exploitation by the British Empire in the Opium Wars. Likewise, the failure of the late-Qing reforms starting in the 1860s — often called the Self-Strengthening Movement 自强运动 or Western Affairs Movement 洋务运动 — saw China miss the Second Industrial Revolution and lose the First Sino-Japanese War (1894–1895) that resulted in Taiwan coming under Japanese control. That is, the loss of Taiwan itself is directly connected to China's historical failure to, in the party's language, 'occupy the strategic high ground' in advanced technology.

Since the turn of the twenty-first century, the party has identified developments in information technology, biotechnology, new materials, and new energy as an emergent technological revolution on the scale of the

Industrial Revolution.[10] The opportunity to seize the unfolding technological revolution is 'fleeting'[11] and the spoils of history await those who can successfully translate technology into power and prosperity. For Beijing, against the backdrop of China's history of missed opportunities, US actions to deny its access to TSMC are freighted with a sense of foreboding that likely informed Xi's prediction of 'high winds and even stormy seas' in his report to the Twentieth Party Congress.[12] That is, for China's leaders, acquiring world-leading capabilities in science and technology is central to the broader goal of 'recovering' national strength, dignity, and prosperity — an objective described by Xi as 'growing strong' 强起来 and achieving national rejuvenation. Taiwan, by offering a version of Chinese modernity that differs from Xi's 'Chinese-style modernisation'[13] but has also successfully developed world-leading capabilities in a technology central to the new technological revolution (that is, semiconductors), represents an existential threat to the party's claim to being the sole steward of Chinese civilisation. In this respect, power and history converge in the 'problem' of TSMC.

Towards Decoupling

The Biden administration's move on 7 October 2022 to significantly broaden technology export restrictions on Chinese semiconductor firms was the latest major step in an unravelling in relations over a decade or more.[14]

Since at least the issuance of the US White Paper on China in 1949, Beijing has been concerned about US subversion, which evolved into a fear of containment during the Cold War.[15] This translates into a longstanding discomfort with its dependence on foreign, and especially US, technology. This discomfort informed China's renewed drive for technological self-sufficiency in 2006 with the issuance of its National Medium and Long-Term Plan for the Development of Science and Technology (2006–2020), the techno-nationalist ideas of which took shape in the Made in China 2025 initiative.

Since the release of the State Council's 2014 *Outline*, China has intensified its campaign to increase self-sufficiency in semiconductor technology. The first major pillar of this effort was the establishment of the two so-called Big

Semiconductor chips
Source: Maxence Pira, Unsplash

Funds, capitalised in 2014 and 2019 with a total of 343 billion yuan.[16] These are state-funded investment vehicles designed to support China's domestic semiconductor industry. They were complemented by generous tax, land-use, and financing policies. The second pillar was an aggressive international mergers and acquisitions drive, often funded by capital from the Big Funds, to acquire overseas talent and technology. These strategies, combined with China's willingness to use its increasing economic and military power in ways potentially damaging to US interests, alarmed business, political, and military constituencies in the United States and elsewhere, leading to a US policy response with two dimensions.

The first is a strategy to constrain China's advanced semiconductor capabilities for the stated reason of safeguarding US national security. Starting in 2019, the United States utilised its dominance of the research and development that underlie the global semiconductor supply chain to target China's two most important semiconductor companies: the semiconductor design company HiSilicon (a Huawei subsidiary) and foundry player Semiconductor Manufacturing International Corporation (SMIC). Both firms were added to the US Bureau of Industry and Security's Entity List,[17] which names companies and individuals subject to licence-based trade restrictions. The US Foreign Direct Product Rule (FDPR), meanwhile, restricted HiSilicon's access to third-nation suppliers that use US technology, including TSMC, for advanced manufacturing.[18]

The United States' diplomatic strategy to convince allies and partners to constrain China's advanced semiconductor capabilities has scored key victories. Most recently, Japan announced — without naming China — that it plans to impose export restrictions on twenty-three types of semiconductor manufacturing equipment.[19] Dutch company ASML, the world's monopoly supplier of extreme ultraviolet (EUV) lithography, has withheld or restricted the sale of key manufacturing equipment to Chinese firms.[20] Without EUV lithography machines, SMIC will be unable to manufacture commercially at leading-edge nodes of five nanometres and below. Logic chips of that complexity — over which TSMC has a near production monopoly — are vital to advanced industrial economies because they enable the most powerful computational capabilities.

The second US policy response is a state-led effort to ensure US leadership in semiconductor technology and the reshoring of production of advanced semiconductors, for which the United States currently depends on Samsung and TSMC. The enactment of the *CHIPS and Science Act* on 9 August 2022 appropriated US$52.7 billion dollars to this end, of which US$39 billion is for manufacturing incentives.

In an important speech on 16 September 2022, National Security Advisor Jake Sullivan signalled an expansion of US technological containment of China. He discarded the previous approach of maintaining 'relative' advantages over competitors in a small subset of critical technologies: 'Given the foundational nature of certain technologies, such as advanced logic and memory chips, we must maintain as large of a lead as possible.'[21] He also conceptualised technology export controls as 'a new strategic asset in the US and allied toolkit to impose costs on adversaries'. On 7 October 2022, the Department of Commerce's Bureau for Industry and Security issued a set of rules that restrict China's ability to obtain advanced computing chips, develop and maintain supercomputers, and manufacture advanced semiconductors.[22] At the core of these rules is a broadening of the scope of companies and persons restricted from selling to China and the deployment of the FDPR against a further twenty-eight Chinese advanced computing companies, preventing them from benefiting from US-origin technology that would enable access advanced semiconductors (defined as sixteen nanometres or below) for logic chips.[23]

As the decoupling of US and Chinese supply chains continues, there are implications for TSMC and its function as a deterrent to war.

Declining Deterrent: Taiwan's 'Silicon Shield'?

In her article in the November–December 2021 issue of *Foreign Affairs*, entitled 'Taiwan and the fight for democracy', Taiwanese president Tsai Ing-wen referred to her country's semiconductor industry as 'a "silicon shield" that allows Taiwan to protect itself and others from aggressive attempts by authoritarian regimes to disrupt global supply chains'.[24] There was a degree of consensus among technologists and those engaged with global trade that TSMC acted as a strong deterrent to a hot war over Taiwan.[25] Before the United States severed China's access to TSMC's manufacturing capabilities, both Chinese and US corporations were dependent on TSMC for the production of their leading-edge logic chips. TSMC's factories operate under specific conditions and depend on uninterrupted sources of materials, water, and energy, as well as the highly trained scientists and professionals that operate them. A hot war would imperil these conditions and prove disastrous for both US and Chinese technological ambitions. But US measures to cut off China from TSMC's advanced logic-chip manufacturing capabilities reduce the costs to China of any disruption to TSMC caused by war, thereby decreasing the deterrent effect of the 'silicon shield'.

If technologists approached the question of war over Taiwan in terms of the stabilising role of TSMC, military planners saw the problem in terms of relative military capabilities. While the enormous costs of any war are obvious, some military experts are expressing concern about the deterrent effect of US military capabilities. Oriana Skylar Mastro of Stanford University has written that, in late 2020, her contacts in the Chinese military expressed for the first time the belief that the People's Liberation Army (PLA) could successfully invade Taiwan.[26] A March 2023 piece by veteran defence intelligence officer Lonnie Henley offered a sobering assessment of US military capabilities to overcome a sustained Chinese blockade of Taiwan.[27] If the Chinese side perceives a favourable military balance or tentative US resolve, it will only further destabilise an already fragile status quo.

The strategic situation surrounding Taiwan is deteriorating, as longstanding and irreconcilable Chinese and US strategic interests with respect to the island move to the surface. The visit to Taiwan of Nancy Pelosi's delegation on 2 August 2022 precipitated extensive military exercises by the PLA Eastern Theatre Command that effectively blockaded the island and triggered an increase in military activity in the Taiwan Strait.[28] In his report to the Twentieth Party Congress in October, President Xi reaffirmed that unification with Taiwan 'will certainly be realised, and can certainly be realised', preferably by peaceful means, but by other means if necessary.[29] Around the same time, the US secretary of state, Antony Blinken, and the chief of naval operations, Admiral Mike Gilday, both asserted the possibility that China's timeline for unification with Taiwan had been brought forward.[30] While the looming danger of US power is a constant in the party's collective psyche, at the Two Sessions in March 2023, Xi for the first time squared off against the United States directly. He named the 'unprecedentedly severe' threat of US-led containment, foresaw a deteriorating international environment in which 'the risks and challenges China faces will only become more and more severe',[31] and used a more decisive formulation to signal that reunification with Taiwan is absolutely integral to the destiny of the Chinese nation.[32] Xi's carefully chosen words matter, and these rhetorical shifts indicate that Beijing's strategic posture is hardening against the perceived Western threat. The gravity of such pronouncements should not be underestimated.

Wartime Stories

Amid worsening relations and as the fabric of the globally integrated supply chain in advanced technology continues to fray, both Washington and Beijing are employing wartime metaphors and rhetoric to inspire national efforts for strategic security in semiconductors.

President Xi Jinping delivers a speech in 2017
Source: UN Geneva, Flickr

In his remarks delivered on 16 September 2022, Jake Sullivan referred to the *CHIPS Act* as 'an investment larger than the real cost of the Manhattan Project' — the United States' era-defining acquisition of the atomic bomb, which ended the Pacific War and laid the foundation for the postwar order that China sees as preserving US interests.[33] China's leaders, state media, and the scientific community have long touted the Two Bombs, One Satellite 两弹一星 achievement of the Mao Zedong era as the model for China's proven ability to realise technological breakthroughs that dramatically improve its security situation.[34] China's successful testing of an atomic bomb through the Two Bombs, One Satellite program in 1964 provided an effective deterrent to US encroachment into Asia and attack from the Soviet Union, with which it had severed relations. In a January 2021 interview, the prominent scientist and fellow of the Chinese Academy of Engineering Li Guojie 李国杰 referred to lithography machines, etching technology, and EDA semiconductor design software as the 'Two Bombs One Satellite project for the new era'.[35]

Achieving self-sufficiency in core technologies that convey strategic advantage now sits at the centre of China's economic model. This was reinforced by bureaucratic reforms announced at the Two Sessions that restructured the Ministry of Science and Technology to focus on breaking technological chokepoints. China's quest for strategic autonomy in a febrile geopolitical context recalls the 1950s and early 1960s: it signifies a broadened role for the party-state and a likely return to major national technology projects led by scientists who will devote their efforts to the patriotic cause. Mao called such reliable technocrats 'red and expert' 又红又专.[36]

Despite SMIC's reported breakthrough in manufacturing at seven nanometres,[37] the medium-term prospects for China's advanced semiconductor capabilities are not bright. It is uncertain how the US Department of Commerce's rules will be implemented, but the stated intention of the Biden administration, building on the strategy of the Trump administration, is to utilise its extraterritorial reach to contain China's development in advanced semiconductor technology to the greatest possible extent. The wheel of decoupling is now turning with its own internal momentum.

Conclusion

> Since the 16th century, the world has gone through several revolutions in science and technology, each of which has profoundly shaped the structure of global power. In a sense, strength in science and technology determines the changes in the balance of political and economic forces in the world, and also determines the future and destiny of all countries and nations.[38]
>
> — Xi Jinping, 9 June 2014

The lessons of history are never far from President Xi's mind. He gave the above speech in 2014, which he observed was a *jiawu* 甲午 year in the traditional Chinese calendar of sixty-year cycles — one of 'special meaning'. The most famous *jiawu* year in modern Chinese history was the disastrous year of 1894 when the Sino-Japanese War broke out, resulting in a humiliating peace treaty that granted sovereignty over Taiwan to the Japanese Empire. Xi's mention of the *jiawu* year freights China's pursuit of technology with existential significance and indirectly links it to the fate of Taiwan.

From his recent language at the Two Sessions, President Xi appears to perceive that the party's protracted struggle against the US-led capitalist West has entered a new and potentially decisive phase. In attempting to deny China the very lifeblood of the new technological revolution — advanced semiconductors — the United States has struck at the heart of both Beijing's anxieties and its ambitions. For US policy not only threatens China's ability to rectify its history of missed technological revolutions; in doing so, it also imperils Xi's vision for a rising Chinese world order that would use control over Taiwan to break through the US postwar 'island chain' containment strategy. In the narrow battle for technological primacy and the broader contest of systems between Beijing and Washington, history, power and destiny converge on Taiwan.

Buckle Up: Pelosi's Visit and the

Fourth Taiwan Strait Crisis

ARTHUR DING

Psyops and Cyberwar in Taiwan

LENNON CHANG

BUCKLE UP: PELOSI'S VISIT AND THE FOURTH TAIWAN STRAIT CRISIS

Arthur Ding

AMID TAIWANESE aspiration, Chinese rage, and regional concern about whether the Speaker of the US House of Representatives, Nancy Pelosi, would visit Taiwan, she arrived on 2 August 2022. The most senior US official to travel to Taiwan in a decade and the first sitting House Speaker to do so in twenty-five years, her itinerary was busy and full. She spoke with Mark Liu 劉德音, the chairman of the Taiwan Semiconductor Manufacturing Corporation (TSMC); had breakfast at the American Institute in Taiwan (an unofficial agency that functions as a de facto embassy); addressed the Legislative Yuan (Taiwan's parliament) and met President Tsai Ing-wen 蔡英文 there; toured the Jing-Mei White Terror Memorial Park;[1] hosted an exchange with Taiwan-based dissidents from Hong Kong and the People's Republic of China (PRC); and held a press conference. Her visit was high profile and widely covered by global media.

It infuriated Beijing. Before her flight even took off for Taipei, on 30 July, China announced a live-fire zone in Fujian province across the Taiwan Strait,[2] along with temporary import bans on certain Taiwan-manufactured foods on the grounds that they had not been registered in the PRC.[3] More retaliatory measures were adopted after Pelosi's flight landed in Taipei. PRC Foreign Ministry spokesperson Hua Chunying 华春莹 expressed her government's position: the United States and Taiwan were the first to act provocatively, whereas China was compelled to act in self-defence. Any countermeasure taken by the PRC would be a justified and necessary response to the United States' obliviousness to Beijing's repeated démarches and to the United States' unscrupulous behaviour.

The People's Liberation Army (PLA) carried out military exercises in six zones on all sides of Taiwan for a week, continuing after Speaker Pelosi left Taiwan for Seoul.[4] The government placed more bans on Taiwanese agricultural and fishing products,[5] halted exports of sand (needed for infrastructure construction), and sanctioned individuals[6] and organisations for 'secession'.[7]

The Communist Party of China (CPC) also released a White Paper titled 'The Taiwan Question and China's Reunification in the New Era',[8] which expresses Beijing's long-term policy towards Taiwan. It describes 'resolving the Taiwan question' as 'indispensable for the realisation of China's rejuvenation' and a 'historic mission' of the CPC. It describes Taiwan's ruling Democratic Progressive Party (DPP) as having an agenda of 'independence' and warns that while 'peaceful reunification' is the CPC's goal, yet: 'We will always be ready to respond with the use of force or other necessary means to interference by external forces or radical action by separatist elements.'

The PLA's Retaliation

The military retaliation measures demonstrated certain things about the PLA's enhanced military capabilities. First, the PLA imposed six zones in this exercise, signalling that it could mobilise sufficient force to encircle the island. In comparison, during the 1995–96 Taiwan Strait Crisis, the PLA imposed six zones in the Taiwan Strait but did not carry out activities in all six at the same time.

Second, the size of some of the August 2022 military exercise zones was double or triple those imposed between 1995 and 1996, implying a prioritised area of operations. Third, some of the zones overlapped the waters of Taiwan's 24-nautical-

Then US Speaker of the House Nancy Pelosi and President Tsai Ing-wen wave to the camera
Source: Chien Chih-Hung, Wikipedia

mile or territorial sea baselines; in the 1995–96 crisis, all were outside these areas. As a result, the PLA's activities affected Taiwan's shipping and civil aviation routes, signalling that the PLA could launch a blockade to choke off Taiwan's external communications.

This shows that after four decades of military modernisation since the 1980s, the PLA can launch a variety of military operations against Taiwan, ranging from coercive quarantine and total blockade to all-out invasion. The number of zones and their size speak to the PLA's capability.

It is not an exaggeration to say that this exercise served to test the PLA's future operation plans. That the large-scale exercise was announced only several hours after Speaker Pelosi had departed Taiwan indicates it had been long in the planning and the PLA had simply been waiting for the right time to carry it out.

It also shows that the PLA's anti-access/area denial (A2/AD) operations — a military tactic that holds that 'the best way of prevailing over a distant adversary, especially if it is superior in overall military power, is to prevent it from deploying its forces into the theatre of conflict in the first place' — are being factored into China's military plans.[9] What's more, they can execute this operation against possible US forces simultaneously with a military operation against Taiwan, because one zone is located to the east of Taiwan, where any US force is expected to pass.

The exercises also sent a warning to Japan to not cooperate with US forces in the event of a conflict in the Taiwan Strait; some of China's ballistic missiles fell into Japan's claimed exclusive economic zone (EEZ). It has been reported that Chinese president Xi Jinping deliberately chose the EEZ as the target.[10]

There is no doubt that Australia is probably also factored into mainland military calculations, because one zone is located south–south-east of Taiwan. In the framework of the strategic defensive alliance agreed to in September 2021 by Australia, the United Kingdom, and the United States, known as AUKUS, it is expected that Australia will play a role in a Taiwan Strait contingency.

In addition to its military function, the August 2022 military exercise carried a strong political message—namely, that the Taiwan Strait had been 'internalised' by the PRC and the PLA could cross it whenever it saw fit.

Since 1949, there has been a median line in the Taiwan Strait to separate the PRC and Taiwan. This line was set unilaterally by the United States during the Cold War, when the historical feud between Taiwan's then ruling Kuomintang (KMT) and the CPC precluded the two parties from communication. Both Taiwan and the PRC had observed this median line as a de facto border between them, though Beijing did not explicitly endorse it.

Starting in 2022, Beijing began to argue more frequently that, based on its long-held claim that Taiwan is an inseparable part of China, the PRC has sovereignty, sovereign rights, and management rights over the whole Taiwan Strait.

Analysis

The military exercise created serious repercussions for US–China relations. First, it worsened the already fragile relationship and heightened strategic competition:

China, considering Taiwan as its core interest, must push further to bring reunification with Taiwan within reach, while the United States must do its utmost to help defend Taiwan to safeguard its credibility. Any concession by either side would come with a political price tag.

Second, the exercises created a new normal in the Taiwan Strait. PLA military jets crossed the median line and its missiles landed within 24 nautical miles of Taiwan, nearly penetrating its sovereign waters. In other words, it is possible for the PRC to enforce its maritime claim over the Taiwan Strait. That could involve denying US warships future freedom of navigation operations there.[11]

In such circumstances, further militarisation of US–China competition in the Taiwan Strait is conceivable. To reach its goal of reunification with Taiwan, China will likely stage its military exercises even closer to Taiwan in the future. This would serve two purposes: to damage Taiwan's morale and confidence, and simultaneously discredit the United States.

Political leadership must be factored into any assessment of the risk of military escalation in the strait. In seeking a third term, breaking long-established norms in China since the 1980s, Xi Jinping staked his legitimacy in part on progress on Taiwan's reunification. His performance over the past two terms shows he is an ambitious leader eager to establish his legacy. Backed by China's growing military capability, he will likely push toward this goal.

Xi's assessment of the external environment may embolden him. The United States is spread thin with conflicts on many fronts globally while internal rifts over some political issues could weaken its national power. Russia, stuck in its long war with Ukraine, meanwhile, needs China more than ever and, for these reasons, is unlikely to attempt to constrain China from the north.

The likelihood of a large-scale invasion of Taiwan at this stage is low. Organising such an action, including coordinating naval, air force, and infantry combat troops, as well as the logistical support they would require across the Taiwan Strait, remains too difficult a task for the near future. Its cost, both in material terms and in potential casualties under Taiwanese retaliation, would damage China's global standing and jeopardise Xi's dream of great national rejuvenation.

In contrast, the 'salami-slicing' grey-zone operations in which, according to the Lowy Institute's definition, 'no individual provocation is large enough to force the other side to respond militarily', along with enhanced disinformation, better serve Xi's purposes.[12] The PRC can incrementally exhaust Taiwan's resources, reduce Taiwan's self-confidence, and drive a wedge between the government and the Taiwanese people. Doing it this way will not give the United States an excuse to intervene militarily, and there will be little else it can do to directly support Taiwan.

Taiwan will not sit idle. Aware of the consequences of inaction, Taiwan is very likely to push back so that the PRC is unable to sustain the new normal established in this military exercise.[13] This also involves Taiwan changing the rules of engagement for its military forces. Of course, any pushback

runs the risk of conflict breaking out between the Taiwanese and Chinese militaries.

US involvement of some sort in the Taiwan Strait would then be inevitable. The *Taiwan Relations Act* requires the US government to act (it is, however, up to the US president to make the ultimate decision), stipulating that 'any effort to determine the future of Taiwan by other than peaceful means, including by boycotts or embargoes, [is] a threat to the peace and security of the Western Pacific area and of grave concern to the United States'.

China's military exercises and grey-zone operations are a threat to 'the peace and security of the Western Pacific area'.[14] I would argue that the United States must react to help safeguard its own credibility. In the wake of growing Chinese military capability and the subsequent asymmetric situation between the Taiwanese and Chinese militaries, US involvement will inevitably be extensive, and at least include providing more arms and combat training. Even short of a commitment to defend Taiwan militarily, its involvement will infuriate China, which will take further action as a result, creating a vicious cycle.

The United States must also take a stance on China's legal claim over the Taiwan Strait. Here, as in the South China Sea, the United States must continue to execute freedom of navigation operations to push back against China's claim of exclusive sovereignty. Helping Taiwan maintain its de facto independence will indirectly help the United States maintain its image as the only power in the world capable of upholding the 'rules-based order' on which so much of global economic, political, and other cooperation depends.

Taiwan has become the focal point of US–China geopolitical competition and has ensured that this competition will be militarised. With relations spiralling, we must all buckle up.

PSYOPS AND CYBERWAR IN TAIWAN

Lennon Chang

CYBERATTACKS TARGETING Taiwan are nothing new. Every day, there are both attempted and successful attacks targeting government and private sector websites. But during former US House Speaker Nancy Pelosi's visit to the island in August 2022, we saw a drastic increase in cyberattacks and cybercrime generally.

The Taiwanese government recorded twenty-three times more cyberattacks than usual on 2 August. Government websites, including those of the Office of the President and the Ministry of Foreign Affairs, came under especially serious attack. It was reported that a significant number of attacks came from internet protocol (IP) addresses in Russia and China.[1]

One popular type of attack that occurred during Pelosi's visit, but which happens with less intensity in normal times, is the distributed denial-of-service (DDoS). By sending a huge number of messages to a website at the same time, a DDoS attack can be used to disable the website. This happened to the websites of the Office of the President, the Ministry of Foreign Affairs, and the Ministry of National Defence multiple times during this period. For example, the Ministry of Foreign Affairs' website received,

A man stands in front of a projection
Source: Alvan Nee, Unsplash

within a single minute, more than 8.5 million requests for access, which was significantly more than the site's capacity. This sort of attack leaves the government unable to communicate with its citizens through its websites. Website defacement is another popular approach by hackers, and one used intensively during Pelosi's visit. Hackers even replaced the webpages of some government departments and universities[2] and screens at train stations[3] were replaced with messages such as 'There is only one China' 世界只有一個中國 and 'The old witch's visit to Taiwan is a

serious provocation to the Chinese government' 老巫婆竄訪台灣，是對祖國的嚴重挑釁. Significantly, screens at convenience stores also came under attack, their content replaced with similar messages. This caused serious concern as cyber-defence for Taiwan's private sector, which is not on the critical infrastructure list, has not previously been considered a priority but now emerges as a worrying vulnerability.

The timing and intensity of these attacks raise concerns that what was previously thought of as 'cybercrime' or isolated 'cyberattacks' should instead be seen as a concerted strategy of 'cyberwarfare'.

The use of DDoS and website defacement as tactics of cyberwarfare can go further than simple disruption of business. These measures can also facilitate the dissemination of fake news and enable extended disinformation campaigns.

War in the digital era can be very different from traditional warfare in that it can be launched without its victims even being aware they are being targeted. Indeed, as outlined in the Australian government's 2022 *Defence Strategic Update*, disinformation campaigns have already been used to achieve strategic goals without provoking conflict. In Australia and the Indo-Pacific, especially among democratic nations, there is growing concern about disinformation campaigns, especially those believed to originate in China and from the Chinese government.

Some people might associate a disinformation campaign with 'fake news' or 'misinformation', but, these things are better thought of as *mis*information. In a misinformation campaign, people share false or misleading information that they think is true, without intending to mislead others. A disinformation campaign is different. As defined by the Australian Department of Foreign Affairs and Trade, it is

> the intentional creation and dissemination of wholly or partly false and/or manipulated information that is *intended to deceive and mislead* audiences and/or obscure the truth for the purposes of causing strategic, political, economic, social, or personal harm or financial/commercial gain.[4]

(Emphasis in original)

The purpose of disinformation is to deliberately mislead others. The creation and distribution of disinformation can cause great harm to a society or government.

The information distributed in a disinformation campaign may not necessarily be entirely fake. Even verifiable information can be presented in a misleading way to target certain people. An example of a disinformation campaign of this sort involves allegations that the Taiwanese government spent NTD94 million lobbying Pelosi to visit the country. Taiwan's Ministry of Foreign Affairs clarified that money was paid to a lobbying company to expand ties with the US government, not to lobby Pelosi to visit Taiwan, nor to pay for her trip.[5]

We see disinformation disseminated not only through government channels but also in collaboration with individuals, groups, or even criminal organisations. Some examples of such collaboration include the voluntary participation of 'Little Pinks' 小粉红 — typically young self-identified Chinese patriots, including students; the '50 cents party' 五毛党, the predecessors of the Little Pinks, who it is alleged receive a small payment for each post or repost of desired content; and 'content farms', which are organised groups that receive support from companies to disseminate information to the public but also to create content. Disinformation can also be spread through official channels, including official Twitter accounts, Facebook pages, websites, television, and radio.

The crucial lesson is that war might already have appeared in a new guise — one that we do not even recognise as war. Psychological operations ('psyops') are an integral part of the contemporary military strategy of many countries including the United States and Australia. By influencing public opinion, fomenting political polarisation, and otherwise causing conflict within a country, hostile objectives can be accomplished with little effort and no bloodshed. Taiwan has long been a target of psyops over the past decades and has built good countermeasures. However, technologically facilitated psyops are spreading faster and wider than before. While it is important that

Taiwan's government continues to improve its measures against psyops, it is also crucial that it adopts new technologies and ideas to provide genuine information in real time. The tactic of 'humour over rumour' used by the Taiwanese government during the COVID-19 pandemic successfully reduced fear and panic-buying of items such as toilet paper among the public.[6] However, there is a risk in times of disaster that the use of humour as a tactic might not be appropriate and careful consideration must be given to ensure its effectiveness. To protect the country, it is important to study how disinformation campaigns are created and disseminated, and how people are influenced by disinformation, with particular attention to the role of culture and language.

Countering cyberattacks and disinformation campaigns must involve the public and private sectors, as well as individual effort — that is, co-production is critical to tackling cyberattacks and disinformation campaigns.

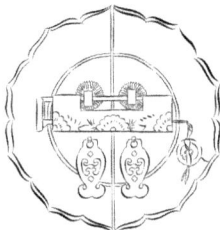

六

CHAPTER 6 —
PACIFIC LINKS

THE CHINA–SOLOMON ISLANDS SECURITY AGREEMENT: CLEAR AND PRESENT DANGER

Sean Kelly

Revelations during the 2022 Australian federal election that the Solomon Islands government was in the process of concluding a secret security agreement with the People's Republic of China (PRC) sounded alarm bells in security circles. It generated dire predictions of a future Chinese naval base and permanent deployment of Chinese troops in the Solomons, seriously affecting Australia's national security. Alarmist voices predicted Solomon Islands was becoming a 'Cuba' off our coast[1] and the then prime minister, Scott Morrison, gave ominous warnings about 'red lines' that must not be crossed.[2] This politically driven rhetoric shifted attention away from very real concerns about the broad potential application of the agreement.

The leaked draft text of the *Framework Agreement between the Government of the People's Republic of China and the Government of Solomon Islands on Security Cooperation*,[3] which knowledgeable sources advise is not significantly different from the final text, only sets out mechanisms by which Chinese security forces (military, armed police, or police) could be deployed to Solomon Islands. It says nothing about cooperation, training, providing equipment, exchanges, or other modes of cooperation. These are covered in a separate 2019 agreement.[4]

This is not out of order; Australia has the *Agreement between the Government of Australia and the Government of Solomon Islands Concerning the Basis for Deployment of Police, Armed Forces, and other Personnel to Solomon Islands*,[5] signed on 14 August 2017. This was the only other such security agreement Solomon Islands had at the time. (An agreement with Papua New Guinea was signed on 8 February 2023 to formalise the deployment of Royal Papua New Guinea Constabulary members for policing duties there,[6] details of which are not yet known but are unlikely to have the implications raised by the agreement with China.) The agreement with China enables a much broader range of Chinese deployments but is scant on details — just over four pages, compared with more than twelve pages in the Australian agreement. The Australian agreement sets out clear formal procedures for Solomon Islands to initiate and terminate deployments, as well as command and control arrangements, legal arrangements, and authorities — all designed to preserve Solomon Islands' sovereign control over any deployments. The agreement with China lacks such details or protections.

The broad scope of potential application of the agreement with China is of particular concern. The scope of cooperation is set out in Article 1[7] in two distinct parts.

Solomon Islands–Initiated Chinese Deployments

The first half of Article 1 provides for the Solomon Islands government, for 'its own needs', to request China send police, armed police, military personnel, and other law enforcement and armed forces to the Solomons 'to assist in maintaining social order, protecting peoples' lives and property, providing humanitarian assistance, carrying out disaster response, or to provide assistance on other tasks agreed upon by the parties'. The term 'maintaining social order' has a much broader meaning in China, and the provision for 'other tasks agreed upon by the parties' opens a wide range of possibilities.

It is likely the agreement was conceived by China with one eye on diplomatic competition with Taiwan for influence in the Pacific. Until 2019, Solomon Islands recognised Taiwan rather than the PRC, and the switch has been controversial; it was identified as a trigger for the targeting of ethnic Chinese businesses in the November 2021 riots.[8] Significant elements in the Solomon Islands opposition are unhappy with this decision and remain supportive of Taiwan; indeed, the government of Malaita Province, the most populous of Solomon Islands' nine provinces, continues to maintain links with and accepted COVID-related aid from Taiwan in 2020, ignoring Chinese protests.[9] The security agreement could be seen as helping to bolster the government of Manasseh Sogavare against pro-Taiwan elements.

The most obvious application of the agreement is in the case of civil conflict or serious breakdown of law and order such as during the riots in 2021. These are the kind of circumstances in which the Solomons would have traditionally turned to Australia, with support from other Pacific nations. Why, then, did the Solomon Islands government look elsewhere for such assistance? It is likely that the Chinese side offered this assistance, pointing to the targeting of ethnic Chinese businesses in the 2021 riots, and asserting its understandable interest in helping protect fellow Chinese.

In this context, it is important to recognise that there are some circumstances in which Australia would be unwilling to send troops to help the Solomon Islands government. For example, should the Solomons experience a constitutional crisis whereby a government was trying to hold on to power illegally, or if it faced a largely peaceful popular uprising, Australia might have qualms about being called on to help forcefully 'restore order', whereas China might not. At the same time, there is concern that China might be more inclined to provide support under the agreement to help prevent the return to government of a pro-Taiwan party.[10] While I am not suggesting this came into the thinking of the Sogavare government, the agreement could be used to underpin a drift to more authoritarian rule.

China-Initiated Deployments

The second half of the scope of cooperation set out in Article 1 allows China, 'according to its own needs', to make ship visits, stopovers, or transits, carry out logistical replenishment, and use Chinese forces 'to protect the safety of Chinese personnel and major projects in Solomon Islands'. There are no equivalent provisions in the agreement with Australia. It is very unusual — if not an infringement of sovereignty — for an agreement of this kind to allow a country to undertake military or security activities in another country 'according to its own needs'.

Previous attention has mostly focused on the provision for ships' visits, but the text allowing Chinese forces to 'protect the safety of Chinese personnel and major projects in Solomon Islands' is equally alarming. As China rolls out increasing numbers of projects under the Belt and Road Initiative (BRI), the scope to activate this provision to deploy Chinese security forces to Solomon Islands to protect its investments increases. The agreement potentially allows China to station security personnel in Solomon Islands for an open-ended period to protect any projects it is building or operating. In northern Laos and Myanmar, the BRI has led to the establishment of special economic zones that appear to exercise a form of extraterritoriality[11] in which China administers all aspects of the zone, including security.

It is striking that the agreement lacks any details for the processes or constraints on Chinese-initiated deployments, with only a vague requirement for 'consent'. This contrasts with requirements for Solomon Islands–initiated deployments set out in Article 3 of the same agreement, which include formal written requests from Solomon Islands, including details of the security situation, the type and number of forces requested, the duties of the personnel to be sent, and the duration of the mission. No such provisions apply to China-initiated deployments; there is only some form of 'consent', which can come from the Solomon Islands Foreign Ministry, the Ministry of Police, or the National Security and Correctional Services.

The vagueness of the wording even leaves open the possibility of a blanket consent — for example, for Chinese vessels to come and go as they please. Given China's well-known proclivity to use inducements to secure support for its objectives, and the leverage that China's increasing investments in the Solomons will give it, gaining such consent would seem to be not difficult. As things stand, this is a fundamentally unequal agreement that heavily favours China's interests without protecting Solomon Islands' sovereignty.

A Chinese Naval Base

Much has been made of the potential establishment of a formal Chinese naval base under the security agreement, though Prime Minister Sogavare has ruled out such a possibility.[12] Yet, China could gradually establish a de facto base under the current provisions of the agreement. It enables Chinese naval ship visits at China's discretion — unlike naval ship visits by the United States and Australia, which are conducted on the explicit invitation of the host government. The agreement with China provides for port visits to carry out unspecified logistical replenishments (opening the possibility of armament replenishments). This is no small thing; during World War II, the ability to replenish in friendly neutral countries like Spain[13] was invaluable to the German navy. To support such visits, it is reasonable to assume China will invest in docks, fuel resupply, and warehousing, which could end up being effectively 'dual-use' facilities, designed to support Chinese naval vessels alongside commercial ones. The agreement could then enable China to deploy security forces to protect these facilities, creating a de facto base without the need to formally create one.

The agreement should also be seen in the context of the draft 'Blue Economy' agreement[14] now being discussed between China and the Solomons, which inter alia encourages cooperation on 'distant water fishing'. The Solomons could become a forward base for China's distant water fishing fleet, which is notorious for its noncompliance with regional and global fisheries agreements. This also opens the possibility that Chinese maritime security vessels could operate deep in the Pacific to protect the illegal activities of their fishing fleet, as they do in the South China Sea.[15]

A Question of Intent?

Some may question whether China intended the agreement to have such broad potential application; however, China has a large and highly skilled foreign ministry with vast experience in negotiating international agreements, and an agreement of this significance would have attracted high-level scrutiny. The language is deliberately vague and open-ended. It is not credible that this was unintended.

A good indicator of the intent of the agreement can be found in its secrecy provisions. Article 5 provides that '[w]ithout written consent of the other party, neither party shall disclose the cooperation information to a third party'.[16] This means that, without Beijing's approval, the details of the agreement must be withheld from not only foreign governments like Australia, but also the Solomon Islands parliament and people (as releasing information to either the parliament or the public would mean

US Military Personnel onboard a high-speed vessel in Honiara, Solomon Islands
Source: US Pacific Fleet, Flickr

third countries automatically had access). The secrecy provisions extend to 'cooperation information', which could apply to the very existence of a Chinese deployment. This kind of opacity does not suggest benign intent.

The potential strategic importance of some of China's targeted investments also casts doubt on its intent. For example, in 2019, China and Solomon Islands signed a memorandum of understanding providing for a Chinese state-owned company, AVIC Commercial Aircraft, to upgrade nearly three dozen airfields across the Solomons.[17] While it is doubtful there is a sensible business case for such large investments, this would potentially enable China to assess and upgrade airfields to a level sufficient for military use — and deploy Chinese security personnel to protect them. As China invests in other strategically important infrastructure, from ports to underwater optical-fibre cables, its security presence has the scope to continue growing — in a country that has no formal armed forces of its own.

The Broader Pacific Context

The security agreement forms part of a broader geostrategic push. China's state councillor and minister for foreign affairs, Wang Yi 王毅, conducted an eight-nation visit to the Pacific from 26 May to 4 June 2022, bearing a string of bilateral agreements for signing, as well as proposals for broad regional cooperation agreements intended to substantially alter the balance of influence in the Pacific in China's favour.

The security agreement, which was formally signed with Solomon Islands during Wang's visit, drove a wedge between Australia and one of its erstwhile closest security partners in the Pacific. At the same time, the agreement probably bolstered Sogavare's prominence in the Pacific, positioning him as an advocate for expanded regional engagement with China.

There is no evidence Wang sought to replicate this agreement in the other Pacific nations on his itinerary, although secrecy provisions in such agreements mean it is unknown whether China had already sought or been granted similar rights from other Pacific countries. Officials from several countries on Wang's itinerary ruled out a similar security agreement, with their focus on collaboration spanning economic development — in particular, fisheries and tourism, COVID-19 response, and police training — collaboration plans similar to those that preceded the China–Solomon Islands Security Agreement. Still, through its security agreement with Solomon Islands, China may have established a benchmark for progressing relations under the BRI requiring its Pacific partners to agree to arrangements that enable access for Chinese military and security forces as the price of investment.

On 20 May 2022, the president of the Federated States of Micronesia, David Panuelo, wrote a letter to fellow Pacific Island leaders, clearly reflecting this concern.[18] He expressed alarm at the draft *China–Pacific Island Countries Common Development Vision*[19] and *China–Pacific Island Countries Five-Year Action Plan on Common Development*[20] circulated by China in advance of the second PRC–Pacific Island Countries Foreign Ministers Meeting, held via video-conferencing from Suva on 30 May. He warned that China was seeking 'control of traditional and non-traditional security', including law enforcement training, supply, and joint enforcement efforts, as well as cooperation on cybersecurity and network governance, collection of biodata through smart customs, and Chinese marine spatial mapping. The vision statement does not (as Panuelo wrote) specifically refer to 'the protection of Chinese assets and citizens', as in the Solomons agreement, but the projects detailed in it and the action plan would provide ample basis for China to press for similar access. Panuelo warned of China's 'intent to shift those of us with diplomatic relations with China very close into Beijing's orbit, intrinsically tying the whole of our economies and societies to them', and linked this directly to drawing Pacific Island nations into a potential future war over Taiwan. Despite the very lucrative proposals on the table, the ten Pacific Island countries participating in the Suva meeting declined to sign the proposed documents, primarily due to concerns about economic sovereignty and security.[21]

This, combined with Fiji's decision on 27 May to be the first Pacific Island nation to sign on to the United States–initiated Indo-Pacific Economic Framework[22] — the Biden Administration's answer to the BRI — has taken the wind out of the sails of China's Pacific push. But Chinese largesse remains a powerful temptation for Pacific nations frustrated with the pace of their economic development. China can be expected to regroup and press forward with these countries — more likely on a bilateral basis, with security cooperation continuing to feature.

A 27 May article on Wang Yi's visit to Kiribati in the *Global Times*, which is famous for giving 'unofficial' voice to Chinese threats and warnings, offered insight into current strategic thinking in Beijing about the Pacific. The article quotes a Chinese academic, who, referring to US military bases in the north-west Pacific, said: 'If China sets up a military base in Kiribati, the US's first and second island chains would be meaningless.'[23] China is pursuing plans to upgrade an almost two-kilometre-long World War II–era military airstrip on the remote and virtually uninhabited island of Kanton, nearly 1,800 kilometres east of the Kiribati capital, ostensibly to support commercial air travel between the capital, Tarawa, and other islands,[24] but with obvious strategic value to China.

The security agreement with Solomon Islands also serves to extend Beijing's influence in overseas Chinese communities, both in Solomon Islands and elsewhere in the Pacific. China has been increasingly asserting its responsibility to protect all ethnic Chinese, not just PRC citizens. Seen in the context of the 2021 anti-Chinese riots, the Solomons security agreement represents a concrete step towards protecting these communities, creating a greater sense of psychological dependency on China, and increasing China's political influence through Chinese communities.

What Should Australia Do?

Solomon Islands is a sovereign nation well within its rights to enter any agreement with anyone it wishes. Australia could have done something to forestall the security agreement if it had cultivated a good enough relationship with the Solomons to ensure sufficient foreknowledge and consultation. At this point, the agreement is a *fait accompli*. Australia must focus its efforts on limiting any negative impacts of the agreement, both in the Solomons and across the Pacific, and restoring Australia's position as partner of first choice.

The election of the Albanese government provided an excellent opportunity for a substantial reset of Australia's relations with the Pacific that will also help to address the challenge posed by China's diplomatic offensive. Australian Foreign Minister Penny Wong's decision to make her first bilateral visit — just four days after being sworn in — to Fiji was well received in the Pacific. Fiji is one of the largest and most influential Pacific Island nations and home to the Pacific Islands Forum (PIF) Secretariat. Equally important was Prime Minister Anthony Albanese's attendance at the PIF Leaders Meeting in Suva in July.[25] In her first nine months as foreign minister, Wong made eight visits to the Pacific, visiting twelve of Australia's seventeen PIF partners. Australia concluded a security agreement with Vanuatu in December 2022, and announced the Pacific Engagement Visa to facilitate greater labour mobility in the Pacific in February 2023. Continuing this intensive engagement at the highest levels will be essential to Australia restoring and maintaining its position as partner of first choice for the Pacific.

The key themes articulated during Wong's visits to the Pacific resonated well: recognition of the centrality of climate change to the security and economies of the Pacific, commitment to taking real action domestically on the climate crisis, and to cooperative action through the new Australia–Pacific Climate Infrastructure Partnership; a respectful and supportive relationship that listens to the concerns of Pacific partners; valuing the contribution Pacific Island peoples have made to Australian society; and concrete measures to support Pacific aspirations, ranging from increased

Solomon Islands Parliament House, Honiara
Source: DFAT, Flickr

aid to deeper defence and maritime cooperation to expanding opportunities for Pacific workers in Australia. Wong pointedly noted during her first visit to Fiji that closer relations with Australia came 'without strings attached'.[26] The then Fijian prime minister, Frank Bainimarama, described his meeting with Wong as 'wonderful'.[27] Maintaining this very positive response will depend on continuing action to give substance to the positive atmosphere — in particular, strong action on climate change.

The Labor government's commitment to spend an additional A$525 million on development cooperation in the Pacific[28] was also a good start towards improving relations and establishing Australia as a partner of choice. But Australia will never win a dollar-for-dollar competition with China. It must focus on areas of comparative advantage, governance, and systems resilience to minimise the scope for Chinese investment to turn into political leverage, and where it can, try to deny China control over strategically important assets and infrastructure. And Australia must do a better job of mobilising aid and investments from like-minded countries to give ballast to its efforts.

Australia must carefully examine what led the Solomon Islands government to conclude its secret security agreement with China — to enable it both to take remedial action and to learn lessons for the future. From the Solomons' perspective, the agreement not only facilitates greater Chinese investment, but also provides leverage with Australia and other traditional partners to demand more aid, unconditional security assistance, and greater diplomatic clout (evidenced by the United States' announcement in Fiji on 12 February 2023 that it would reopen its embassy in the Solomons' capital of Honiara).[29]

Neutralising the Chinese security agreement with Solomon Islands, which remains the most advanced potential Chinese strategic foothold in the Pacific, should remain a high priority for the Australian government. While respecting the Solomons' sovereign right to enter into such arrangements and the economic development aspirations that underpin it, Australia must explain — both to Solomon Islands and to other Pacific nations — the specific reasons for its concern and encourage the Solomons to limit the agreement's application to protect its sovereignty. This must happen behind closed doors; Pacific Island countries do not respond well to megaphone diplomacy.

Australia could encourage Solomon Islands to consider implementing legislation that requires clear definition of the scope of any Chinese deployments and sets out processes to ensure the rigorous assessment of any proposals. The Solomons could also consider mandating transparency for any requests for the deployment of Chinese military or security forces on its soil under the agreement — or even require explicit, case-by-case parliamentary approval of any China-initiated deployments.

Australia should give more substance to its rhetoric about the strategic importance of its relationships with the Pacific by establishing serious high-level strategic consultations with every Pacific country, and even some low-level intelligence-sharing arrangements, so that each fully understands Australia's perspective, knows its own views are understood and respected in turn, and is well equipped to make fully informed decisions. Australia must make it clear that it no longer thinks of the Pacific as its 'backyard'.

Australia should also explore with Pacific Island countries how to help strengthen the capacity of their governments to navigate this increasingly complex and contested strategic environment. Capacity-building in strategic analysis and policy development, and on international law and treaty drafting, could assist Pacific countries to protect their sovereignty when entering into any future agreements.

Finally, Australia must encourage the United States, the United Kingdom, France, and other partners to become much more engaged in the South Pacific. That the United States previously had no embassy in the Solomons, allowing China to build influence, is as much an Australian foreign policy failure as it is a US one.

The security agreement between China and Solomon Islands is a fundamentally unequal one. It has the potential to significantly alter the strategic environment in the South Pacific. It is essential that Australia and other concerned nations work with the Solomon Islands government to limit its application and minimise the possibility of it being replicated elsewhere in the Pacific.

.

BEIJING RESHAPES ITS PACIFIC STRATEGY

Denghua Zhang

THE PEOPLE'S REPUBLIC of China (PRC) and traditional regional powers such as the United States, Australia, New Zealand, and Japan are jockeying for influence in the Pacific. There are signs that China is now recalibrating its strategy in response to this newly energised competition, which was triggered by China's growing activities in the region. In the past, China's regional approach was largely limited to attendance at annual Pacific Islands Forum (PIF) dialogues, small donations to the PIF and the Pacific Tourism Organisation, and Chinese government scholarships (twenty per year) delivered through the PIF. Although China established the high-level China–Pacific Islands Economic Development and Cooperation Forum in 2006, it is not an annual event. So far, only three summits have been held, in 2006, 2013, and 2019.

The recent recalibration presents itself in three main aspects. The first involves adopting a dual strategy of competition and engagement, with a focus on competition. In a rare move, Chinese foreign minister Wang Yi convened two China–Pacific Foreign Ministers' meetings (in October 2021 and May 2022) in less than eight months.[1] The International Department of the

Communist Party of China (CPC) has also been busy establishing ties with major political parties in the Pacific and sharing ideas on enhancing state governance. These activities send a clear message that China is ramping up its competition with the traditional powers.

Interestingly, during his trip, Wang also said China was 'open-minded about carrying out more tripartite cooperation with other countries inside and outside the region'.[2] This is best interpreted as a temporary tactic to reduce traditional powers' concerns about China's activities in the region rather than a long-term policy change. Gone is the golden age of about a decade ago when China and traditional donor countries had a genuine interest in piloting trilateral cooperation in third countries, as typified by the Australia–China–Papua New Guinea malaria project and the New Zealand–China–Cook Islands water project. These experiments reveal that high-level political trust between China and traditional donors is a crucial element in China's trilateral cooperation, which is clearly now lacking.[3] Affected by the growing tensions in its bilateral

relations with China, it has also become increasingly difficult for Australia to hold regular diplomatic consultations with China on Pacific affairs. Even when they do, such as the recent video conference on the subject in May 2022, it was more a formality than an opportunity to have fruitful discussions.

Second, China is piloting an approach of 'driving with two steering wheels' 双轮驱动, which includes both bilateral and regional engagement with Pacific Island countries, although bilateral engagement will remain the focus.[4]

During Wang Yi's visit, he proposed two broad agreements to the region's leaders: the *China–Pacific Island Countries Common Development Vision* and the *China–Pacific Island Countries Five-Year Action Plan on Common Development (2022–2026)*. The agreements were intended to be the main achievement of the second foreign ministers' meeting and to represent China's new effort to boost its engagement with the Pacific. In the end, however, neither of the two agreements was adopted.[5] A possible reason is that Pacific Island states are becoming increasingly sensitive to policing and security cooperation with

China in the context of heightened geostrategic rivalry in the region.[6] Such concerns are exacerbated by the China–Solomon Islands security pact signed in March 2022, which has caused concerns about its implications for regional security.[7] According to some reports, there was also inadequate consultation between China and the region on the two proposed agreements.[8]

The third aspect of China's recalibration of its approach in the Pacific is the creation of institutional structures for systematic engagement. In particular, Beijing will rely heavily on six new China–Pacific cooperation centres, as well as tasking three provinces with promoting its Pacific diplomacy.[9] The six centres will focus, respectively, on climate change, poverty alleviation, disaster prevention and mitigation, agriculture, *juncao* (fungus grass, 菌草) technology, and the reservation of emergency supplies. Although China has previously cooperated with the Pacific Islands in these areas, the establishment of the cooperation centres highlights its desire to deepen engagement with Pacific countries. For example, the Pacific research centre at Liaocheng University will manage the China–Pacific climate change centre, conduct related research, and promote exchanges and cooperation.

The Chinese government has also tasked the coastal provinces of Guangdong, Fujian, and Shandong with leading China's provincial diplomacy in the Pacific. Compared with other provinces, these three have rich experience, resources, and expertise in cooperating with the Pacific. All have established Pacific research centres within their universities, including Sun Yat-sen University and Guangdong Foreign Studies University in Guangdong, Fujian Agriculture and Forestry University, and Shandong's Liaocheng University. These centres have established close relations with Pacific Islands through scholarships, volunteer teachers, and agricultural cooperation.

China has been adjusting its Pacific strategy in response to the growing determination of other powers — including the United States, Australia, New Zealand, and some Pacific countries — to counterbalance its influence in the region. The United States has responded to the China 'challenge' in a systematic way, including releasing its Indo-Pacific Strategy,[10] conducting diplomatic visits (Secretary of State Antony Blinken to Fiji in February 2022, White House Coordinator for the Indo-Pacific Kurt Campbell to Solomon Islands in April 2022, and Vice-President Kamala Harris's virtual address to the 2022 PIF in July and hosting of the first US–Pacific Islands Countries Summit in Washington, DC, in September), providing economic, financial, and technical assistance, and bolstering people-to-people links. To Beijing, these actions are aimed at containing China's rise — a challenge that must be met head-on. Xie Feng 谢锋, the Chinese vice-foreign minister in charge of China–Oceania relations, slammed traditional powers' opposition to the China–Solomon Islands security pact, asking: '[W]hat rights do these countries have to make unwarranted comments on China and Solomon Islands? How is Australia in any position to draw a "red line" between Solomon Islands 2,000 kilometres away and China ten thousand miles away?'[11] There is alarm among some traditional powers and the opposition party in Solomon Islands that the China–Solomon Islands security pact could pave the way for China to establish a military base in the islands. Despite this alarm, China is deepening policing cooperation with the country, including donating twenty-two police vehicles, thirty motorcycles, two police water cannons, eight police drones, and advanced close personal protection equipment.[12] In August 2022, the Solomon Islands government took out a ninety-six-million-dollar concessional loan from the Exim Bank of China to contract Huawei to build 161 telecommunications towers, sparking further controversy about security and debt risks.[13] Some Chinese scholars suggest that in reacting to Australia's 'Pacific Step-Up' and to reduce pressure from Australia over its Pacific diplomacy, China should 'take advantage of the fundamental contradiction between Australia's Monroe Doctrine and Pacific Island countries' independent foreign policies'.[14]

Pushback from Pacific nations themselves to China's growing activities poses a further challenge to its Pacific policies. Pacific Island nations do not wish to be pawns in a geostrategic power struggle, but have their own agendas on climate change, marine conservation, and development. The growing tensions between China and traditional powers have made it an imperative for Pacific Islands to manage their relations with China in a more cautious manner. Many are seemingly comfortable with the existing security arrangements, including partnerships with powers such as the United States and Australia that date back to World War II. They want, in the words of the PIF Secretariat's *2050 Strategy for the Blue Pacific Continent*, 'inclusive and enduring partnerships based on mutual accountability and respect'.[15] Pacific civil society stakeholders' views on China are complex and often divided.[16]

China is recalibrating its Pacific strategy to prevent Pacific Island nations forging closer links with its strategic competitors (including Taiwan). But Beijing is also aware of its limits. As China's economic growth slows and foreign reserves shrink, it is prioritising 'small but beautiful' 小而美 aid projects.[17] What remains unchanged in China's Pacific strategy is that Beijing sees Pacific Island nations in strategic terms, as more than just partners in areas like climate change or trade: for China, Pacific Island nations play an integral role in its South–South cooperation, which represents its attempt to strengthen relations with other developing countries to resist the pressure placed on it by the United States and others.

BUILDING A WORLD-CLASS NAVY: THE STORY OF CHINA'S FIRST AIRCRAFT CARRIER

Edward Sing Yue Chan

THE PEOPLE'S LIBERATION Army Navy (PLAN) is increasingly making its presence felt regionally and globally. The security pact between the People's Republic of China (PRC) and Solomon Islands signed in April 2022 opens the possibility for Chinese maritime security vessels to operate deep into the Pacific.[1] In May, a Chinese surveillance ship was spotted in the Indian Ocean near the West Australian coast, which then defence minister Peter Dutton described as 'an act of aggression'.[2] On 17 June 2022, the PRC launched its third aircraft carrier, the *Fujian* 福建舰, which is named for the mainland coastal province directly opposite Taiwan. This is the first aircraft carrier to be fully designed in China.[3] Compared with China's previous two carriers, the *Fujian* has a larger displacement, of approximately 85,000 tonnes, and is fitted with advanced technologies such as an electromagnetic catapult system for launching aircraft, putting it almost on par technologically with the carriers of the United States.[4]

The launch of the *Fujian* was a defining moment for the PLAN, marking its rise as a world-class navy. The story of how the PLAN acquired its first aircraft carrier —

a second-hand Soviet ship bought from Ukraine — is filled with plot twists worthy of a good spy novel.

Admiral Liu Huaqing's Vision

Liu Huaqing 刘华清 (1916–2011), who served as navy commander-in-chief from 1982 to 1988, was the first to articulate the dream of a Chinese-built aircraft carrier. During his term in office, Liu laid down two fundamental strategies for the PLAN: 'near sea active defence' 近海防御 and the development of a Chinese aircraft carrier. The 'near sea active defence' strategy shifted the PRC's geostrategic focus from land borders and coastlines to the maritime domain. It emphasised defence against immediate maritime threats, especially offshore territorial disputes.[5] Moreover, the strategy regarded the East and South China seas and Taiwan as a buffer zone to protect China's mainland. To prevent foreign intervention, the PLAN aimed to gain anti-access/area denial capacity in the maritime zone, which is a military strategy to control access to and within an operating environment. The

doctrine remains influential and was cited in the most recent National Defence White Paper, in 2019.

Liu stipulated that China should build an aircraft carrier by 2000. He saw this as necessary to manage security in the Taiwan Strait, assert Chinese sovereignty over the Spratly Islands (which are also claimed by the Philippines, Malaysia, Vietnam, and Brunei), and generally safeguard China's maritime rights and interests.[6] The navy set up a research institute in Shanghai in the early 1980s to design an aircraft carrier.[7] In 1985, Chinese shipbreakers purchased the HMAS Melbourne, a damaged light aircraft carrier, from the Royal Australian Navy. According to some observers, the Australian government did not oppose the sale at that time because China was seen as an important strategic counterweight to Soviet expansion in the Asia-Pacific. Chinese naval architects were able to study the design and build of the HMAS Melbourne and the PLAN used its flight deck for pilot training.[8]

However, Liu's vision met with some resistance. Some military officers argued that there was no need for China to have such a

Ships patrol the ocean
Source: Vidmarsimon, Pixabay

powerful warship. The Ministry of Foreign Affairs also raised concerns about the profound impact this would have on China's foreign relations, especially with the Association of Southeast Asian Nations (ASEAN) countries, as well as New Zealand and Australia.[9] More critically, the West imposed bans on military technology transfers after the 4 June massacre in 1989. Research and development stalled.

Getting the *Varyag* Home

The turning point in the achievement of Liu's vision came after the collapse of the Soviet Union in 1991. Ukraine had inherited two unfinished carriers, the Ulyanovsk and the *Varyag*. As the new Ukrainian government lacked the funding to complete their construction, it scrapped the Ulyanovsk and searched for potential buyers for the *Varyag*, which was about 70 percent complete. Both China and India expressed interest in acquiring it.[10] The United States and Japan, however, put pressure on Ukraine not to sell to China, accusing it of engaging with a state that was under an arms embargo. Beijing was also unable to pay the US$2 billion price tag the Ukrainians had put on the vessel.[11]

In 1998, the *Varyag* was put up for auction. A Chinese businessman, Xu Zengping 徐增平, bid US$20 million.[12] He bought the vessel under the name of the Chong Lot Tourism and Entertainment Company 长乐旅游与娱乐公司, which was registered in Macau. Even though the Chinese government denied any association with Chong Lot, newspapers in Hong Kong reported that Xu was a retired PLA soldier and most of those on Chong Lot's board were former naval officers and Chinese nationals from the province of Shandong, which was home to the North Sea Fleet.[13]

In November that year, Chong Lot unveiled plans to turn the *Varyag* into a floating casino and entertainment complex anchored in Macau harbour — supposed evidence that it was not intended for military use.[14] However, the Macanese authorities never received an application to operate such a casino. It would also have been impossible for the *Varyag* to dock in Macau's shallow harbour.[15]

Getting the *Varyag* to China proved slow and costly. Some design blueprints went missing, and Xu had to request a new copy from the Ukrainian government, which took months of waiting. Then, Türkiye refused the *Varyag* permission to pass through its territorial waters as the ship 'had not taken certain technical measures' required for such a large vessel without an engine.[16] Turkish authorities

were also concerned about sea lane safety. It was not until Beijing promised to boost trade and tourism links with Ankara that the eighteen months of deadlock ended.[17] During this time, Xu had to pay Ukraine approximately US$272,000 a month for mooring and towing costs. When the *Varyag* finally passed out of the Black Sea, it was denied entry to the Suez Canal by Egypt for the same reasons. In the end, the *Varyag* had to detour through the Strait of Gibraltar and around the Cape of Good Hope to reach the Indian Ocean. It was 3 March 2002 when it finally arrived in the port of Dalian in Liaoning province.[18]

The Chinese government secretly reimbursed Xu for his expenses and ownership of the *Varyag* was transferred to the PLAN. It took another nine years to transform the vessel into China's first aircraft carrier, the *Liaoning* 辽宁舰, which was launched in 2012. Five years later, the first domestically built carrier, the Shandong 山东舰, which was based on the Liaoning, entered active service, in 2019. Fourth and fifth aircraft carriers are currently in the planning stage, but activity has stalled because of a lack of training staff and pilots.[19]

Building a World-Class Navy

Addressing a parade of naval forces in April 2018, Xi Jinping, as chairman of the Central Military Commission, announced the goal of constructing a world-class navy.[20] His speech clearly signalled to the world that China intended to expand its influence across the oceans in the coming decades.

Three years before Xi's speech, in the PRC's National Defence White Paper of 2015, the Ministry of Defence proposed extending its naval strategy to 'far sea protection' 远海护卫 in addition to 'near sea defence'. The role of the PLAN would no longer be limited to defending Chinese maritime territory. Far sea protection is about safeguarding China's expanding interests overseas, including the protection of sea lines of communication, maritime cargo, ships, and trade routes as well as the security of its citizens and businesses overseas.[21]

From 2005 to 2021, the PLAN added eighty-six ships to its fleet, many of which were missile-equipped rapid patrol craft, corvettes, and cruisers. It also acquired new classes of submarines,

destroyers, frigates, and amphibious ships, most of which were put into operation after 2019.[22] To accommodate the expansion of its naval force, China's shipyards are also expanding. The Jiangnan Shipyard 江南造船厂 in Shanghai — one of the most important for the PLAN — occupies more than 7.3 square kilometres, while the neighbouring Hudong-Zhonghua Shipyard 沪东中华造船厂 will be expanding its shipbuilding area by about 50 percent.[23] Such significant shipbuilding development — all the vessels were constructed in China — allowed the PLAN to enhance its maritime defence capability in both near and far seas.

As defined by military leaders and official media, a 'world-class navy' will play a more crucial role in national rejuvenation than other parts of the military because of its international reach. Robert Ross, a professor at Boston College, describes China's maritime ambition as 'naval nationalism', following the historical pattern that great powers turn seaward with the growth of mass nationalism and nationalistic leadership.[24] Although initially the goal of building an aircraft carrier was to enhance the PRC's naval capability, Chinese state media now typically portray its construction as a symbol of great-power status, showcasing the country's technological capacity and resources. It presents the deployment of warships, on the other hand, as representing China's ability to defend its own territory and prevent foreign intervention in Chinese affairs — an antidote to the bitter history of the century of humiliation. Indeed, the PLAN has become more assertive since Xi Jinping took power: militarisation and land reclamation in the South China Sea, an increase of navigation in the Western Pacific Ocean, and the series of military exercises across the Taiwan Strait since August 2022.[25]

The party also views the navy as a tool for power projection. Hu Jintao made 'constructing a strong maritime state' 建设海洋强国 a national objective close to the end of his term as party and state leader in 2012. The PLAN supports this national goal by increasing its presence in the open ocean.[26] In 2017, it established the PRC's first overseas base, in Djibouti, in the Horn of Africa. Although state media claim that the base is only for logistical

support, it is certainly strategically advantageous. As part of the Belt and Road Initiative, China has been purchasing overseas ports for commercial purposes, which some Western analysts worry could serve the PLAN's military objectives.[27] The concern is valid, given China's need to protect its overseas interests and build a China-led security network. However, according to analysis by RAND Corporation, many factors must be considered for the PLAN to pursue bases in the Indian Ocean, such as the ability to obtain land and access, their utility for overseas military operations, and potential provocation of counterbalancing behaviours. Ultimately, it could take ten to twenty years (that is, until the 2030s) to turn ports into military bases; Cambodia, Myanmar, Bangladesh, and Pakistan are the four countries with highest desirability and feasibility.[28]

In addition, before the COVID-19 pandemic, the PLAN had conducted port visits and joint exercises with foreign navies, including those of the United States, Russia, Pakistan, and Thailand, as a type of naval diplomacy. It has also been involved in non-military operations — such as search and rescue, escort, and anti-piracy — in the Indian Ocean, through which run some of the world's busiest trade routes. By January 2023, forty-three Chinese fleet groups had conducted anti-piracy escort missions in the Gulf of Aden. The PLAN has also been training civilian vessels to act as maritime militias when necessary, such as escorting other Chinese civilian vessels for fishing activities and tracking and monitoring foreign vessels in disputed waters.[29] It also provides professional guidance to several domestic maritime law enforcement agencies, such as the China Coast Guard. Clearly, the PLAN has become more than a warfighting tool.

A world-class navy also helps protect the PRC's regional interests. Since 2012, the Chinese government has largely employed non-military measures to increase its maritime influence in the East and South China seas, such as law enforcement operations and land reclamation (reef building). China perceives itself as encircled by regional naval powers, including Russia, Japan, and India, as well as the presence of the global US Navy in nearby waters. Beijing believes a world-class navy is required to prevent the United States and its allies from contravening its interests in the Asia-Pacific.

Challenges Ahead

Despite investing considerable resources to become world-class, the PLAN still faces many challenges. Like the country's other armed forces, the Chinese Navy lacks modern combat experience. The last time the PLAN was involved in a military confrontation was the Johnson South Reef Skirmish with Vietnamese forces in 1988. Even though it has conducted much training and many exercises throughout the years, its ability to operate modern warships and weaponry systems in a sea battle remains untested.

A lesson of the Russia–Ukraine war is that a weakness in modern joint operations is coordination between land, sea, air, cyber, and space forces.[30] Most strategists would still describe the Chinese Navy as a semi–blue-water navy with the capability to navigate globally but lacking operational experience. In addition, the expansion of the carrier fleet is yet to offer a direct challenge to the United States' dominant global sea power. The *Fujian* demonstrates that China is catching up with US naval technology, but the PLAN is still unable to compete with the US Navy in fleet size and capability. As Sam Roggeveen, the director of the International Security Program at the Lowy Institute, points out: 'Carriers are a sign of Chinese power — but that doesn't mean Beijing has to rule the waves.'[31]

A complicated geopolitical environment hinders further expansion of the PLAN. Blocked from projecting its influence beyond the near seas by Japan, Taiwan, the Philippines, India, and the United States, the PLAN does not have direct access to the open ocean — one reason for the PRC's push for security cooperation with other developing states in the Indian and Pacific oceans, such as Cambodia and Sri Lanka.[32] Moreover, because of the ongoing territorial disputes in the East and South China seas, neighbouring countries tend to view China's assertive naval expansion, especially any build-up of forces in the Asia-Pacific, as a security threat. Such a view was echoed in a March 2022 report by the US Congressional Research Service, which stated: 'In an era of renewed great power competition, China's military modernization effort, including its naval modernization effort, has become the top focus of US defense planning and budgeting.'[33] Regardless, as China's overseas interests increase, its maritime ambition will continue to expand. The goal, as President Xi has stated, is nothing less than the PRC's transformation into a 'true maritime power' 海洋强国.

七

CHAPTER 7 —
CHINA'S RUSSIA
PROBLEM

A 'NO LIMITS' PARTNERSHIP?

CHINA–RUSSIA STRATEGIC COOPERATION

Alexander Korolev

On 4 February 2022, the opening day of the Winter Olympic Games in Beijing and only twenty days before Russia's invasion of Ukraine, the People's Republic of China (PRC) and Russia declared a 'no limits' partnership that 'surpasses an alliance'.[1] Given the two countries' geopolitical ambitions and boundaries, a tighter alignment could significantly change the power structure of the contemporary international system and fundamentally challenge the existing liberal order.

This chapter takes stock of recent developments in the China–Russia strategic alignment from three often neglected angles. The first is the consistency of Chinese–Russian cooperation. The second is growing military–technical cooperation. The third deals with the structural shifts in great-power politics that drive Chinese–Russian relations. The chapter also addresses the main weaknesses of China–Russia strategic cooperation and the impact on it of Russia's invasion of Ukraine.

Consistent Consolidation of Bilateral Cooperation

The relatively high level of China–Russia strategic cooperation is not an ad hoc phenomenon. Nor is it a knee-jerk reaction to the deterioration of US–Russia relations in the aftermath of the Ukraine crisis or recent US–China tensions in South-East Asia and beyond. It is a continuation of a consistent consolidation of the strategic partnership between China and Russia since the breakup of the Soviet Union. The steady expansion of China and Russia's comprehensive mechanism of strategic cooperation has proven immune to episodical perturbations, progressing into what in alliance studies is defined as an advanced form of strategic cooperation.[2]

This consistent trend is reflected in official statements, according to which the relationship has progressed from 'good neighbourliness' in the early 1990s to 'constructive cooperation' in the late 1990s, to a 'comprehensive strategic partnership' in 2001, a 'comprehensive strategic partnership of coordination' in 2012, and a 'comprehensive strategic partnership of equality, mutual trust, mutual support, common prosperity and long-lasting friendship' in 2019.[3] On 5 June 2019, Chinese president Xi Jinping and Russian president Vladimir Putin upgraded China–Russia relations to 'a comprehensive strategic partnership of coordination for a new era'. This progression highlights consistent consolidation of the alignment, its immunity to exogenous shocks, and the willingness of both sides to deal together with future challenges.[4]

The consolidation materialised mostly in military–strategic terms, including the introduction of a comprehensive mechanism for military consultations at different levels. The number of joint military exercises involving the two countries' armies, air forces, and navies in different parts of the world, as well as regular computer-simulated missile defence drills, significantly increased coordination between them. The critique and condemnation of US policies in Asia and elsewhere as 'increasingly threatening', as well as China and Russia's proclamation to jointly resist the growing US threat, became an embedded norm of Chinese–Russian security dialogue. Cooperation across economic and diplomatic dimensions, while not yet as strong, has also steadily increased.

There have been ups and downs. Examples include a temporary stagnation in military–technical cooperation in the mid-2000s and the occasional suspension of otherwise regular bilateral consultations. However, the overall trend is upward; viewed in its entirety, the relationship shows itself immune to short-term fluctuations. It is in this context that on 4 February 2022 the two leaders announced a 'no limits partnership' that 'surpasses an alliance' because it has 'no forbidden areas'.[5]

Then came Russia's invasion of Ukraine. Beijing has carefully tried to distance itself from Russia over Ukraine to avoid being affected by the global sanctions, which suggests at least one limit to the partnership — an unwillingness to be partners in economic adversity. However, China has procured more energy resources from Russia since the latter's aggression against Ukraine. Amid the sanctions imposed on it over the war, Russia has become China's biggest supplier of oil. In May 2022, imports of Russian oil rose by 55 percent from a year earlier, reaching a record level and displacing

A train enters China from Russia
Source: Jack01, Wikipedia

Saudi Arabia as China's biggest provider.[6] Moreover, the continuing bilateral military exercises and joint air patrols over the Western Pacific, especially recent incidents of Chinese and Russian warplanes together entering the South Korean air defence zone from the Sea of Japan,[7] suggest that China is not distancing itself from Russia when it comes to the strategic aspects of the bilateral cooperation, even though China's voting decision on Ukraine at the UN Security Council suggests more neutrality than support.[8]

Growing Military–Technical Cooperation

Military–technical cooperation (MTC) relates to the degree of military alignment between China and Russia and is ultimately a question of how technically prepared the two countries are for a hypothetical fully fledged alliance, including united military action.

China and Russia have travelled a long way in terms of strategic cooperation since the early 1990s. Currently, they carry out twenty to thirty high-level security-related consultations every year, which is at the level of a functional alliance. This number excludes regional consultations between Chinese and Russian provinces and cities and exchanges between military academies.[9]

Russia's attitude towards a more comprehensive and interdependent MTC with China has evolved, with Moscow increasingly less wary of relying on China in this area. Political factors that used to constrain Russia in its MTC with China — which included concerns about China's unlicensed reverse-engineering of weapons, potential competition from cheaper China-made weapons on international markets, and worries about excessive dependence on China — have disappeared and interconnectedness is becoming the dominant tendency.[10] Russia has begun to rely on China for such things as electronic components for its space program, composite materials and technologies used in drone construction, and engines for warships — all of which result in closer military–technical interdependence.[11] Russia's tendency to consider China as not only a target market for its weapons but also a source of critical equipment and technologies has only consolidated in the context of its war in Ukraine. Willingly or not, Russia has reconsidered its previous defence-equipment-for-cash model of cooperation with China. The imposition of global sanctions on Russia, however, has made China more cautious about sending it supplies and has incentivised the use of more complex and less traceable schemes in bilateral transactions.[12]

China and Russia have undertaken a growing number of joint military exercises in different parts of the world. For example, 'Joint Sea-2015' was held in the NATO-dominated Mediterranean and 'Joint Sea-2016' became the first major exercise of its type to include China and a second country in the disputed South China Sea after the Hague tribunal overruled China's claims over the waters within its Nine-Dash Line. The increasing operational complexity of these joint exercises has laid the foundation for potential simultaneous joint military actions in multiple theatres of operation. This could enable China and Russia to draw the attention and capabilities of the United States and its allies to a specific region, reducing their ability to react to, for example, Chinese actions in the Pacific or Russia's in western Eurasia.[13] This is one of the reasons, in the context of Russia's ongoing war in Ukraine, the United States has paid so much attention to China's potential military invasion of Taiwan.[14] As some recent congressional reports specified, the United States could struggle to win a war against China or Russia if forced to fight on two or more fronts simultaneously.[15]

The degree of interoperability between Chinese and Russian forces has increased: recent joint military exercises have involved the creation of temporary joint command centres, tactical groups under a single command, and air groups jointly implementing simulated attacks. China and Russia have also started integrating their satellite navigation systems, Beidou and GLONASS, respectively. Huawei Technologies Group has been facilitating China–Russia cyber integration by opening data centres in Moscow, St Petersburg, Kazan, Novosibirsk, and Nizhny Novgorod.[16]

A new level of military cooperation came with the announcement by President Putin in October 2019 that Russia was actively helping China to create an early warning radar system for missile attack.[17] According to some assessments, the new system will be based on the Russian 'Tundra' satellites and 'Voronezh' modular ground-based radar stations set up in Chinese territory.[18] The system will provide advance warning of incoming missiles' potential trajectory, speed, time-to-target, and other critical information needed for effective interception. Missile early warning systems constitute one of the most critical aspects of any country's defence capability. Potential integration of the two countries' systems would facilitate the convergence of their defence strategies, in which case their military integration and interdependence would potentially match that of US alliances with such countries as France and the United Kingdom.[19]

Structural Shifts in Great-Power Politics

To understand the third aspect of the relationship, the structural balance of power, requires looking into the structural shifts in great-power politics. There are strong factors within the international system that drive China–Russia alignment. Historical research suggests that of sixteen great-

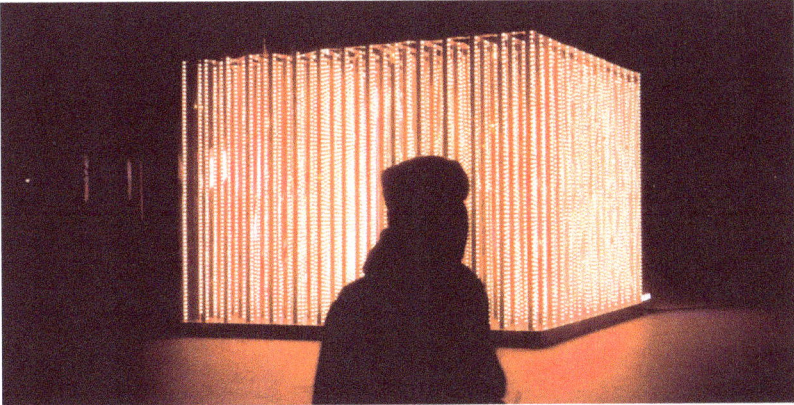

'Cage of Wonders' art installation
Source: Alexander Muller, Wikipedia

power transitions (shifts in the global balance of power in which a rising power catches up with or surpasses the dominant great power in terms of comprehensive capabilities), only four were peaceful.[20]

In the contemporary international system, a transition of power is occurring between China and the United States. According to the World Bank, in 1991, the total US gross domestic product (GDP) of US$6.2 trillion was more than sixteen times that of China (US$383.4 billion). By 2020, China's GDP reached almost 70 percent of that of the United States (US$14.3 trillion versus US$21.4 trillion).[21] History shows that an established superpower (the United States, in this case) represents the greatest threat to states that are on the cusp of becoming superpowers (in this case, China).[22] In this context, China has every reason to develop its strategic alignment with Russia, which, given Russia's anti-US foreign policy orientation, military, and geopolitical characteristics, and its permanent seat on the UN Security Council, presents the most effective counterbalance against US power.

At the same time, the United States explicitly identifies China and Russia as major strategic threats — an assessment that drives its defence decisions and allocation of military resources. As the United States' main strategic rival, China is given a primary place in US defence strategy.[23] Russia, in turn, is dubbed a 'revitalised malign actor' that must be contained through comprehensive sanctions (increased since its invasion of Ukraine).[24] A simultaneous US focus on China and Russia contributes to a situation in which the latter two start to view the US the same way the US views them: as the greatest threat to their national security and the primary focus of defence policy.

This tendency was exacerbated on 27 October 2022, when the Biden administration unveiled a new defence strategy that effectively puts the US military in Cold War mode towards both China and Russia. The new strategy details the United States' plan to confront the two nuclear peers and potential adversaries with a historic multi-year buildup of modernised weaponry, enhanced foreign alliances, and a complete overhaul of its nuclear arsenal.[25] The issue is complicated by the fact that while the United States and Russia have negotiated on nuclear weapons, China has never agreed to any such talks. As a result, the power balance in the international system that is conducive to China–Russia alignment is buttressed by their shared perception of external threats: both increasingly feel that the United States jeopardises their geopolitical interests, national identity, and domestic political regimes.

The current behaviour of the United States suggests a lack of questioning within its strategic establishment of whether adopting a hostile attitude towards both China and Russia makes strategic sense. According to some assessments, the approach does not bode well for the United States' long-term strategic interests because it encourages China–Russia alignment.[26] In the context of the evolving power balance, this deterioration removes any remaining political barriers to closer alignment.[27]

'Unfavourable Complementarity' in Economic Relations

Economic cooperation remains the Achilles heel of Chinese–Russian strategic alignment. The two countries have become more complementary economically and more interdependent in the energy sector. However, as

China and Russia's relative shares in each other's external trade indicate, Russia depends much more on China than China depends on Russia in terms of trade. China ranks as Russia's top trading partner, but Russia is only China's fourteenth-largest trading partner. Moreover, Russia has ended up in a role that it is reluctant to embrace. The so-called complementarity of China and Russia's economic models — allegedly conducive to closer cooperation — creates unfavourable geopolitical pressures on the relationship.

The rapid growth of the total China–Russia trade volume — from a meagre US$5.6 billion in 1992 to US$153.9 billion in the first 10 months of 2022 — has been accompanied by the emergence of a bilateral trade structure that is too unbalanced to be healthy for the relationship and reflects the degradation and primitivisation of Russia's economy since the breakup of the Soviet Union. Russia's manufacturing sector has all but collapsed and the country has become a petrostate. Meanwhile, China has become the world's factory on a gargantuan scale, producing more than 20 percent of global manufacturing output. Between 2001 and 2021, the share of machinery and equipment in China's exports to Russia rose from less than 10 percent to almost 50 percent, but Russia's exports of the same to China dropped from almost 30 percent to less than 1 percent. Simultaneously, the share of oil and oil products in Russia's exports to China soared, from 10 percent in 2001 to more than 70 percent by 2020.[28] Despite this, China, unlike Europe, does not strongly depend on Russian resources, which represent only 19 percent of its total energy/oil consumption. In contrast, for some European countries such as Germany, Russian resources accounted for more than 50 percent of total energy/oil consumption in 2021. The war in Ukraine and the comprehensive sanctions imposed on Moscow will most likely accelerate the technological degradation of the Russian economy, reducing Russia's significance to China, from a true economic partner to little more than an energy provider.

The deterioration of Russia's economic standing vis-a-vis China has various implications. Except for the Russian military-industrial complex, China perceives Russia less as a source of innovation and new technologies and more as simply a source of energy resources and a market for finished manufactured products. For Russia, which only twenty years ago was ahead of China on many economic development indicators, this is a disappointing outcome that thins the otherwise strong foundations of and support for strategic cooperation with China.

On a psychological level, China's increasing perception of Russia as a net energy exporter discomfits many Russians, including political elites, and makes the Russian government cooler on China than it might otherwise be.

These tendencies consolidated after Russia invaded Ukraine. Barred from access to Western technologies by comprehensive economic sanctions that are unlikely to ease in the foreseeable future, Moscow has rushed to extend its energy exports to Asia at discounted prices — a situation of which China has taken advantage. Thus, the pattern of unequal bilateral economic transactions is likely to continue. This in turn will lead to demands within Russia for protection of national markets and producers from Chinese economic expansion, and to prevent Russia from turning into little more than China's resource appendage.

The Test of the Ukraine War

The war in Ukraine is stress-testing China–Russia strategic cooperation. By not distancing itself from Moscow, Beijing has incurred serious reputational costs and potentially risks becoming a target of secondary economic sanctions. Yet, the war is unlikely to significantly reverse the strategic alignment because of Beijing's growing recognition that it is on a long-term collision course with the United States.

US policies towards China indicate that Washington has embarked on a strategy of containing China, though its official rhetoric favours use of the word 'competition'. On top of de facto economic containment — enforced through such measures as restricting exports of microchip technologies to China and pressuring partners to ban Chinese companies Huawei and ZTE from involvement in building 5G network infrastructure — the United States continues to back Taiwan with arms sales and high-profile visits by top officials. These measures place serious stress on China–US relations and make China increasingly reluctant to distance itself from Russia.

Ten days after Russia invaded Ukraine, former US secretary of state Mike Pompeo travelled to Taipei and urged Washington to 'take necessary and long-overdue steps to do the right and obvious thing', by which he meant recognise 'free and independent' Taiwan.[29] Former House Speaker Nancy Pelosi's visit to Taiwan on 2 August 2022 (five months after Russia's invasion of Ukraine), despite Beijing's vehement criticism and the staging of live-fire exercises off Taiwan's coast, added fuel to the fire.[30] For Beijing, any proclamation of Taiwanese independence is a red line. Washington could have tried to use the Ukraine war to pull China away from Russia, but actions such as those of Pompeo and Pelosi have made this difficult.[31] An argument can be made that neither Pelosi's visit nor Pompeo's words represent US policy and that, thanks to the nature of its political system, both are independent actors. However, if this was the case — that is, Pelosi's visit was the pursuit of her personal political interest — and the United States was interested in minimising tensions with China, the Biden administration should have criticised Pelosi's visit.

President Xi has continued to speak directly with President Biden, including for three hours in Bali, as the two leaders affirmed their mutual opposition to any use of tactical nuclear weapons in Ukraine. Nonetheless, Beijing remains suspicious that Washington is promoting a new Cold War. These suspicions were exacerbated significantly by, among other things, the recently minted AUKUS initiative that former Australian prime minister Scott Morison claimed was a way to push back against a China-led 'arc of autocracy'.[32]

Another factor that contributes to China's unwillingness to openly criticise Putin's war in Ukraine is Western hypocrisy in not making much noise about India's friendship with Russia. Like China, India has never condemned Russia's invasion of Ukraine and, through its purchases of crude oil from Russia, is supporting Moscow no less than is China.[33] In March 2022, India was preparing a rupee–ruble trade arrangement with Russia that will allow the two countries to continue trade despite Western sanctions against Russia.[34] Attempts to warn India of the consequences if it tries to circumvent the sanctions have only been mild and delivered with nowhere near as much pressure and hostile rhetoric as those targeted at China.[35]

From Beijing's perspective, this behaviour appears to confirm that US criticism of it is not about the war in Ukraine, but about using the war to contain China. In such a hostile context, then, Beijing has been reluctant to condemn Russia and risk undermining their strategic alignment.

Conclusion

China and Russia's alignment is not a formal military alliance and may not become one. Moreover, it is not impossible for Chinese–Russian military cooperation to unravel. For all its reluctance to condemn Russia directly, China remains ambivalent about the war in Ukraine and its position on the issue of state sovereignty does not fully coincide with Moscow's. Economic factors could also hinder the upgrading of relations to the level of a fully fledged alliance. The different economic roles of China and Russia in the global division of labour remains another challenge for bilateral strategic cooperation.

Yet, the China–Russia strategic alignment is solid, institutionalised, and comprehensive, and it should be taken seriously. It is also trending incrementally upward. Their shared great-power hostility towards US hegemony in world politics suppresses the most likely centrifugal forces that could pull them apart. The simultaneous deterioration of China–US and Russia–US relations after Russia's invasion of Ukraine prevents the Ukraine war from becoming a factor that will slow or undermine the China–Russia strategic alignment. An alliance is possible, although if one is in the works, China and Russia may delay an official announcement or not make an announcement at all.

Chinese Social Media and

the War in Ukraine

KECHENG FANG

CHINESE SOCIAL MEDIA AND THE WAR IN UKRAINE

Kecheng Fang

IN A RARE SURVEY of Chinese public opinion on the Russia–Ukraine war conducted by the Carter Center in March–April 2022, we can identify two highly significant findings: first, the majority (about 75 percent) of respondents believed that supporting Russia was beneficial to the national interest of the People's Republic of China (PRC); and second, the consumption of state media and the use of social media were the top two predictors of a pro-Russia attitude.[1]

Outside observers and some China researchers once believed that social media was a place where the Chinese public could express diverse opinions, especially those alternative to or even critical of the dominant narrative of state propaganda. Contrary to this expectation, we see convergence between state and social media on the issue of the Russia–Ukraine war. This pattern is the product of a decade-long process of political censorship, cooption, commercial incentives, and transnational flows of disinformation, and reveals a much more complicated Chinese social media landscape than the traditional picture of top-down propaganda.

Pro-Russia as a 'Secret Code to Wealth'

On the YouTube-like video platform Bilibili, the most-watched video about the Russia–Ukraine war was not published by state media. Titled 'What kind of big power game is hidden behind the strange Russia–Ukraine conflict?', it was published by the *zimeiti* 自媒体 ('self-media') account Lu Kewen Studio 卢克文工作室 on 24 February 2022.[2] Arguing that Ukraine was a puppet of the United States and the war was the result of US provocation and the 'aggressive eastward expansion' of the North Atlantic Treaty Organisation (NATO), this was the top trending video on the site the day after its publication, and accumulated more than 9.5 million views by the end of August 2022.

Another top video on this issue is titled 'Emergency deletion, mysterious virus, biochemical experiments ... What exactly did the US do in Ukraine?', which was posted by another *zimeiti*, Sai Lei Hua Jin 赛雷话金, on 25 March 2022.[3] It had more than seven million views by the end of August 2022.

As the title suggests, it is a video promoting conspiracy theories about US biolaboratories.

Both Lu Kewen Studio and Sai Lei Hua Jin are notorious *zimeiti* accounts that have built extremely large followings by publishing sensationalist, nationalistic content, including articles on WeChat's public platform and *Jinri Toutiao* 今日头条 (China's leading news aggregator and a core product of the company ByteDance), and videos on Bilibili, Xigua Video, and Weibo. And they are far from the only prominent actors in this business; other big *zimeiti* accounts include Zhan Hao 占豪, Wuheqilin 乌合麒麟 (who created the infamous computer-generated image of an Australian soldier slitting the throat of an Afghan child that was promoted by Chinese foreign affairs official Zhao Lijian in November 2020), and Digua Xiong Laoliu 地瓜熊老六, among others. All harvest and monetise user attention on social media by waving the nationalistic flag, which includes rooting for Russia — the 'friend without limits', as proclaimed in the joint statement issued by the Chinese and Russian

Chinese programmer
Wang Jixian in Odessa
Oblast, Ukraine
Source: Wang Jixian, Wikipedia

governments during the meeting between Presidents Vladimir Putin and Xi Jinping in February.

Some may wonder whether *zimeiti*, like Lu Kewen Studio, Sai Lei Hua Jin, and Zhan Hao, are affiliated with the party-state. For example, Sai Lei Hua Jin's video pushing the US biolabs conspiracy theory was a collaboration between Sai Lei Hua Jin and the Henan Provincial Committee of the Communist Youth League. Zhan Hao is a member of the Hubei Provincial Committee of the Chinese People's Political Consultative Conference. However, the emergence of nationalistic influencers is more about commercial incentives than political manipulation. As I have argued in

a previous paper on *zimeiti*, the industry is enabled by social media platforms and the business model of the attention economy and focuses on strategies to attract traffic that can translate into advertising revenue.[4] Nationalistic content, while politically safe and unlikely to be censored, is highly effective in generating attention due to its highly emotional nature. Not surprisingly, many astute businesspeople have chosen this path.

Lu Kewen and his peers have, to use a popular online catchphrase in China, found a 'secret code to wealth' 财富密码. Praising Russia and President Putin, denouncing the United States and NATO, and mocking Ukraine and its actor-turned-president has proven a fruitful way to activate the 'secret code'. Seeing the influencers' huge follower bases on social media platforms, the state has chosen to collaborate with them, offering the political connections the entrepreneurs crave, while piggybacking on their popularity to spread pro-government messages.

Strategic Filtering and Imports of Information

The party-state closely monitors and censors information about the Russia–Ukraine war on Chinese social media. A few days after Russia's invasion of Ukraine, five renowned Chinese historians published an open letter online, denouncing Russia and calling for peace. 'In the midst of all the noise, we felt the need to make our voices heard,' the letter said. 'We are concerned that Russian military action will lead to turmoil in Europe and the entire world, and trigger a wider humanitarian disaster.'[5]

Censors took down the letter after two hours and forty minutes. Although the authorities never provide the reasons for censorship, in this case, we can speculate that what triggered the alarm was not

only the writers' anti-Russia stance — in contrast with the Chinese government's position — but also the nature of collective action in the drafting and public release of the co-signed letter.

However, the party-state does not simply block all information about the war that is not published by its official sources. Rather, it strategically allows certain messages from outside the 'Great Firewall' to be introduced into Chinese cyberspace.

The Russian government's mouthpieces RT and Sputnik both have official accounts on Weibo, with tens of millions of followers collectively. They are two of the main providers of pro-Russia narratives on Weibo, which also amplify their voices through algorithmic recommendation and putting their posts on the trending list. The public WeChat account of the *China Daily* interviewed the deputy chief editor of RT in March, who argued that the Western world was waging a war of information and public opinion 信息舆论战 to isolate and censor Russia's voice.[6] An underlying message of the interview was that, unlike Western audiences, who were 'blinded' by Western media, Chinese readers could get 'comprehensive' information about the war thanks to their access to Russian media on Chinese platforms.

Under such arrangements, the Russian government and media can easily export disinformation to Chinese social media. Sai Lei Hua Jin's US biolab story — originally disseminated by the Kremlin — chimed with conspiracy theories that had already spread across the Chinese internet about the origins of COVID-19. It was reported by multiple state media outlets and promoted to the trending topics list by Weibo. No wonder about half the respondents to the Carter Center's survey had seen the conspiracy theory, and only 13 percent deemed it inaccurate.

There is also a large group of Chinese social media users spontaneously importing pro-Russia information from the outside; many are military enthusiasts with nationalistic attitudes. The dynamic resembles that of the importation to Chinese platforms of Western (anti-Black) racism and Islamophobia by influencers — the subject of a previous study of mine.[7] The influencers selectively translate messages from foreign media and social media sites such as Twitter. If the messages are not favourable to Russia, they are interpreted as fake news or evidence that the West is targeting Russia (and China) for political reasons. For example, when an influencer posted a video of destroyed Russian military equipment on Ukraine's Independence Day, he added a comment that Russian people questioned why there were no visible 'Zs' or 'Vs' (Russian symbols of its military actions in Ukraine) and figured that 'they might be Ukraine's own stuff'. His followers commented on the video: 'It's natural for an actor to borrow some props.'[8] A wide range of information can find its way on to China's social media platforms, but it is largely twisted and used to support, rather than challenge and diversify, the mainstream narrative.

The Small Yet Important Group Sympathising with Ukrainians

Although pro-Russia attitudes and content prevail on Chinese social media, there is a small yet important group of people who openly express their support for Ukraine, despite heavy censorship and possible offline retaliation.

As well as the open letter published by the historians, there have been other notable initiatives. For example, a group of Chinese internationalists launched an 'alternative news agency' 替代性通讯社 named hxotnongd 与此同时 ('*Meanwhile*') that publishes articles on WeChat with a firm anti-war stance and expressing solidarity with Ukraine.[9] Although censors eventually deleted the content and the WeChat account, the group's articles managed to circulate among some young and well-educated people in China (see their Facebook page).[10]

Videos published by Wang Jixian 王吉贤, a software engineer living in Ukraine's third-largest city, Odessa, reached a large audience on WeChat's video channel before being censored. In the videos, Wang shared his fear of living in a country at war and his anger at his fellow Chinese citizens who supported Russia. Although we do not know how many people followed his WeChat video account before it was

blocked, his YouTube channel had more than 110,000 followers by the end of August 2022.[11]

Some of the more subtle voices sympathising with Ukrainians have survived on the Chinese internet. For example, Guyu 谷雨, a media account focusing on non-fiction storytelling, published a story in late March, in which the author described her experience of volunteering at Berlin's central railway station to help Ukrainian refugees.[12] The podcast *The Weirdo* 不合时宜 produced two episodes about the war, one in February and the other in August.[13] The host and the guests on both episodes expressed a clear pro-Ukraine stance. The second episode also featured a Chinese student studying in Ukraine, who volunteered in the community by teaching painting to children in a shelter and raised money from his Chinese friends and followers to help Ukrainians. Another podcast, *Story FM* 故事FM, released an episode in June about how museum staff in Ukraine protected artefacts and preserved culture and history.[14] The message of the brutality of war and the impressive efforts to save culture was clear.

It should be noted that such voices mostly appear on platforms that do not allow public comments and limit direct interactions among users. Such platforms, like the WeChat public platform and podcasts, make it hard for trolls to harass and attack the authors. It is much more difficult to express anti-Russia opinions on relatively open platforms such as Weibo and Bilibili, which are more vulnerable to cyberbullying. That said, the official Weibo account of Ukraine's embassy in Beijing, which constantly publishes anti-Russia posts, has a moderate number of followers (roughly 136,000 at the end of August) and an average post will receive hundreds of comments and shares. Comments like 'Go Ukraine!' and 'Support for Ukraine' can be easily found on this account, despite the obvious risk associated with such open expression.[15]

Although publicly audible anti-Russia voices are understandably fewer than those supporting the invasion, they demonstrate that discussions of and opinions about the Russia–Ukraine war in China are far from black and white.

八

CHAPTER 8 — CHINA–AUSTRALIA AT FIFTY

TAKING STOCK AT FIFTY

Yi Wang and Linda Jaivin

The first four decades of diplomatic relations between Australia and the People's Republic of China (PRC) proceeded largely along an upward trajectory. Increasing institutional, economic, cultural, and other links drew the two countries and peoples closer. There have been times of friction, including a period of several years after the killing of prodemocracy protesters on the streets of Beijing in 1989. But these have generally been followed by periods of rebuilding: Deng Xiaoping's reaffirmation of the economic reforms in 1992 led to an economic resurgence that saw a boom in Australian exports to China of iron ore, among other things, and with them, Australian goodwill towards the PRC. The thrust of the most recent decade, however, has been downwards.

Decade of Deterioration

Marking the fortieth anniversary of diplomatic relations in 2012, the Australian embassy in Beijing declared the relationship with China to be one of its most important. The bilateral relationship, it said, was 'based on shared interests and mutual respect, an approach which offers the best prospects to maximise shared economic interests, advance Australia's political and strategic interests, and manage differences in a sensible and practical way'.[1] Two years later, the relationship was looking stronger than ever. The then prime minister, Tony Abbott, even invited China's new leader, Xi Jinping, to address the Australian Parliament. Together, they witnessed the signing of a declaration of intent for a free-trade agreement between the two countries, while other bilateral agreements signed at the same time enhanced Australian–Chinese cooperation in Antarctica, agreed to establish a renminbi clearing bank in Sydney, and boosted cooperation in investment and education. The leaders upgraded the relationship to a 'comprehensive strategic partnership'.[2]

Within four years, the bilateral relationship had turned tense. Canberra, still under a coalition government, had come to perceive China's rise as a threat. Among the concerns were political influence operations. Acting on Australian Security Intelligence Organisation (ASIO) advice, in 2018 the government passed nine laws intended to prevent foreign interference. Although China was not explicitly named, it was no secret that concerns about the PRC prompted the hurried drafting of the bills. Among other things, it had been revealed that a Chinese businessman and long-time resident, Huang Xiangmo 黄向墨, who had made millions of dollars in political donations, was connected with the Communist Party of China (CPC) through various United Front organisations; he was barred entry to Australia on national security grounds the next year. Australia also banned Huawei from its 5G networks in 2018.

Beijing was openly displeased and relations soured. In 2019, the writer and Australian citizen Yang Hengjun 杨恒均 was arrested at an airport in China (he has maintained his innocence and alleges he has been tortured; as of early 2023, he had been convicted but not yet sentenced on charges of espionage). Other reasons for strained relations included ongoing Australian criticism of human rights abuses in Xinjiang.

After the Morrison government made its unilateral demand for an independent investigation of the origins of COVID-19 in early 2020, which Beijing characterised as Australia playing 'political games', the relationship began a further rapid downward slide. Beijing applied de facto trade sanctions against selected Australian exports including wine, lobsters, beef, barley, and coal worth more than A$5.4 billion. It also suspended high-level official contacts. Towards the end of the year, a Chinese official presented a list of fourteen 'grievances' the country had with Australia to a journalist from Channel 9 at a meeting in Canberra. Predictably, these included unhappiness with the Huawei ban, the call for an inquiry into the origins of COVID-19, the foreign interference laws, limits on foreign investment, and Canberra's criticism of human rights abuses in Xinjiang. The list also cited 'unfriendly or antagonistic' media reports about China that it claimed were poisoning relations.

Other Chinese officials, meanwhile, threw fuel on the fire by responding to the official inquiry into possible Australian war crimes in Afghanistan by tweeting a mocked-up picture of an Australian soldier slitting the throat of an Afghan child, sparking widespread outrage.[3] Attitudes towards the PRC hardened among politicians and the public at large. The following year, Australia signed up to the AUKUS security pact with the United Kingdom and the United States.

The AUKUS pact, under which the Australian Navy will acquire nuclear-powered submarines, went far beyond the Australia, New Zealand, United States Security Treaty (ANZUS Treaty) of 1951. That had served as a general assurance against the possibility of a militaristically resurgent Japan as well as any communist threat from the north. The AUKUS pact was created specifically (if never explicitly) against the perceived threat from a rising and assertive China in the Indo-Pacific, where China was ramping up military activities around disputed islands in the South China Sea and the Taiwan Strait, among other things. In joining AUKUS, Australia not only compromised its long-held stance against nuclear proliferation, but also tied itself more firmly to the US war chariot. Because it integrates Australian troops with UK and US forces to 'move beyond interoperability to interchangeability', critics question whether Australian forces will potentially be subject to the command of US-led military operations in the future, though both sides deny this is the case.[4]

By ditching its original deal with France to build conventional submarines in favour of nuclear ones, Australia not only incurred French fury, but also provoked anxieties among regional neighbours, including its closest partner, New Zealand, which pursues a nuclear-free policy. The lengths to which Australia has gone to secure the AUKUS pact indicate the threat to national security it sees in the growing power of the PRC.

Antecedents and Precedents

Laws and regulations to prevent foreign influence have historical precedents in both countries, including Australia's *Immigration Restriction Act* of 1901, known as the White Australia Policy. Imperial China also imposed closed-door and seclusion policies, including those aimed at shutting ports 海禁 or closing passes in the Great Wall 闭关自守 to ward off 'barbarian' infiltration.

Both Australia and the PRC had previously suspended bilateral political contacts. Canberra cancelled official exchanges in response to the 4 June crackdown in 1989 and Beijing called off high-level visits to protest what it regarded as 'unfriendly acts' by the Howard administration in 1996 including increasingly close alignment with the United States.[5] Howard's assurances towards the end of 1996 that this alignment had not changed Australia's China policy defused those tensions. Beijing again suspended high-level visits over irritation with various actions of the Rudd government. Still, towards the end of 2009, then vice-premier Li Keqiang 李克强 visited Australia and the two countries signed a joint statement affirming their desire for an increasingly comprehensive, mutually beneficial, respectful, and cooperative relationship.[6] By then, China had become Australia's single largest trading partner (relegating Japan to third place).

Beijing's trade punishments of 2020 were the first major sanctions since 1971, when the PRC suspended wheat imports from Australia to register its displeasure with the McMahon government's refusal to normalise relations.

Ingrained in History

Fear of their surroundings was a central part of the experience of European settlers in Australia in the eighteenth century. This was true for the alien land in which they found themselves, with its unfamiliar flora and fauna, harsh environment, and the First Nations peoples whose languages, laws, and customs they did not understand (or respect).

It was also true of the broader region. The nineteenth-century gold rush saw the China-born population of Australia swell to more than 38,000 by 1861, or 3.3 percent of the total population,[7] sparking fears of being overrun by 'Mongol hordes'. Yet, it was not an uninflected story, featuring such figures as the Guangzhou-born tea trader Quong Tart, who became a leading businessman and society figure in Sydney in the late nineteenth century.

Australia stationed a trade commissioner in China from 1921 to 1922 and, in 1934, the deputy prime minister, John Latham, led a trade mission there. Two years earlier, Chinese residents of Australia founded a lecture series named for the Australian China correspondent George E. Morrison that aimed to further cultural understanding of China in Australia (based at The Australian National University, the Morrison lectures are still going nine decades on).

Australia first came into focus for, especially southern, Chinese in the late Qing dynasty (1644–1911 CE) as 'New Gold Mountain' 新金山 (San Francisco was 'Old Gold Mountain' 旧金山). Despite the racist exclusionary laws of the twentieth century, Melbourne hosted a Chinese consul-general in 1909 and, in 1930, the Republic of China's soon-to-be president Lin Sen 林森 visited Australia.

In 1941, Australia appointed its first official envoy to the Nationalist government in its wartime capital of Chongqing, three years after the Japanese invaded China. The Department of External Affairs argued that establishing a legation 'at a most unfavourable time and when few reciprocal material benefits can result, will probably create a profound impression on Chinese minds, and have incalculable consequences in our future relations'. Frederic Eggleston, the first envoy, maintained that China 'held the key' to peace in the Pacific.[8]

The establishment of the PRC under the CPC changed everything. The historical fear of the 'yellow peril' that had inspired the White Australia Policy evolved into terror of the 'red menace' of communism. Australian soldiers followed the US soldiers into the Korean War. Canberra maintained formal relations with the Nationalists, who had relocated the Republic of China to Taiwan after 1949.

Then, while still in opposition, Gough Whitlam led a delegation to China, where he met with Mao Zedong; in 1972, as prime minister, he normalised relations with the PRC.

During the first two decades after the normalisation of diplomatic relations, and especially after Deng's determination to modernise and reform China and open its doors to the world, the business, academic, and cultural communities of both nations responded with enthusiasm to the opportunities for exchange and engagement, including in the economic sphere. Trade and investment grew. Deng's reform and open-door policies

Gough Whitlam during his visit to China in 1973
Source: National Archives of Australia, Wikipedia

gave some in Australia and elsewhere in the West (misplaced) hope that the CPC was also heading down the path to liberal democracy. The violent crushing of the prodemocracy protests of 1989 dashed this hope.

Several years later, after Deng made it clear that China would not reverse the course of reforms and expanded the role of the market, China's economy boomed. Its need for massive amounts of iron ore gave the Australian economy a huge boost as well. Soon one of every three export dollars earned, including from tourism and education, came from China.

However, the old anxieties never entirely went away. When asked in 2015 by German chancellor Angela Merkel to sum up Australia–China relations, prime minister Abbott famously responded, 'fear and greed'. Yet, there was still significant cooperation and perceived opportunity on both sides: in 2016, Australia became a founding member of China's Asian Infrastructure Investment Bank (the United States and Japan declined to join).

It did not take long for fear to trump greed. By the middle of the 2010s, unease was growing about Beijing's increasing assertiveness in the region, including the Pacific, which Australia considered its natural sphere of influence. The rapid modernisation and empowerment of the People's Liberation Army (PLA) and Australia's growing economic dependency on trade and investment with China fed the unease.

Recent Baggage

Not long after Donald Trump was elected US president in 2016, Washington launched a virtual trade war with China. As prime minister of Australia, Malcolm Turnbull banned Huawei from Australia's 5G networks and introduced the foreign interference laws. Beijing once more suspended high-level contacts with Canberra in protest. Turnbull's successor, Scott Morrison, who took office in 2018, had several opportunities to restore direct dialogue with Beijing. He met with Premier Li Keqiang in Singapore during the Association of Southeast Asian Nations (ASEAN) summit in November 2018 and again in Bangkok on the sidelines of the East Asia Summit in November 2019. He also met with Vice-President Wang Qishan in Jakarta at Indonesian president Joko Widodo's inauguration in October 2019. But the distrust between the two sides was so deep that no progress was made.[9]

As discussed above, the bilateral relationship worsened when Beijing took offence at Canberra's call for an international inquiry into the origins of the COVID-19 pandemic, imposing de facto trade sanctions. Canberra hardened its stance and the AUKUS pact was born.

Present Reality: Glimmer of Hope?

In January 2022, a new Chinese ambassador, Xiao Qian 肖千, arrived in Canberra, declaring that Beijing was ready to 'actively develop friendship and cooperation with Australia' and 'willing to work with Australia to meet each other halfway'.[10] But with Yang Hengjun and another Chinese Australian journalist, Cheng Lei 成蕾, still in prison in China, where their health was said to be deteriorating, and other bilateral tensions unresolved, Morrison refused Xiao's offer of a meeting — a stance supported by then opposition leader Anthony Albanese.[11] Russia's invasion of Ukraine the next month, not long after Xi Jinping and Russian president Vladimir Putin met in Beijing and declared that the friendship between their two nations had 'no limits', further stressed relations.

The main entrance to the Chinese embassy in Canberra
Source: Nick-D, Wikipedia

With a federal election looming, the coalition government focused attention on the issue of national security, including the threats posed by China. The defence minister, Peter Dutton, fronted the press a week before the election in May 2022 to make an issue of a sighting of PLA Navy vessel *Haiwangxing* 250 nautical miles off the coast of Western Australia.[12]

By the time the prime-ministerial baton was passed to Anthony Albanese in May 2022, Australia's political relationship with the PRC had reached its lowest point in fifty years of diplomatic relations. Premier Li sent Albanese a congratulatory message along with a wish for 'sound and steady' relations with Australia. The Albanese government, with Penny Wong as foreign minister, had a similar goal. It set a different tone in its rhetoric towards China: firm on principle but minus the aggressive edge.

Albanese insisted, however, that there would be no reset of relations without Beijing ending its trade punishments. Before long, significant meetings were taking place. In June, the new Australian defence minister, Richard Marles, met with his Chinese counterpart, Wei Fenghe, at the Shangri-La Dialogue in Singapore. In July, Foreign Minister Wong met her counterpart, Wang Yi 王毅, at the G20 Foreign Ministers' Meeting in Bali — 'an important first step', in her words.[13]

In August, Ambassador Xiao addressed the National Press Club in Canberra, calling for a reset in the relationship based on a return to mutually beneficial economic relations and less argument over values — or, as journalist Katharine Murphy summed it up in *The Guardian*: '[M]ore trade and less trash talk.'[14] Xiao warned Australia not to pick sides between the United States and the PRC, and to stay out of the Taiwan issue.

In November, President Xi met Prime Minister Albanese on the sidelines of the G20 Summit in Bali. It was the first such high-level meeting in six years. No great announcements followed, but, as Laura Tingle wrote in the *Australian Financial Review*, 'the most important thing to be said about the meeting was that it took place at all'.[15] Albanese observed: 'There are many steps yet to take. We will cooperate where we can, disagree where we must, and engage in our national interest.'

In December, Penny Wong travelled to Beijing for the fiftieth anniversary of relations, where she and her counterpart, Wang Yi, met for 90 minutes and agreed to reopen structured, regular dialogue on issues ranging from trade to consular affairs, climate change, defence, and regional affairs, and to maintain 'high-level engagement'. Wong remarked: '[T]he ice thaws, but slowly.'[16]

While politicians took their first steps, business made strides. In September, Australian mining giant Rio Tinto and China's largest steelmaker, Baowu 宝武 Steel, announced a two-billion-dollar joint venture to develop the Western Range iron ore project in the Pilbara region of Western Australia. With Rio Tinto owning 54 percent and Baowu 46 percent, the joint venture would begin construction in 2023 and produce about 275 million tonnes of iron ore over thirteen years, generating 1,600 jobs in Australia. The project would cement long-term cooperation in this key sector.

From the time of the imposition of the trade punishments in 2020, Australian businesses had worked hard to diversify their customer base to reduce dependency on the Chinese market. Chinese enterprises similarly strove to reduce their own dependency on Australian goods and inputs and increase their bargaining power over key commodities. Two months before its joint venture with Rio Tinto was announced, Baowu had joined with other major Chinese steel producers, including Ansteel, Minmetals, and Shougang, to form the China Mineral Resources Group 中国矿产资源集团. Headquartered in the Xiong'an New Area 雄安新区 about 100 kilometres south-west of Beijing, this supersized new entity, with twenty billion yuan in registered capital, is being closely watched by Australian mining companies, which regard it as an attempt to centralise China's iron ore purchasing. The impact of this will soon be apparent.

Looking Ahead

At the time of writing, diplomats from both countries are working towards the resumption of regular high-level dialogue between Canberra and Beijing and stabilised relations. How future relations pan out will depend on several key factors. Beijing responded angrily to Foreign Minister Wong's criticism of the live-fire exercises conducted by the PLA around Taiwan in response to US congresswoman Nancy Pelosi's visit in August as 'disproportionate and destabilising'. Beijing viewed Wong's criticism as part of an orchestrated Western campaign to contain China rather than the expression of legitimate concern over action with the potential to destabilise the region and even provoke war.

One reason for this is that given Australia's historical alliance with the United States, plus the Quadrilateral Security Dialogue (Quad), and the AUKUS pact, Beijing is wary of Australia joining what it sees as an orchestrated, US-led campaign to contain China. A more independent foreign policy could allow Australian leaders, following the tradition of prime ministers from Bob Hawke to John Howard, to play a useful mediatory role between Washington and Beijing.

In the absence of a fundamental shift of US policy towards China, however, Australia–China relations are unlikely to recover the warmth with which they began fifty years ago.

The relationship is not just a matter of governments, of course; it also rests on public perceptions. Chinese officials like Foreign Ministry spokesman Zhao Lijian and media including the *Global Times* have not done Beijing many favours with the 'wolf warrior' rhetoric of recent years, including comparing Australia to 'gum stuck on China's shoes' and a 'paper kitten' (versus the United States as a 'paper tiger'), and tweeting the offensive doctored image of the Australian soldier in Afghanistan. Public sentiment is also influenced by such things as the ongoing imprisonment of Yang Hengjun and Cheng Lei, the absence of Australian journalists in China (the last two left in 2020 after threats and interrogation),[17] widely reported human rights abuses in Xinjiang and elsewhere, and incidents such as the one in June 2022 in which a Chinese military aircraft cut across the path of an Australian maritime patrol plane and released metal chaff into the Australian plane's engines.[18]

Not surprisingly, Lowy Institute polling in 2022 revealed that only 12 percent of those surveyed said they trusted China 'somewhat' or a great deal — a forty-point decrease since 2018. The same surveys, interestingly, revealed that a decreasing percentage of Australians aged eighteen to forty-four believed Australia should support the United States in a conflict with China, and an increasing percentage of that same cohort believed Australia should remain neutral.[19]

There has been disagreement among China watchers about the extent to which the language used by the media has affected Australian attitudes towards China. The list of fourteen grievances presented in 2020, for example, was often mistranslated as fourteen 'demands'. Media reports also used the word 'demands' in translating the four 'points for consideration' or 'suggestions' 四点建议 of Chinese foreign minister Wang to Penny Wong in July 2022.[20] Another, widely discussed example related to Xiao's address to the National Press Club. Former ambassador and China scholar Stephen FitzGerald was among those who criticised reporters for focusing not on what FitzGerald characterised as 'a friendly, conciliatory and constructive' speech, but on the ambassador's answers to journalists' questions on Taiwan.[21] On the other hand, those answers were the most newsworthy aspect of an otherwise platitudinous speech, especially when Xiao denied that an attack on the island could be characterised as an 'invasion' and addressed the issue of potential Taiwanese resistance to forced reunification with what many observers found to be a chilling warning: '[T]here might be a process for the people in Taiwan to have a correct understanding of China, about the motherland.'

The Way Ahead: Back to Basics

Some thirty-six universities across China have Australian studies centres. In contrast, only twenty-odd tertiary institutions in Australia offer Chinese studies of one kind or another, and this number includes universities where the only courses on China or the Chinese language are taught by Confucius Institutes (controversial organs of Chinese 'soft power', answerable to the Chinese government).[22] In 2019, then opposition frontbencher Chris Bowen claimed that there were only about 130 people in Australia of non-Chinese background who spoke Mandarin well enough to do business in China. The ABC fact-checked his claim and concluded it was a reasonable guess. The point is, whatever the exact number, there is a very small pool of non-Chinese Australians who can read, write, and speak Mandarin proficiently. In China, hundreds of millions of people study English, and it is estimated that at least ten million are conversant in it. If knowledge is power, this is a power imbalance. Unlike imbalances that arise out of geopolitical or economic circumstances, this one should not be hard for Australia to remedy. Cultivating greater China expertise in Australia is not a magic pill that will solve the substantial and ongoing issues in the relationship. But it can help in the search for solutions.

A Contentious Friendship

GEREMIE R. BARMÉ

A CONTENTIOUS FRIENDSHIP

Geremie R. Barmé

IT IS FIFTEEN YEARS since I suggested to Kevin Rudd that he use the expression *zhengyou* 諍友 in a speech he was to give at Peking University (PKU) in April 2008. *Zhengyou* means a friend or an adviser who dares give voice to unpleasant truths, one who offers discomforting opinions and counsels caution. The expression has ancient origins, though today it might be glibly rendered as 'speaking truth to power'.

Rudd at the time was Australia's newly elected prime minister. The speech at PKU was on the itinerary of his first overseas trip in the office, which included courtesy calls on political leaders in Washington, London, Paris, and Berlin, as well as those in Beijing. The People's Republic of China (PRC) leg of the trip was particularly fraught because of controversies surrounding the international Olympic Torch Relay and the recent uprising in 'Tibetan China', which the Beijing media dubbed the '3.14 [14 March] Riots'.[1] These were mostly peaceful protests against Chinese rule that had broken out in March, not just in the official 'autonomous region' of Tibet, but also in other areas with sizeable numbers of Tibetans. The ban on foreign journalists visiting the region coupled with the draconian repression of protesters had caused consternation around the world. Western political leaders were particularly anxious to see China's vaunted 'coming-out party' at the 2008 Summer Olympics in Beijing that August go off without a hitch. Hopeful international politicians, academics, media commentators, and China watchers speculated that China's further integration into the international community as symbolised by its hosting of the Olympics might be matched with a greater openness and relaxation within the People's Republic itself.

On 14 February 2008, Rudd had led a historic parliamentary apology for the devastating impact of past government policies on Australia's Indigenous peoples. In the fraught atmosphere of the country's racial politics, it was a moment of tremendous symbolism. Not long after, when the Tibet protests were rocking the international community, I saw him at a business forum in Sydney where he gave an after-dinner speech on East Asia and Australia's engagement with the region. As we chatted, he proudly told me that he had written the Apology himself. He also said he would soon be travelling overseas.

Among other things, he would be addressing an audience at PKU. Would I be willing to offer some 'Sino-babble' that he could use in the speech? (Rudd was not being flippant; it was a jocular shorthand for cultural and historical colour that might impress his audience.)

Rudd felt that in his public PKU speech he had to address the question of the widely reported and egregious human rights abuses in Tibet. Relations between China and the West were fraught and, as the first Western leader to visit Beijing since the uprising, Rudd's words and actions would be under intense scrutiny.

Despite the care taken in composing it, Kevin Rudd's 8 April 2008 speech at PKU proved controversial.[2]

The subsequent Chinese media discussion of his use of *zhengyou* (the true friend who dares to disagree) was considerable. The phrase *zhengyou* radically departed from the milksop *pengyou* 朋友 ('friend') of official Communist Party of China (CPC) discourse. Mao Zedong observed in one of his most famous and oft-quoted writings: 'The first and foremost question of

Kevin Rudd addresses an audience in 2011
Source: DFAT, Flickr

the revolution is: who is our friend and who is our foe?' 誰是我們的敵人? 誰是我們的朋友? 這個問題是革命的首要問題. It is a question that has underpinned official Chinese attitudes to outsiders since 1949. 'Friendship' 友誼 was and remains the unmovable cornerstone of Chinese diplomacy and Sino-foreign exchange.

To be an official friend of China, the Chinese people, the party-state, or, in the reform period, even a business partner of a mainland enterprise, the foreigner is expected to stomach unpalatable situations as well as keep silent in the face of egregious behaviour. A 'friend of China' or an 'old friend' 中國的老朋友 might enjoy the privilege of offering the occasional word of caution in private; in the public arena, however, he or she is expected to have the strategic nous, good sense, and courtesy to be 'objective' 客觀 — that is, to toe the line, whatever the line happens to be. To be regarded and feted as *pengyou*, but to voice errant views about China, meant that you were 'not friend enough' 不夠朋友. The concept of 'friendship' had long degenerated into being little more than an effective tool employed by the party-state for emotional blackmail and enforced complicity. The Chinese authorities have their own formulation to accommodate disagreement, which is summed up in the four-word expression *qiu tong cun yi* 求同存異: 'to seek common ground while recognising existing differences'. This provides a pragmatic rationale for dealing with ideological and strategic competitors, but really is little more than that: a verbal sleight of hand allowing for mutually beneficial accommodation.

Rudd's tactic was to sidestep the vice-like embrace of the model of friendship imposed by the Chinese authorities by substituting another. 'A strong relationship and a true friendship,' he told the students, 'are built on the ability to engage in a direct, frank, and ongoing dialogue about our fundamental interests and future vision.'

The distinction was not lost on the Chinese government. The official news agency *Xinhua* reported: 'Eyes lit up when [Rudd] used this expression ... [I]t means friendship based on speaking the truth, speaking responsibly. It is evident that to be a *zhengyou* the first thing one needs is the magnanimity of pluralism.'[3] Of course, in the land of linguistic slippage, it is easy to see that while for some *zhengyou* means speaking out of turn, for others, it could simply become an updated and practical way to allow pesky foreigners to let off steam.

In many ways, 2008 was a year of great significance. During that year, the careful observer would also have noted evidence of Xi Jinping's heavy hand as he was the security tsar of the Olympic Games, overseeing the torch relay, stage-managing the politics behind the opening ceremony, coordinating security, limiting protests, and hamstringing internet access for foreigners and Chinese alike. The hints of China's unfolding 'assertiveness' were also increasingly evident at that time. For his part, Rudd, the prime minister of a not-insignificant liberal democracy in the Asia-Pacific, by introducing the term *zhengyou* with all its potential into dealings with the People's Republic, was attempting to do something of significance. Today, only those who are in constant engagement with China can gauge whether the term *zhengyou* and the demeanour of canny interaction with the People's Republic that it connotes still have a place in lived reality.

In *The Avoidable War: The Dangers of a Catastrophic Conflict between the US and Xi Jinping's China* (2022), Rudd continues his efforts as a *zhengyou*, but this time one who cautions both the People's Republic and the United States.[4] He warns that cultural misunderstandings, historical grievances, and ideological incompatibilities, combined with geopolitical and commercial competition between the two powers, are now a matter of inescapable and global concern. For Australia, the pursuit of principled yet amicable disagreement with China appears even more distant than when he addressed that audience at PKU.

In an international environment in which borders, walls, and paranoia inform public opinion as well as political action, principled friendship may be nothing more than the nostalgic luxury for an imagined past. In Xi Jinping's China, there is no room for principled disagreement, let alone dissent; nurtured by decades of hypernationalistic propaganda and education, a vast army of online xenophobes cheers on official 'wolf-warrior' intransigence. As for Australia–China relations, both sides have abiding mutual interests but contradictory approaches to how those interests can be pursued in an era of 'strategic competition'. Now, as was the case in 2008, to be a principled friend who dares to disagree, one first and foremost needs principles, and not merely transactional tactics. The challenge for Australia, therefore, is twofold: to put its own house in order and to assume a role in dealing with China and with the US–China conflict. In this new age of extremes, in which red lines are readily drawn and offence is easily taken, marrying principles and pragmatism is a challenge. To be a *zhengyou* rather than merely a pliant *pengyou* to China is today well nigh impossible; nor is it particularly easy when dealing with the United States.

NOTES

INTRODUCTION

1. 'Wang Sir's News Talk: The secret of film censorship in China', *YouTube*, premiered 30 September 2022, online at: https://www.youtube.com/watch?v=CyRz4PzqDhc

2. Yitong Wu, Chingman, and Qiao Long, 'Chinese censors delete post hitting out at mass, high-tech pandemic surveillance', *Radio Free Asia*, [Washington, D.C.], 26 May 2022, online at: https://www.rfa.org/english/news/china/COVID-professor-05262022144728.html

3. David Cowhig trans., '2022: Chinese law prof's lament and encouragement', 高大伟 *David Cowhig's Translation Blog*, 29 January 2022, online at: https://gaodawei.wordpress.com/2022/01/29/2022-chinese-law-profs-lament-and-encouragement/

4. Translation of *People's Daily* opinion piece by Geremie R. Barmé, 'When zig turns into zag the joke is on everyone', *China Heritage*, 11 December 2022, online at: https://chinaheritage.net/journal/when-zig-turns-into-zag-the-joke-is-on-everyone/

5. 'Wu Guoguang on the 20th Party Congress and the future of China' 吴国光: 20大结局与中国未来走向, Bumingbai 不明白, 24 October 2022, online at: https://podtail.com/podcast/0ca23212/--20-20/

6. Zichen Wang and Jinhao Bai, 'Full text & analysis: Central Economic Work Conference 2022', *Pekingnology*, 17 December 2022, online at: https://www.pekingnology.com/p/full-text-and-analysis-central-economic

7. Zichen Wang, 'Six high-profile economists call for "opening up economic activities"', *Pekingnology*, 4 December 2022, online at: https://www.pekingnology.com/p/six-high-profile-economists-call?utm_source=post-email-title&publication_id=47580&post_id=88388853&isFreemail=true&utm_medium=email

8. Zhao Yuanyuan, 'In the name of stooping, picking up trash is suddenly cool among young Chinese', *The China Project*, [New York], 6 October 2022, online at: https://thechinaproject.com/2022/10/06/in-the-name-of-stooping-picking-up-trash-is-suddenly-cool-among-young-chinese/

9. Reuters, 'China approves 15GW of new coal-fired power in HI — research', *Channel NewsAsia*, [Singapore], 28 September 2022, online at: https://www.channelnewsasia.com/business/china-approves-15-gw-new-coal-fired-power-h1-research-2970561

10. Jinglin Gao and Jiang Jiang, 'Q&A: How China can meet its carbon reduction targets — Part 1', *Ginger River Review*, [China], 3 October 2022, online at: https://www.gingerriver.com/p/q-and-a-how-china-can-meet-its-carbon

11. National Working Committee on Children and Women, *Outline for Chinese Women's Development (2021–2030)*, Beijing: State Council of the People's Republic of China, online at: https://www.nwccw.gov.cn/2021-09/27/content_295246.htm

12. All translations from 'PRC Law on the Protection of the Rights and Interests of Women', *China Law Translate*, 30 October 2022, online at: https://www.chinalawtranslate.com/en/law-on-protection-of-wome-2022/; or summary at 'China passes new women's protection law, revamped for first time in decades', Reuters, 30 October 2022, online at: https://www.reuters.com/world/china/china-passes-new-womens-protection-law-revamped-first-time-decades-2022-10-30/

13. Zhao Yuanyuan, 'China's revised law on women's protection: What you need to know', *The China Project*, [New York], 2 November 2022, online at: https://thechinaproject.com/2022/11/02/chinas-revised-law-on-womens-protection-what-you-need-to-know/

14. Luis Zheng, 'Feminists and LGBTQ activists at China's COVID protests', *The China Project*, [New York], 14 December 2022, online at: https://thechinaproject.com/2022/12/14/feminists-and-lgbtq-activists-at-chinas-COVID-protests/

15. Christopher Rowland, 'COVID shutdowns in China are delaying medical scans in the U.S.', *The Washington Post*, 11 May 2022, online at: https://www.washingtonpost.com/business/2022/05/11/medical-scans-dye-shortage/

16. Peter Hasenkamp quoted in Christian Schuh, Wolfgang Schnellbächer, Alenka Triplat, and Daniel Weise, 'The semiconductor crisis should change your long-term supply chain strategy', *Harvard Business Review*, 18 May 2022, online at: https://hbr.org/2022/05/the-semiconductor-crisis-should-change-your-long-term-supply-chain-strategy

17. Election Study Center, National Chengchi University, 'Taiwanese/Chinese identity (1992/06–2022/06)', *Data Archives*, Taipei: Election Study Center, National Chengchi University, 12 July 2022, online at: https://esc.nccu.edu.tw/PageDoc/Detail?fid=7800&id=6961

18. Ben Wright, 'We risk backing China into a corner over Taiwan', *Sydney Morning Herald*, 24 August 2022, online at: https://www.smh.com.au/world/asia/we-risk-backing-china-into-a-corner-over-taiwan-20220823-p5bbx6.html

19. A.A. Bastian, 'China is stepping up its information war on Taiwan', [Washington, D.C.], 2 August 2022, online at: https://foreignpolicy.com/2022/08/02/china-pelosi-taiwan-information/

20. Jessica Jones, 'China's extreme cancel culture and increasingly hostile online environment', *The China Story*, 14 June 2022, online at: https://www.thechinastory.org/chinas-extreme-cancel-culture-and-increasingly-hostile-online-environment/

21. The Japan Times, 'Well-armed Chinese ship enters Japanese waters near Senkakus', *The Japan Times*, [Tokyo], 25 November 2022, online at: https://www.japantimes.co.jp/news/2022/11/25/national/armed-china-ship-senkakus/

22. For links to translations of both Lee Yee's and Ni Kuang's writings, see Geremie Barmé, 'Hong Kong apostasy', *China Heritage*, [Wairarapa], online at: https://chinaheritage.net/hong-kong-apostasy/

The Year of the Tiger

1. Cao Zhenfeng, *The Tiger Culture* 虎文化, Shanghai: Shanghai jinxiu wenzhang chubanshe, 2009, p.22.

2. Chris Coggins, *The Tiger and the Pangolin: Nature, Culture, and Conservation in China*, Honolulu: University of Hawai'i Press, 2003, p.53.

3. Chi Hsu-Sheng, *New Verifications of the Shuowen* 說文新證, Taipei: Yiwen yinshuguan, 2014, p.408.

4. 'Tan Gong II' 檀弓下, The Book of Rites 禮記, translation slightly modified based on James Legge, *The Sacred Books of China: The Li Ki*, online at: https://ctext.org/liji/tan-gong-ii

5. Kathy Huang, '"Runology": How to "run away" from China', *Council on Foreign Relations Blog*, 1 June 2022, online at: https://www.cfr.org/blog/runology-how-run-away-china

6. Li Yuan, 'The army of millions who enforce China's zero-Covid policy, at all costs', *The New York Times*, 12 January 2022, online at: https://www.nytimes.com/2022/01/12/business/china-zero-covid-policy-xian.html

7. John C. Wang (trans.), *Chin Sheng-t'an*, New York, NY: Twayne Publishers, 1972, p.79.

8. Elijah Coleman Bridgman and Samuel Wells Williams, *The Chinese Repository. Volume 7: From May 1838 to April 1839*, Canton: Printed for the Proprietors, 1839, pp.596–597.

9. Javier C. Hernández, 'China, after outcry, reinstates ban on rhino and tiger parts in medicine', *The New York Times*, 12 November 2018, online at: https://www.nytimes.com/2018/11/12/world/asia/china-rhino-tiger-ban.html

10. Beatrice Hodgkin, 'The tiger who came to Ai Weiwei', *Financial Times*, [London], 18 October 2022, online at: https://www.ft.com/content/cbd098a6-fa5e-4657-8bd8-5b6a460adb72

11. Mao Tse-tung, 'On the People's Democratic Dictatorship', in *Selected Works of Mao Tse-tung. Volume IV*, Peking: Foreign Languages Press, 1960, online at: https://www.marxists.org/reference/archive/mao/selected-works/volume-4/mswv4_65.htm

12. Jay Taylor, *The Generalissimo's Son: Chiang Ching-kuo and the Revolutions in China and Taiwan*, Cambridge, MA: Harvard University Press, 2000, p.157.

In This Whirlpool of Chaotic Jumble, 'Your World' Is Also 'My World'

1. Stochastic Volatility, '[Stochastic Mailbox] Quarantine, incoming letters: "There is no distinction between "Your World" and "My World"' 【随机信箱】隔离来信: "再没有 '你的世界' 和 '我的世界' 的区分", *Stochastic Volatility*, 17 April 2022, online at: https://www.stovol.club/post04

2. Fan Yiying, '"Group-buying" becomes a lifeline for hungry Shanghai residents', *Sixth Tone*, [Shanghai], 10 April 2022, online at: https://www.sixthtone.com/news/1010087/group-buying-becomes-a-lifeline-for-hungry-shanghai-residents

3. The writer is most likely referring to a collection of essays by the famous essayist Lu Xun, *A Call to Arms* 呐喊, literally meaning to 'Cry out!'. Lu took to writing to expose the ugliness of reality in the hope of awakening the spirit of his fellow citizens and bringing about hope for the future.

FOCUS — The Twentieth Party Congress

The Twentieth Party Congress: A Primer

1. 'Brief #126: 20th Party Congress Report: Keywords Analysis', *Neican*, 18 October 2022, online at https://www.neican.org/brief-126-20th-party-congress-report-keywords-analysis/?ref=translations-newsletter

A Matter of Perspective: Insider Accounts of Xi Jinping and the Twentieth
Party Congress

1. Minxin Pei, 'China's Governance Crisis', *Foreign Affairs*, 1 September 2002, online at: https://carnegieendowment.org/2002/09/01/china-s-governance-crisis-pub-1057

2. Jessica Batke and Oliver Melton, 'Why Do We Keep Writing About Chinese Politics As if We Know More Than We Do?', *ChinaFile*, 16 October 2017, online at: https://www.chinafile.com/reporting-opinion/viewpoint/why-do-we-keep-writing-about-chinese-politics-if-we-know-more-we-do

3. Yuen Yuen Ang, *China's Gilded Age: The paradox of Economic Boom and Vast Corruption*, Cambridge, UK: Cambridge University Press, 2020.

4. Michael Smith, 'Inside the hidden fortunes of China's red aristocrats', *Australian Financial Review*, 16 September 2021, online at: https://www.afr.com/world/asia/inside-the-hidden-fortunes-of-china-s-red-aristocrats-20210915-p58rr2

5. Cai Xia, 'The Party That Failed: An Insider Breaks With Beijing', *Foreign Affairs*, 4 December 2020, online at: https://www.foreignaffairs.com/articles/china/2020-12-04/chinese-communist-party-failed; and Cai Xia, 'The Weakness of Xi Jinping: How Hubris and Paranoia Threaten China's Future', *Foreign Affairs*, 20 September 2022, online at: https://www.foreignaffairs.com/china/xi-jinping-china-weakness-hubris-paranoia-threaten-future

6. Desmond Shum, *Red Roulette: An Insider's Story of Wealth, Power, Corruption, and Vengeance in Today's China*, New York, NY: Scribner, 2021, pp.265–266.

7. ibid, p.282.

8. Cai, 'The Weakness of Xi Jinping'.

9. Cai Xia, 'China-US Relations in the Eyes of the Chinese Communist Party: An Insider's Perspective,' Hoover Institution, 29 June 2021, online at: https://www.hoover.org/research/china-us-relations-eyes-chinese-communist-party-insiders-perspective-zhong-gong-yan-zhong

10. Lingling Wei, 'China's forgotten premier steps out of Xi's shadow as economic fixer', *The Wall Street Journal*, 11 May 2022, online at: https://www.wsj.com/articles/china-premier-li-keqiang-xi-jinping-11652277107

11. Cai, 'The Weakness of Xi Jinping'.

12. Nicholas D. Kristof, 'Looking for a jump-start in China', *The New York Times*, 6 January 2013, online at: https://www.nytimes.com/2013/01/06/opinion/sunday/kristof-looking-for-a-jump-start-in-china.html

13. Shum, *Red Roulette*, p.251.

14. ibid.

15. Frederick C. Teiwes, 'The study of elite political conflict in the PRC: politics inside the "black box"', in David S.G. Goodman ed., *Handbook of the Politics of China*, Cheltenham, UK: Edward Elgar Publishing, 2015, p.21.

16. George Walden, 'Zhao's Tiananmen memoir bares infighting, offers hope: review', *Bloomberg*, [New York City], 5 June 2009, online at: https://www.bloomberg.com/news/articles/2009-06-05/zhao-s-tiananmen-memoir-bares-infighting-offers-hope-review

17. Lily Kuo, 'China's Xi Jinping facing widespread opposition in his own party, insider claims', *The Guardian*, [London], 18 August 2020, online at: https://www.theguardian.com/world/2020/aug/18/china-xi-jinping-facing-widespread-opposition-in-his-own-party-claims-insider

18. CNN Staff, 'China's Communist Party is a threat to the world, says former elite insider', *CNN*, 22 August 2020, online at: https://edition.cnn.com/2020/08/22/asia/chinas-communist-party-threat-world-intl-hnk/index.html

19. Hoover Institution, 'The Hoover Institution releases essay by former Chinese Communist Party insider about Beijing's perspective on relationship with the United States', Press release, 29 June 2021, Hoover Institution, Stanford, CA, online at: https://www.hoover.org/press-releases/hoover-institution-releases-essay-former-chinese-communist-party-insider-about

20. Batke and Melton, 'Why Do We Keep Writing About Chinese Politics As if We Know More Than We Do?'.

21. ibid.

22. Gloria Davies, 'Destiny's Mixed Metaphors', *The China Story*, 4 November 2015, online at: https://www.thechinastory.org/yearbooks/yearbook-2014/chapter-4-destinys-mixed-metaphors/

Ghosts of Mao and Deng

1. Joseph Fewsmith, *Rethinking Chinese Politics*, Cambridge, UK: Cambridge University Press, 2021; Frederick C. Teiwes, 'The Paradoxical Post-Mao Transition: From Obeying the Leader to "Normal Politics"', *The China Journal*, no.34 (July 1995): 55–94.

2. Joseph Torigian, *Prestige, Manipulation, and Coercion: Elite Power Struggles after Stalin and Mao*, New Haven, CT: Yale University Press, 2022; Frederick C. Teiwes and Warren Sun, *Hua Guofeng, Deng Xiaoping, and the Dismantling of Maoism: From Restoration toward Reform, 1976–1981*, London: Routledge, forthcoming.

3. Ezra Vogel, *Deng Xiaoping and the Transformation of China*, Cambridge, MA: Harvard University Press, 2011; Barry Naughton, 'Deng Xiaoping: The Economist', *The China Quarterly*, no.135 (September 2013): 495–514.

4. For an English-language translation of the resolution, see 'Resolution of the CPC Central Committee on the Major Achievements and Historical Experience of the Party over the Past Century', *Xinhua*, 16 November 2021, online at: http://www.news.cn/english/2021-11/16/c_1310314611.htm

5. Neican, 'Brief #96: Historic resolution, rally round the flag, Wang Liqiang, beauty standards', *China Neican*, 26 November 2021, online at: https://www.neican.org/brief-96/

Chapter 1 — Economy and Supply Chains

The Chinese Economy: Bursting Bubbles, Terminal Troubles?

1. The Economic Times, 'World Bank slashes China growth forecast over Covid damage', *The Economic Times*, [Mumbai, India], 8 June 2022, online at: https://economictimes.indiatimes.com/news/international/business/world-bank-slashes-china-growth-forecast-over-covid-damage/articleshow/92074329.cms

2.   The Straits Times, 'World Bank slashes East Asia 2022 growth outlook, citing China slowdown', *The Straits Times*, [Singapore], 27 September 2022, online at: https://www.straitstimes.com/business/economy/world-bank-cuts-east-asia-2022-growth-outlook-citing-china-slowdown

3.   Martin Farrer, 'A Ponzi scheme by any other name: The bursting of China's property bubble', *The Guardian*, [London], 25 September 2022, online at: https://www.theguardian.com/business/2022/sep/25/china-property-bubble-evergrande-group

4.   Peh Hong Lim, 'China's strict zero-COVID policy creates supply chain chaos', *VOA News*, [Washington, D.C.], 26 May 2022, online at: https://www.voanews.com/a/china-s-strict-zero-covid-policy-creates-supply-chain-chaos-/6591227.html

5.   Suranjana Tewari, 'Five reasons why China's economy is in trouble', *BBC News*, 5 October 2022, online at: https://www.bbc.com/news/world-asia-china-62830775

6.   Fitri Wulandari, 'China consumer confidence reflects deepening gloom as world's most populous nation grapples with zero-Covid, property crisis', *Capital.com*, 28 October 2022, online at: https://capital.com/china-consumer-confidence

7.   Carl Minzner, 'China's doomed fight against demographic decline: Beijing's efforts to boost fertility are making the problem worse', *Foreign Affairs*, 3 May 2022, online at: https://www.foreignaffairs.com/articles/china/2022-05-03/chinas-doomed-fight-against-demographic-decline

8.   Laura He, 'US curbs on microchips could throttle China's ambitions and escalate the tech war', *CNN Business*, 31 October 2022, online at: https://edition.cnn.com/2022/10/31/tech/us-sanctions-chips-china-xi-tech-ambitions-intl-hnk/index.html

9.   News18, 'Pak, Sri Lanka, Bangladesh, Laos and more: China's "debt-trap" pushing vulnerable countries to economic crisis? News18 explores', *News18*, [New Delhi], 4 September 2022, online at: https://www.news18.com/news/world/pak-sri-lanka-bangladesh-laos-more-chinas-debt-trap-pushing-vulnerable-countries-to-economic-crisis-news18-explores-5722627.html

10. Ruchir Sharma, 'China's economy will not overtake US until 2060, if ever', *The Financial Times*, [London], 21 October 2022, online at: https://www.ft.com/content/cff42bc4-f9e3-4f51-985a-86518934afbe

11. Gordon G. Chang, 'Gordon Chang: China's economy is in deep trouble', *The National Interest*, [Washington, D.C.], 27 May 2020, online at: https://nationalinterest.org/feature/gordon-chang-chinas-economy-deep-trouble-158011; and Luca Cacciatore, 'Gordon Chang predicts China's economy headed for collapse', *Newsmax*, [West Palm Beach, FL], 6 September 2022, online at: https://www.newsmax.com/newsfront/gordon-chang-china-economy/2022/09/06/id/1086280/

12. Tom Orlik, 'The China bubble is losing air but won't burst', *Bloomberg*, [New York City], 7 October 2022, online at: https://www.bloomberg.com/news/articles/2022-10-06/china-s-economic-bubble-is-losing-air-but-won-t-burst

13. For a case in point, see 'Can China Keep Rising?', *Foreign Affairs*, July–August 2021, online at: https://www.foreignaffairs.com/issue-packages/can-china-keep-rising

14. Michael Beckley and Hal Brands, 'The end of China's rise: Beijing is running out of time to remake the world', *Foreign Affairs*, 1 October 2021, online at: https://www.foreignaffairs.com/articles/china/2021-10-01/end-chinas-rise

15. Jude Blanchette, 'Xi's confidence game: Beijing's actions show determination, not insecurity', *Foreign Affairs*, 23 November 2021, online at: https://www.foreignaffairs.com/articles/asia/2021-11-23/xis-confidence-game

16. Macrotrends, 'China population 1950–2023', Seattle, WA: Macrotrends, 2023, online at: https://www.macrotrends.net/countries/CHN/china/population

17. Fang Cai and Yang Lu, 'Take-Off, Persistence and Sustainability: The Demographic Factor in Chinese Growth', *Asia and the Pacific Policy Studies*, vol.3, no.2 (2016): 203–225.

18. Owen Haacke, 'China's mandatory retirement age changes: Impact for foreign companies', *News*, Washington, D.C.: The US–China Business Council, 1 April 2015, online at: https://www.uschina.org/china%E2%80%99s-mandatory-retirement-age-changes-impact-foreign-companies

19. Luna Sun, 'China to delay retirement ages "gradually" by 2025, after holding firm for seven decades', *South China Morning Post*, [Hong Kong], 22 February 2022, online at: https://www.scmp.com/economy/china-economy/article/3167985/china-delay-retirement-ages-gradually-2025-after-holding-firm

20. International Labour Organization, 'Labor force participation rate, female (% of female population ages 15+) (modeled ILO estimate): China', *Data*, Washington, D.C.: The World Bank, 2023, online at: https://data.worldbank.org/indicator/SL.TLF.CACT.FE.ZS?locations=CN

21. The Global Gender Gap Index provides an international comparison of gender equity across four dimensions (economic participation and opportunity, educational attainment, health and survival, and political empowerment). See World Economic Forum (WEF), *Global Gender Gap Report 2022: Insight Report July 2022*, Geneva: WEF, 2022, online at: https://www3.weforum.org/docs/WEF_GGGR_2022.pdf

22. Bloomberg News, 'China youth jobless rate hits record 20% in July on Covid woes', *Bloomberg*, [New York City], 15 August 2022, online at: https://www.bloomberg.com/news/articles/2022-08-15/china-youth-jobless-rate-hits-record-20-in-july-on-covid-woes

23. Statista, 'Average annual per capita disposable income of urban and rural households in China from 1990 to 2022', Hamburg: Statista, 2022, online at: https://www.statista.com/statistics/259451/annual-per-capita-disposable-income-of-rural-and-urban-households-in-china/

24. Frank Tang and Orange Wang, 'China's Xi Jinping sends "warning signal" to the wealthy as he opens new front in "common prosperity" push', *South China Morning Post*, [Hong Kong], 20 October 2022, online at: https://www.scmp.com/economy/china-economy/article/3196510/chinas-xi-jinping-sends-warning-signal-wealthy-he-opens-new-front-common-prosperity-push

25. Maria Ana Lugo, Martin Raiser, and Ruslan Yemtsov, 'What's next for poverty reduction policies in China?', *Brookings Blog*, [Washington, D.C.] 24 September 2021, online at: https://www.brookings.edu/blog/future-development/2021/09/24/whats-next-for-poverty-reduction-policies-in-china/

26. For example, this paper claims that 13 percent of people who were not classified as living in poverty before the COVID pandemic could fall into poverty post pandemic, due to the significant drop in rural migrant remittances. See Yumei Zhang, Yue Zhan, Xinshen Diao, Kevin Z. Chen, and Sherman Robinson, 'The Impacts of COVID-19 on Migrants, Remittances, and Poverty in China: A Microsimulation Analysis', *China and World Economy*, vol.29, no.6 (2021): 4–33.

27. For this and all other quotes attributed to Ang here, see Yuen Yuen Ang, 'Decoding Xi Jinping: How will China's bureaucrats interpret his call for "common prosperity"?', *Foreign Affairs*, 8 December 2021, online at: https://www.foreignaffairs.com/articles/china/2021-12-08/decoding-xi-jinping

28. Scott Rozelle and Natalie Hell, *Invisible China: How the Urban–Rural Divide Threatens China's Rise*, Chicago, IL: University of Chicago Press, 2020.

29. Giulia Interesse and Frank Ka-Ho Wong, 'China's hukou reform: Zhengzhou could become first megacity to relax *hukou* restrictions', *China Briefing*, 23 September 2022, online at: https://www.china-briefing.com/news/chinas-hukou-reform-zhengzhou-could-become-first-megacity-to-relax-hukou-restrictions/

30. Cao Chen, 'Shanghai relaxes *hukou* rules to attract more talent', *China Daily*, 9 June 2022, online at: https://www.chinadaily.com.cn/a/202206/09/WS62a15fdba310fd2b29e61aa6.html

31. Lee Jones and Shahar Hameiri, *Debunking the myth of 'debt-trap diplomacy': How recipient countries shape China's Belt and Road Initiative*, Research Paper, London: Chatham House, August 2020, online at: https://www.chathamhouse.org/sites/default/files/2020-08-19-debunking-myth-debt-trap-diplomacy-jones-hameiri.pdf

32. Farrer, 'A Ponzi scheme by any other name'.

33. James Kynge, Sun Yu, and Thomas Hale, 'China's property crash: "A slow-motion financial crisis"', *Financial Times*, [London], 4 October 2022, online at: https://www.ft.com/content/e9e8c879-5536-4fbc-8ec2-f2a274b823b4

34. Orlik, 'The China bubble is losing air but won't burst'.

35. Geoff Raby, 'The bubble that never pops', *APAC News*, [Sydney], 16 January 2020, online at: https://apac.news/the-china-bubble-that-never-pops/

36. Jude Blanchette, 'Xi's gamble: The race to consolidate power and stave off disaster', *Foreign Affairs*, 22 June 2021, online at: https://www.foreignaffairs.com/articles/china/2021-06-22/xis-gamble

37. Jude Blanchette, 'Party of one: The CCP Congress and Xi's quest to control China', *Foreign Affairs*, 14 October 2022, online at: https://www.foreignaffairs.com/china/party-one-ccp-congress-xi-jinping

The Untold Story of Chinese Banking and Why It Matters

1. Adam Yao Liu, 'Building markets within authoritarian institutions: The political economy of banking development in China', Doctoral dissertation, Stanford University, Stanford, CA, 2018.

2. Adam Yao Liu, Jean C. Oi, and Yi Zhang, 'China's Local Government Debt: The Grand Bargain', *The China Journal*, vol.87, no.1 (2022): 40–71.

3. Liu, 'Building markets within authoritarian institutions', p.96.

4. ibid.

5. From author's dataset of China's bank branches, collected from official statistics.

6. Nicholas R. Lardy, *Markets Over Mao: The Rise of Private Business in China*, New York, NY: Columbia University Press, 2014.

7. Liu, 'Building markets within authoritarian institutions', p.96.

8. ibid.

9. Liu et al., 'China's Local Government Debt'.

10. Author interview, 2015.

Coal Supply Chains: No Bright Outlook for Australia

1. Jorrit Gosens, Alex B.H. Turnbull, and Frank Jotzo, 'China's Decarbonization and Energy Security Plans Will Reduce Seaborne Coal Imports: Results from an Installation-Level Model', *Joule*, vol.6, no.4 (2022): 782–815.

2. Investing.com, 'Newcastle coal futures streaming chart', *Investing.com*, 2007–2023, online at: https://au.investing.com/commodities/newcastle-coal-futures-streaming-chart

3. The Global Economy, 'Australian coal prices', *theglobaleconomy.com*, n.d., online at: https://www.theglobaleconomy.com/World/australian_coal_prices/

4. J.P. Casey, 'The coal war: Why has China turned its back on Australian coal?', *Mining Technology*, 25 May 2021, online at: https://www.mining-technology.com/features/the-coal-war-why-has-china-turned-its-back-on-australian-coal/

5. Zhao Ziwen, 'China's power crisis: Why is it happening and what does it mean for the economy?', *South China Morning Post*, [Hong Kong], 27 August 2022, online at: https://www.scmp.com/economy/china-economy/article/3190313/chinas-power-crisis-why-it-happening-and-what-does-it-mean

6. Bill Birtles with wires, 'China increasingly expected to drop ban on Australian coal as nation's economic woes deepen', *ABC News*, 15 July 2022, online at: https://www.abc.net.au/news/2022-07-15/china-increasingly-expected-to-drop-ban-on-australian-coal/101242670

7. Jorrit Gosens, 'The short-lived comeback of coal', *East Asia Forum*, 28 June 2022, online at: https://www.eastasiaforum.org/2022/06/28/the-short-lived-comeback-of-coal/

8. Department of Industry, Science and Resources, *Resources and Energy Quarterly: June 2022*, Canberra: Office of the Chief Economist, 4 July 2022, online at: https://www.industry.gov.au/publications/resources-and-energy-quarterly-june-2022

9. Kpler, 'We facilitate efficient and sustainable trade', *Kpler.com*, [London], 2023, online at: https://www.kpler.com/

10. Bloomberg News, 'China coal futures surge to record as flood swamps mine hub', *Bloomberg*, [New York City], 11 October 2021, online at: https://www.bloomberg.com/news/articles/2021-10-11/china-coal-futures-surge-to-record-amid-flooding-in-key-mine-hub#xj4y7vzkg

11. Amanda Lee and Yujie Xue, 'China's power crisis prompts Beijing to liberalise electricity pricing', *South China Morning Post*, [Hong Kong], 12 October 2021, online at: https://www.scmp.com/economy/china-economy/article/3152095/chinas-power-crisis-prompts-beijing-liberalise-electricity

12. Yi-Le Weng, Jenny Ma, and Jessie Li, 'Weakness in China's thermal coal prices may prompt government action: Sources', *S&P Global Commodity Insights*, New York, NY: S&P Global, 4 May 2020, online at: https://www.spglobal.com/commodityinsights/en/market-insights/latest-news/coal/050420-weakness-in-chinas-thermal-coal-prices-may-prompt-government-action-sources

13. Bloomberg News, 'China's "Green Zone" coal price tested as virus fight continues', *Bloomberg*, [New York City], 13 April 2020, online at: https://www.bloomberg.com/news/articles/2020-04-12/china-s-green-zone-coal-price-tested-as-virus-fight-rumbles-on

14. Lee and Yujie, 'China's power crisis prompts Beijing to liberalise electricity pricing'.

15. ibid.

16. David Stanway, Zhang Yan, and Martin Quin Pollard, 'China's scorching southwest extends power curbs as drought, heatwave continue', *Reuters*, 23 August 2022, online at: https://www.reuters.com/world/china/chinas-sichuan-extends-power-curbs-until-aug25-heatwave-drags-caixin-2022-08-22/

17. Helen Davidson, 'China drought causes Yangtze to dry up, sparking shortage of hydropower', *The Guardian*, [London], 22 August 2022, online at: https://www.theguardian.com/world/2022/aug/22/china-drought-causes-yangtze-river-to-dry-up-sparking-shortage-of-hydropower

18. National Bureau of Statistics (NBS), 'Growth of enterprise above designated size rose 3.9% in June 2022' 2022年6月份规模以上工业增加值增长3.9%, Beijing: NBS, 15 July 2022, online at: http://www.stats.gov.cn/sj/zxfb/202302/t20230203_1901514.html

19. Lauri Myllyvirta and Xing Zhang, 'Analysis: What do China's gigantic wind and solar bases mean for its climate goals?', *Carbon Brief*, [London], 3 May 2022, online at: https://www.carbonbrief.org/analysis-what-do-chinas-gigantic-wind-and-solar-bases-mean-for-its-climate-goals/

20. SolarPower Europe, 'World installs a record 168 GW of solar power in 2021, enters solar terawatt age', Press release, Brussels: SolarPower Europe, 10 May 2022, online at: https://www.solarpowereurope.org/press-releases/world-installs-a-record-168-gw-of-solar-power-in-2021-enters-solar-terawatt-age

21. China Electricity Council (CEC), 'Statistics on electric power industry between January and August 2022' 2022年1-8月全国电力工业统计数据一览表, Beijing: CEC, online at: https://www.cec.org.cn/upload/1/editor/1663749637018.pdf

22. National People's Congress (NPC), *Fourteenth Five-Year Plan for National Development*, Beijing: NPC, 13 March 2021, online at: http://www.gov.cn/xinwen/2021-03/13/content_5592681.htm

23. NBS, 'Growth of enterprise above designated size rose 1.3% in December 2022'.

24. ibid.

25. Bloomberg News, 'China's energy game plan features a giant coal-hauling rail line', *Bloomberg*, [New York City], 20 September 2019, online at: https://www.bloomberg.com/news/articles/2019-09-19/china-s-energy-gameplan-features-a-giant-coal-hauling-rail-line

26. Gosens et al., 'China's Decarbonization and Energy Security Plans Will Reduce Seaborne Coal Imports'.

27. Agence France-Presse, 'New Mongolian rail link with China to boost coal exports', *South China Morning Post*, [Hong Kong], 12 September 2022, online at: https://www.scmp.com/news/china/diplomacy/article/3192220/new-mongolian-rail-link-china-boost-coal-exports

28. Gosens et al., 'China's Decarbonization and Energy Security Plans Will Reduce Seaborne Coal Imports'.

29. Clyde Russell, 'Column: China's easing of Australian coal ban is symbolic, not market-shifting', *Reuters*, 10 January 2023, online at: https://www.reuters.com/markets/commodities/chinas-easing-australian-coal-ban-is-symbolic-not-market-shifting-russell-2023-01-09/

CHAPTER 2 — Climate Problem, Tech Solutions

Supercharging China: Cars, Batteries, and Lithium

1. Davide Castelvecchi, 'Electric cars and batteries: How will the world produce enough?', *Nature*, 17 August 2021, online at: https://www.nature.com/articles/d41586-021-02222-1

2. International Energy Agency (IEA), *Net Zero by 2050: A Roadmap for the Global Energy Sector*, Paris: IEA, May 2021, online at: https://iea.blob.core.windows.net/assets/4719e321-6d3d-41a2-bd6b-461ad2f850a8/NetZeroby2050-ARoadmapfortheGlobalEnergySector.pdf

3. Rick Mills, 'Graphite deficit starting this year, as demand for EV battery anode ingredient exceeds supply', *Mining.com*, 22 July 2022, online at: https://www.mining.com/web/graphite-deficit-starting-this-year-as-demand-for-ev-battery-anode-ingredient-exceeds-supply/

4. Pratima Desai, 'Explainer: Costs of nickel and cobalt used in electric vehicle batteries', *Reuters*, 4 February 2022, online at: https://www.reuters.com/business/autos-transportation/costs-nickel-cobalt-used-electric-vehicle-batteries-2022-02-03/

5. Castelvecchi, 'Electric cars and batteries'.

6. Paul Martin, 'How much lithium is in a Li-Ion vehicle battery?', *LinkedIn Pulse*, 29 November 2017, online at: https://www.linkedin.com/pulse/how-much-lithium-li-ion-vehicle-battery-paul-martin/

7. Mills, 'Graphite deficit starting this year, as demand for EV battery anode ingredient exceeds supply'.

8. Desai, 'Explainer'.

9. Hal Hodson, 'Lithium dreams: The surreal landscapes where batteries are born', *New Scientist*, 14 October 2015, online at: https://www.newscientist.com/article/mg22830430-300-lithium-dreams-the-surreal-landscapes-where-batteries-are-born/

10. Maeve Campbell, 'In pictures: South America's "lithium fields" reveal the dark side of our electric future', *Euronews*, [Lyon], 1 February 2022, online at: https://www.euronews.com/green/2022/02/01/south-america-s-lithium-fields-reveal-the-dark-side-of-our-electric-future

11. Desai, 'Explainer'.

12. Campbell, 'In pictures'.

13. Scarlett Evans, 'Lithium's water problem', *Mining Technology*, 27 January 2021, online at: https://www.mining-technology.com/analysis/lithiums-water-problem/

14. Cobus van Staden, 'Green energy's dirty secret: Its hunger for African resources', *Foreign Policy*, [Washington, D.C.], 30 June 2022, online at: https://foreignpolicy.com/2022/06/30/africa-congo-drc-ev-electric-vehicles-batteries-green-energy-minerals-metals-mining-resources-colonialism-human-rights-development-china/

15. Thomas Fox, 'As details of $1b Glencore FCPA settlement show, cooperation pays', *Corporate Compliance Insights*, 15 June 2022, online at: https://www.corporatecomplianceinsights.com/glencore-fcpa-analysis/

16. Walton Pantland, 'Special report: Glencore, the commodities giant with no soul', *IndustriALL Global Union*, 25 April 2018, online at: https://www.industriall-union.org/special-report-glencore-the-commodities-giant-with-no-soul/

17. Todd C. Frankel and Peter Whoriskey, 'Tossed aside in the "white gold" rush', *The Washington Post*, 19 December 2016, online at: https://www.washingtonpost.com/graphics/business/batteries/tossed-aside-in-the-lithium-rush/?tid=batteriesseriesbottom/

18. Peter Whoriskey, 'In your phone, in their air', *The Washington Post*, 4 October 2016, online at: https://www.washingtonpost.com/graphics/business/batteries/graphite-mining-pollution-in-china/

19. Sam Bold, 'Albemarle Bunbury lithium facility facing workplace safety investigation after complaints', *ABC News*, 24 May 2022, online at: https://www.abc.net.au/news/2022-05-24/albemarle-lithium-under-investigation/101081226/

20. Govind Bhutada, 'Visualizing 10 years of global EV sales by country', *Elements: Visual Capitalist*, 7 August 2022, online at: https://elements.visualcapitalist.com/visualizing-10-years-of-global-ev-sales-by-country/

21. Li Jun, 'National car ownership reaches 315 million' 全国汽车保有量达3.15亿辆, *21st Century Business Herald*, [Guangzhou], 8 October 2022, online at: https://m.21jingji.com/article/20221008/herald/96d02e2a892803cf3317fe24c07b6cd6.html

22. Liu Liangwen, 'Passenger federation: Estimated sales of new energy passenger cars of 730,000 in December' 乘联会：预估12月乘联会新能源乘用车厂商批发销量73万辆, *Securities Times*, [Shenzhen], 5 January 2023, online at:https://www.chinanews.com.cn/cj/2023/01-05/9928405.shtml/

23. Barry van Wyk, 'What is China's "double carbon" policy?', *The China Project*, [New York], 16 May 2022, online at: https://thechinaproject.com/2022/05/16/what-is-chinas-double-carbon-policy/

24. Yu Cong, 'Three ministries announce that purchase tax exemption policy for new energy vehicles will continue until the end of 2023' 三部委公告新能源汽车免征购置税政策延续至2023年底, *Caixin*, [Beijing], 26 September 2022, online at: https://www.caixin.com/2022-09-26/101944997.html/

25. Mark Kane, 'World's top 5 EV automotive groups ranked by sales: H1 2022', *InsideEVs*, 2 August 2022, online at: https://insideevs.com/news/601770/world-top-oem-ev-sales-2022h1/

26. Muyu Xu and Norihiko Shirouzu, 'China's BYD ends full combustion engine cars to focus on electric, plug-in hybrids', *Reuters*, 3 April 2022, online at: https://www.reuters.com/business/autos-transportation/chinas-byd-ends-combustion-engine-cars-focus-electric-2022-04-03/

27. Chen Kangliang, 'BYD's market value breaks through 1 trillion yuan, ranking third among global automakers' 比亚迪市值突破1万亿元大关 位居全球车企第三, *China News Service*, 10 June 2022, online at: https://www.chinanews.com.cn/cj/2022/06-10/9776867.shtml

28. Feng Tiwei, 'BYD sales in October exceeded 200,000 units, three times that of Tesla, and its market share may exceed 30 percent' 比亚迪10月销量再破20万辆 三倍于特斯拉、市占率或超30%, *Sina Finance*, [Beijing], 3 November 2022, online at: https://finance.sina.com.cn/stock/s/2022-11-03/doc-imqqsmrp4812443.shtml

29. Kzaobao.com, 'BYD's non-net profit deducted in the third quarter increased by 930 percent year-on-year' 比亚迪三季度扣非净利同比增930%, *Kzaobao.com*, 30 October 2022, online at: https://www.kzaobao.com/shiju/20221030/126867.html

30. Zhu Yanjing, 'BYD held a European conference and launched three models for the European market' 比亚迪召开新能源乘用车欧洲发布会 三款车型推向欧洲市场, *China News Service*, 28 September 2022, online at: https://www.chinanews.com.cn/cj/2022/09-28/9862943.shtml

31. Jill Shen, 'BYD makes expansion moves in Southeast Asia and Europe', *Technode*, 20 October 2022, online at: https://technode.com/2022/10/20/byd-makes-expansion-moves-in-southeast-asia-and-europe/

32. 36Kr, 'BYD: Global car rental company Sixt will purchase at least 100,000 new energy vehicles from the company in the next 6 years' 比亚迪: 全球汽车租赁公司SIXT未来6年内将向公司采购至少10万台新能源车, *36Kr*, [Beijing], 4 October 2022, online at: https://www.36kr.com/newsflashes/1943187065964937

33. TechWeb, 'In order to sell cars overseas, BYD has spent 5 billion yuan on orders to build ships' 为了在海外卖车 比亚迪被曝斥资50亿下单造船, *163.com*, 30 October 2022, online at: https://www.163.com/dy/article/HKU1EMM7051188EC.html

34. Yu Liyan, 'In the first half of the year, the installed volume of domestic batteries increased by 109.8 percent year-on-year, and CATL accounted for 47.67 percent of the total' 上半年国内动力电池装车量同比增长109.8%, 宁德时代占比47.67%居首, *36Kr*, [Beijing], 11 July 2022, online at: https://www.36kr.com/newsflashes/1823005774770056

35. Xu Wei, 'China's CATL tops rank for global EV battery installation', *Yicai Global*, 2 November 2022, online at: https://www.yicaiglobal.com/news/china-catl-tops-rank-for-global-ev-battery-installation

36. Phate Zhang, 'CATL posts Q3 net profit of $1.3 billion, up 188 percent year-on-year', *CnEVpost*, 21 October 2022, online at: https://cnevpost.com/2022/10/21/catl-q3-2022-earnings/

37. Gong Mengze, '"Battery king" CATL Qilin battery against the Tesla 4680, Chinese battery companies are competing to catch up' "宁王"麒麟电池对垒特斯拉4680 中国动力电池企业竞相崛起赶超, *China News Service*, 24 June 2022, online at: https://www.chinanews.com.cn/cj/2022/06-24/9787424.shtml

38. Barry van Wyk, 'CATL's new battery is a leap forward but also a precursor of something radical to come', *The China Project*, [New York], 28 June 2022, online at: https://thechinaproject.com/2022/06/28/catls-new-battery-is-a-leap-forward-but-also-a-precursor-of-something-radical-to-come/

39. ibid.

40. International Energy Agency (IEA), *Global EV Outlook 2022: Securing Supplies for an Electric Future*, Paris: IEA, May 2022, online at: https://iea.blob.core.windows.net/assets/ad8fb04c-4f75-42fc-973a-6e54c8a4449a/GlobalElectricVehicleOutlook2022.pdf

41. Nhlanhla Kunene, 'Top 8 lithium producers in the world by country', *IG*, 12 October 2022, online at: https://www.ig.com/sg/trading-strategies/top-8-lithium-producers-in-the-world-by-country-221012

42. 36Kr, 'Vanadium electricity, a trillion-dollar gimmick or the "new king"?' 钒电, 万亿噱头还是"新王者"?, *36Kr*, [Beijing], 8 October 2022, online at: https://36kr.com/p/1946920206697091

43. Melissa Pistilli, 'Top 9 nickel-producing countries (updated 2022)', *Investing News Network*, 20 September 2022, online at: https://investingnews.com/daily/resource-investing/base-metals-investing/nickel-investing/top-nickel-producing-countries/

44. Cobus van Staden, 'DRC court temporarily halts China Molybdenum's control over massive Tenke Fungurume cobalt mine', *China Global South Project*, 1 March 2022, online at: https://chinaglobalsouth.com/2022/03/01/drc-court-temporarily-halts-china-molybdenums-control-over-massive-tenke-fungurume-cobalt-mine/

45. Rodrigo Castillo and Caitlin Purdy, *China's Role in Supplying Critical Minerals for the Global Energy Transition: What Could the Future Hold?*, Leveraging Transparency to Reduce Corruption Project, Washington, D.C.: Brookings Institution, July 2022, online at: https://www.brookings.edu/wp-content/uploads/2022/08/LTRC_ChinaSupplyChain.pdf

46. IEA, *Global EV Outlook 2022*.

47. ibid.

48. Castillo and Purdy, *China's Role in Supplying Critical Minerals for the Global Energy Transition*.

49. Shanghai Metals Market, 'BYD won the mining right of 80,000 mt of lithium ore in Chile', *Shanghai Metals Market*, 13 January 2022, online at: https://news.metal.com/newscontent/101724947/byd-won-the-mining-right-of-80000-mt-of-lithium-ore-in-chile/

50. Agence France-Presse, 'Chile court freezes multi-million dollar lithium deal', *France24*, 15 January 2022, online at: https://www.france24.com/en/live-news/20220114-chile-court-freezes-multi-million-dollar-lithium-deal

51. Wu Yuli, 'BYD is negotiating the purchase of six African lithium mines that will cover its battery demand for the next ten years' 比亚迪洽购6座非洲锂矿, 将覆盖其未来十余年电池需求, *The Paper*, [Shanghai], 31 May 2022, online at: https://www.thepaper.cn/newsDetail_forward_18350577

52. IEA, *Global EV Outlook 2022*.

53. Castillo and Purdy, *China's Role in Supplying Critical Minerals for the Global Energy Transition*.

54. Zhu Keli, 'The battery industry chain "goes west" and "two-wheel linkage" can win the future' 动力电池产业链"西进" "双轮联动"才能赢在未来, *Hexun*, 28 September 2022, online at: http://news.hexun.com/2022-09-28/206836032.html

55. Fei Xinyi, '100 billion yuan battery expansion tide: Competition accelerates upstream and downstream collaboration' 千亿级电池扩产潮: 竞赛加速 上下游协同, *21st Century Business Herald*, [Guangzhou], 28 September 2022, online at: https://m.21jingji.com/article/20220928/herald/59ef46e098d7eeb7aae4564191c39356.html

56. Liu Yuying, 'In the first half of the year, the revenue of China's lithium-ion battery industry exceeded 480 billion yuan' 上半年中国锂离子电池行业收入突破4800亿元, *China News Service*, 3 August 2022, online at: https://www.chinanews.com.cn/cj/2022/08-03/9819132.shtml

57. TrendForce, 'Power batteries enter period of rapid development with global installed capacity expected to exceed 3TWh in 2030, says TrendForce', *TrendForce*, [Taipei], 14 September 2022, online at: https://www.trendforce.com/presscenter/news/20220914-11381.html

58. Katharina Gerber, 'Why we are probably not running out of lithium', *LinkedIn Pulse*, 22 March 2021, online at: https://www.linkedin.com/pulse/why-we-probably-running-out-lithium-katharina-gerber-ph-d-/

59. Barry van Wyk, 'The battle for lithium: A Chinese mine just sold for 596 times the opening price', *The China Project*, [New York], 23 May 2022, online at: https://thechinaproject.com/2022/05/23/the-battle-for-lithium-a-chinese-mine-just-sold-for-596-times-the-opening-price/

60. Shen Peng, 'Fleeing the lithium mine' 逃离锂矿?, *36Kr*, [Beijing], 19 September 2022, online at: https://36kr.com/p/1922048979771396

61. Shu Yajiang, 'The performance of listed companies in the lithium industry in the first three quarters was "explosive", and a golden period of industry development may be coming' 锂业上市公司前三季度业绩"爆棚"行业发展黄金期或将来, *China News Service*, 1 November 2022, online at: https://www.chinanews.com.cn/cj/2022/11-01/9884245.shtml

62. Lu Yutong, 'Lithium prices fall below 400,000 yuan per ton, a drop of more than 20% year-to-date' 锂价跌破每吨40万元 年初至今跌超20%, *Caixin*, [Beijing], 25 February 2023, online at: https://www.caixin.com/2023-02-25/102001967.html

63. Shen, 'Fleeing the lithium mine?'.

64. Leonardo Paoli and Timur Gül, 'Electric cars fend off supply challenges to more than double global sales', *Commentary*, Paris: IEA, 30 January 2022, online at: https://www.iea.org/commentaries/electric-cars-fend-off-supply-challenges-to-more-than-double-global-sales

65. International Energy Agency (IEA), *The Role of Critical Minerals in Clean Energy Transitions*, World Energy Outlook Special Report, Paris: IEA, May 2021, online at: https://iea.blob.core.windows.net/assets/ffd2a83b-8c30-4e9d-980a-52b6d9a86fdc/TheRoleofCriticalMineralsinCleanEnergyTransitions.pdf

66. Dong Peng, 'Dismantling the "profit chain" of the new energy vehicle industry: Lithium salts dominate the pack, and the diaphragm "makes a fortune"' 拆解新能源车产业"利润链": 锂盐傲视群雄 隔膜"闷声发财", *21st Century Business Herald*, [Guangzhou], 8 September 2022, online at: http://auto.hexun.com/2022-09-08/206727797.html

67. Shu, 'The performance of listed companies in the lithium industry in the first three quarters was "explosive"'.

68. Antonio De la Jara, 'Tianqi buys stake in lithium miner SQM from Nutrien for $4.1 billion', *Reuters*, 3 December 2018, online at: https://www.reuters.com/article/us-chile-tianqi-lithium-idUSKBN1O217F

69. Dong Peng, 'Lithium battery industry chain "holding together" to accelerate: Five companies form an alliance in one day, China Innovation Aviation binds Tianqi Lithium' 锂电产业链"抱团"加速：一天五家公司结盟 中创新航绑定天齐锂业, *21st Century Business Herald*, [Guangzhou], 11 May 2022, online at: https://news.hexun.com/2022-05-11/205914599.html

70. Dave Levitan and Lili Pike, 'How Chinese companies came to dominate the battery supply chain', *Grid News*, [Washington, D.C.], 4 October 2022, online at: https://www.grid.news/story/360/2022/10/04/the-demand-for-electric-vehicles-is-skyrocketing-can-the-supply-of-lithium-and-other-critical-minerals-for-batteries-keep-up/

71. Chris Randall, 'BYD subsidiary FinDreams opens battery factory in China', *Electrive.com*, [London], 16 June 2022, online at: https://www.electrive.com/2022/06/16/byd-subsidiary-findreams-opens-battery-factory-in-china/

72. Dong Peng, 'Leading battery groups lithium "mining" giants end up building batteries, lithium battery industry chain "vertical integration" speeds up' 电池龙头组团"挖矿" 锂矿大佬下场造电池 锂电产业链"纵向一体化"提速, *21st Century Business Herald*, [Guangzhou], 3 October 2022, online at: https://news.hexun.com/2022-10-03/206861274.html

73. Barry van Wyk, 'The future of China's lithium battery industry is in Sichuan province', *The China Project*, [New York], 5 October 2022, online at: https://thechinaproject.com/2022/10/05/the-future-of-chinas-lithium-battery-industry-is-in-sichuan-province/

74. Michelle Lewis, 'How solid state EV batteries could cut emissions by up to 39%', *Electrek*, [Fremont, CA], 19 July 2022, online at: https://electrek.co/2022/07/19/how-solid-state-ev-batteries-could-cut-emissions-by-up-to-39/

75. Guo Yingzhe, 'CATL aims to mass produce sodium-ion batteries in 2023', *Caixin Global*, [Beijing], 25 October 2022, online at: https://www.caixinglobal.com/2022-10-25/catl-aims-to-mass-produce-sodium-ion-batteries-in-2023-101955814.html

76. Zhang Ming and Li Ting, 'Lithium price becoming "highly unaffordable", while the sodium battery is cost-effective and provides new opportunities' 锂价上涨"高攀不起" 钠电池性价比占优迎机遇, *Securities Daily*, [Beijing], 19 September 2022, online at: http://epaper.zqrb.cn/html/2022-09/19/content_877847.htm

77. Barry van Wyk, 'The sodium battery era is coming soon', *The China Project*, [New York], 20 September 2022, online at: https://thechinaproject.com/2022/09/20/the-sodium-battery-era-is-coming-soon

78. Barry van Wyk, 'Great Wall Motors has made a risky and possibly premature bet on hydrogen cars', *The China Project*, [New York], 27 May 2022, online at: https://thechinaproject.com/2022/05/27/great-wall-motors-has-made-a-risky-and-possibly-premature-bet-on-hydrogen-cars/

79. Economic Information Daily, 'Five major urban clusters to explore "hydrogen energy" fuel cell vehicles welcome good news' 五大城市群探路"氢能" 燃料电池汽车迎利好, *Economic Information Daily*, [Beijing], 24 October 2022, online at: http://caijing.chinadaily.com.cn/a/202210/24/WS6355dd3da310817f312f2ef5.html

80. Barry van Wyk, 'The dawn of the vanadium battery age in China', *The China Project*, [New York], 18 October 2022, online at: https://thechinaproject.com/2022/10/18/the-dawn-of-the-vanadium-battery-age-in-china/

81. Maeve Campbell, 'We're facing a lithium battery crisis: What are the alternatives?', *Euronews*, [Lyon], 9 February 2022, online at: https://www.euronews.com/green/2022/02/09/we-re-facing-a-lithium-battery-crisis-what-are-the-alternatives

China's 'Green Steel': Unchaining from Australia

1. State Council, *National Climate Change Adaptation Strategy 2035* 关于印发《国家适应气候变化战略2035》的通知, Beijing: State Council of the People's Republic of China, 10 May 2022, online at: http://www.gov.cn/zhengce/zhengceku/2022-06/14/content_5695555.htm

2. ibid.

3. Belinda Schäpe and Byford Tsang, 'Opinion: China's crucial role in decarbonising the global steel sector', *China Dialogue*, [London], 23 May 2022, online at: https://chinadialogue.net/en/climate/opinion-chinas-crucial-role-in-decarbonising-the-global-steel-sector/

4. Tony Wood and Guy Dundas, *Start with Steel: A Practical Plan to Support Carbon Workers and Cut Emissions*, Grattan Institute Report No.2020-06, Melbourne: Grattan Institute, May 2020, online at: https://grattan.edu.au/wp-content/uploads/2020/05/2020-06-Start-with-steel.pdf

5. Ministry of Industry and Information Technology (MIIT), 'Analysis of "Implementation measures for capacity replacement in the steel industry"' 《钢铁行业产能置换实施办法》解读, Beijing: MIIT, 8 January 2018, online at: https://www.miit.gov.cn/jgsj/ycls/ghzc/art/2020/art_cdc0a47947b84d939aa438704ba9e5fb.html

6. Xinhua, 'China to further cut crude steel output for carbon neutrality goal', *Xinhua*, 29 December 2020, online at: http://www.xinhuanet.com/english/2020-12/29/c_139627279.htm

7. Min Zhang and Dominique Patton, 'China 2021 crude steel output retreats 3% from record high on stringent production curbs', *Reuters*, 17 January 2022, online at: https://www.reuters.com/world/china/china-2021-crude-steel-output-retreats-3-record-high-stringent-production-curbs-2022-01-17/

8. Sina News, 'Mysteel: Can it work without reducing production' 不减产, 能行吗?, *Sina News*, [Beijing], 20 June 2022, online at: https://finance.sina.cn/futuremarket/gypzx/2022-06-20/detail-imizmscu7802549.d.html

9. Zhanxi Li, Fredrik N.G. Andersson, Lars J. Nilsson, and Max Åhman, 'Steel Decarbonization in China: A Top-Down Optimization Model for Exploring the First Steps', *Journal of Cleaner Production*, vol.384 (2023): 135550, online at: https://doi.org/10.1016/j.jclepro.2022.135550

10. Global Times, 'China ramps up recycling of scrap steel amid soaring iron ore prices', *Global Times*, [Beijing], 17 December 2020, online at: https://www.globaltimes.cn/content/1210300.shtml

11. World Steel Association, 'Crude Steel Production November 2022', *Data Viewer*, Brussels: World Steel Association, 22 December 2022, online at: https://worldsteel.org/steel-topics/statistics/steel-data-viewer/

12. Bureau of International Recycling (BIR), *World Steel Recycling in Figures 2016–2020: Steel Scrap — A Raw Material for Steelmaking*, 12th edn, Brussels: BIR, 2021, online at: https://www.bir.org/publications/facts-figures/download/821/175/36?method=view

13. Swarnali Chakraborty and Anjana Sabu, 'Bracing for a surge: Shanghai's net zero emissions target could peak China's ferrous scrap imports', *Recycling Today*, [Valley View, OH], Winter 2022 Scrap Supplement, online at: https://www.recyclingtoday.com/article/bracing-for-a-surge-chinese-ferrous-demand/

14. Baris Bekir Çiftçi, 'Blog: The future of global scrap availability', Brussels: World Steel Association, 2 May 2018, online at: https://worldsteel.org/media-centre/blog/2018/future-of-global-scrap-availability/

15. Bellona Europa, 'Hydrogen in steel production: What is happening in Europe — Part two', *Bellona*, [Oslo], 26 May 2021, online at: https://bellona.org/news/industrial-pollution/2021-05-hydrogen-in-steel-production-what-is-happening-in-europe-part-two

16. Ben Ellis and Wenjun Bao, 'Pathways to decarbonisation episode two: Steelmaking technology', *Prospects*, Melbourne: BHP, 5 November 2020, online at: https://www.bhp.com/news/prospects/2020/11/pathways-to-decarbonisation-episode-two-steelmaking-technology

17. Simon Nicholas and Soroush Basirat, *Iron Ore Quality a Potential Headwind to Green Steelmaking: Technology and Mining Options are Available to Hit Net-Zero Steel Targets*, Report, Lakewood, OH: Institute for Energy Economics and Financial Analysis, 28 June 2022, online at: https://ieefa.org/resources/iron-ore-quality-potential-headwind-green-steelmaking-technology-and-mining-options-are

18. Ministry of Industry and Information Technology (MIIT), *Guiding Opinion on Promoting High-Quality Development of the Iron and Steel Industry* 关于促进钢铁工业高质量发展的指导意见, Beijing: MIIT, 20 January 2022, online at: http://www.gov.cn/zhengce/zhengceku/2022-02/08/content_5672513.htm

19. Jing Zhang, 'For steel sector, China's decarbonization is a costly quest', *S&P Global Commodity Insights*, New York, NY: S&P Global, 19 May 2022, online at: https://www.spglobal.com/commodityinsights/en/market-insights/blogs/metals/051922-green-steel-china-decarbonization-dri

20. Schäpe and Tsang, 'Opinion: China's crucial role in decarbonising the global steel sector'.

21. Kun He, Li Wang, and Xiaoyan Li, 'Review of the Energy Consumption and Production Structure of China's Steel Industry: Current Situation and Future Development', *Metals*, vol.10, no.3 (2020): 302–319.

22. Shell Finance, 'National Development and Reform Commission signals another reduction in reducing coarse steel production' 发改委称今年将继续压减粗钢产量 分析意见认为有助钢企改善盈利, *Toutiao*, [Beijing], 19 April 2022, online at: https://www.toutiao.com/article/7088279141023547941/?wid=1675141931287

23. Pang Wuji, 'Economic watch: Carbon neutrality does not mean blindly reducing steel production' 经济观察: 中国钢铁业碳中和不是盲目减产量, *CNII*, 25 April 2022, online at: https://www.cnii.com.cn/ycl/202204/t20220425_376400.html

24. ibid.

25. David Uren, 'Editors' picks for 2021: "No end in sight for China's dependence on Australian iron ore"', *The Strategist*, [Canberra], 6 January 2022, online at: https://www.aspistrategist.org.au/editors-picks-for-2021-no-end-in-sight-for-chinas-dependence-on-australian-iron-ore/

26. Chen Wenguang, 'A 2021 summary of China's iron ore industry 2021' 年中国铁矿山开采行业概览, *Sina News*, [Beijing], 8 July 2021, online at: https://stock.finance.sina.com.cn/stock/go.php/vReport_Show/kind/search/rptid/679025071836/index.phtml

27. Anil Panchal, 'China to set up centralised iron ore buyer to counter Australia's dominance — FT', *FXstreet*, [Barcelona], 16 June 2022, online at: https://www.fxstreet.com/news/china-to-set-up-centralised-iron-ore-buyer-to-counter-australias-dominance-ft-202206160057

28. Cecilia Jamasmie, 'Guinea halts Simandou iron ore project again', *Mining.com*, 4 July 2022, online at: https://www.mining.com/guinea-halts-simandou-iron-ore-project-again/

29. Sun Yu and Neil Hume, 'China to set up central iron ore buyer to counter Australia', *Australian Financial Review*, 16 June 2022, online at: https://www.afr.com/companies/mining/china-to-set-up-central-iron-ore-buyer-to-counter-australia-20220616-p5au6q

30. Jorrit Gosens and Frank Jotzo, 'China's demand for coal is set to drop fast. Australia should take note', *The Conversation*, [Melbourne], 21 April 2022, online at: https://theconversation.com/chinas-demand-for-coal-is-set-to-drop-fast-australia-should-take-note-181552

31. John Pye, Alireza Rahbari, Emma Aisbett, Frank Jotzo, and Zsuzsanna Csereklyei, 'Red dirt, yellow sun, green steel: How Australia could benefit from a global shift to emissions-free steel', *The Conversation*, [Melbourne], 18 March 2022, online at: https://theconversation.com/red-dirt-yellow-sun-green-steel-how-australia-could-benefit-from-a-global-shift-to-emissions-free-steel-179286

FOCUS — Women in Chains

What Have We Learned from 'the Woman in Chains'?

1. Manya Koetse, 'Mother of eight found chained up in shed next to family home in Xuzhou', *What's On Weibo*, 29 January 2022, online at: https://www.whatsonweibo.com/mother-of-eight-found-chained-up-in-shed-next-to-family-home-in-xuzhou/

2. Li Yuan, 'Seeking truth and justice, Chinese see themselves in a chained woman', *The New York Times*, 1 March 2022, online at: https://www.nytimes.com/2022/03/01/business/china-chained-woman-social-media.html

3. 'Update by Feng county officials on the "mother of eight"' 江苏丰县官方通报"生育八孩女子"情况, *Sina News*, [Beijing], 28 January 2022, online at: https://news.sina.cn/sh/2022-01-28/detail-ikyakumy3181967.d.html

4. 'Response to netizens' queries on the "mother of eight"' 关于网民反映"生育八孩女子"情况的调查通报, *Sina News*, [Beijing], 30 January 2022, online at: https://news.sina.com.cn/s/2022-01-30/doc-ikyamrmz8380928.shtml

5. 'Update by Xuzhou City officials on the "mother of eight"' 江苏徐州公布"丰县生育八孩女子"调查进展, *China News*, 7 February 2022, online at: https://www.chinanews.com.cn/sh/2022/02-07/9670676.shtml

6. CCTV, 'Results from investigation into Feng county's "mother of eight"' "丰县生育八孩女子"事件调查处理情况公布, *Xinhuanet*, 10 February 2022, online at: http://www.news.cn/local/2022-02/10/c_1128353709.htm

7.   Xu Wei, 'Li urges stronger action on abductions', *China Daily*, 30 March 2022, online at: https://www.chinadaily.com.cn/a/202203/30/WS62438e8ba310fd2b29e54035.html

8.   James Z. Lee and Wang Feng, *One Quarter of Humanity: Malthusian Mythology and Chinese Realities, 1700–2000*, Cambridge, MA: Harvard University Press, 1999, p.61.

9.   ibid., p.7.

10. Johanna S. Ransmeier, *Sold People: Traffickers and Family Life in North China*, Cambridge, MA: Harvard University Press, 2017, p.2.

11. Matthew H. Sommer, *Polyandry and Wife-Selling in Qing Dynasty China: Survival Strategies and Judicial Interventions*, Oakland, CA: University of California Press, 2015, p.70.

12. Ida Pruitt and Ning Lao T'ai-t'ai, *A Daughter of Han: The Autobiography of a Chinese Working Woman*, New Haven, CT: Yale University Press, 1945, p.70.

13. Shen Congwen, 'Xiaoxiao', in Joseph S.M. Lau and Howard Goldblatt eds, *The Columbia Anthology of Modern Chinese Literature*, trans. Eugene Chen Eoyang, New York, NY: Columbia University Press, 1995, p.97.

14. Mara Yue Du, 'Reforming Social Customs through Law: Dynamics and Discrepancies in the Nationalist Reform of the Adoptive Daughter-in-Law', *NAN Nü*, vol.21, no.1 (2019): 76–106, at p.87. For the full text of the story by Bing Xin, see online at: http://www. bingxinwang.com/bingxindezuopin/7.html

15. Du, 'Reforming Social Customs through Law', p.78.

16. Ransmeier, *Sold People*, p.20.

17. Mao Tse-tung, 'Report on an investigation of the peasant movement in Hunan', in *Selected Works of Mao Tse-tung*, Peking: Foreign Languages Press, 1927, online at: https://www. marxists.org/reference/archive/mao/selected-works/volume-1/mswv1_2.htm

18. David S.G. Goodman, 'Revolutionary Women and Women in the Revolution: The Chinese Communist Party and Women in the War of Resistance to Japan, 1937–1945', *The China Quarterly*, no.164 (2000): 915–942, at p.919.

19. Central People's Government, *The Marriage Law of the People's Republic of China*, Beijing: Foreign Languages Press, 1950, online at: https://www.bannedthought.net/ China/MaoEra/Women-Family/MarriageLawOfThePRC-1950-OCR-sm.pdf

20. Gail Hershatter, *The Gender of Memory: Rural Women and China's Collective Past*, Berkeley, CA: University of California Press, 2011, p.124.

21. He Qinglian, 'The Xuzhou mother of eight is only a snippet in China's history of human trafficking' 徐州八孩母只是中国人口拐卖的悲惨片段, *Radio Free Asia*, [Washington, D.C.], 7 February 2022, online at: https://www.rfa.org/mandarin/pinglun/heqinglian/hql-02072022111821.html

22. Ansley J. Coale, 'Five Decades of Missing Females in China', *Proceedings of the American Philosophical Society*, vol.140, no.4 (1996): 421–450.

23. United Nations Children's Fund (UNICEF), 'Figure 1.9: Sex ratio at birth, 1982–2017', in *Population Demographics, Beijing: UNICEF China*, online at: https://www.unicef.cn/en/ figure-19-sex-ratio-birth-19822017

24. Xie Zhihong and Jia Lusheng, *An Ancient Crime: A True Account of Trafficking Women* 古老的罪恶: 拐卖妇女纪实, Hangzhou: Zhejiang wenyi chubanshe, 1989, p.12.

25. Tiantian Zheng, 'Human Trafficking in China', *Journal of Historical Archaeology & Anthropological Sciences*, vol.3, no.2 (2018): 171–178, at p.172.

26. Xie and Jia, *An Ancient Crime*, p.19.

27. Wang Jinling, Jiang Jiajiang, and Gao Xueyu eds, *Interview Records of Women Sold into Marriage* 被拐卖婚迁妇女访谈实录, Beijing: Shehui kexue wenxian chubanshe, 2018, pp. 40–65. The author wishes to thank Dr Pan Wang for bringing this source to his attention.

28. ibid., p.36.

29. Greta Lai, 'For women, China's new divorce law is a step back for gender equality', *South China Morning Post*, [Hong Kong], 1 May 2021, online at: https://www.scmp.com/comment/opinion/article/3131461/women-chinas-new-divorce-law-step-back-gender-equality

30. Koetse, 'Mother of eight found chained up in shed next to family home in Xuzhou'.

Violence against Women: Can the Law Help?

1. Manya Koetse, 'What happened in Tangshan? The violent restaurant incident everyone is talking about', *What's on Weibo*, 11 June 2022, online at: https://www.whatsonweibo.com/what-happened-in-tangshan-the-violent-restaurant-incident-everyone-is-talking-about/

2. James Palmer, 'A Brutal Attack Stirs Anger and Shame in China', *Foreign Policy*, [Washington, D.C.], 15 June 2022, online at: https://foreignpolicy.com/2022/06/15/china-tangshan-attack-gender-violence-anger/

3. Louisa Lim, 'American woman gives domestic abuse a face, and voice, in China', *NPR*, 7 February 2013, online at: https://www.npr.org/2013/02/07/171316582/american-woman-gives-domestic-abuse-a-face-and-voice-in-china

4. Manya Koetse, 'Video of assault on woman in Beijing hotel causes urban safety concerns amongst netizens', *What's on Weibo*, 6 April 2016, online at: https://www.whatsonweibo.com/video-assault-woman-shocks-weibo/

5. 'Chinese vlogger dies after "set on fire by ex during live stream', *BBC*, [London], 2 October 2020, online at: https://www.bbc.com/news/world-asia-china-54380148

6. Manya Koetse, 'Shaanxi domestic violence incident caught on home security camera, sparks online outrage', *What's on Weibo*, 23 January 2022, online at: https://www.whatsonweibo.com/shaanxi-domestic-violence-incident-caught-on-home-security-camera-sparks-online-outrage/

7. Pan Wang, '(Wo)men's voices, rights, and the vision of the state', *The China Story*, [Canberra], 8 March 2022, online at: https://www.thechinastory.org/womens-voices-rights-and-the-vision-of-the-state/

8. Manya Koetse, 'The "green tea bitch" — stereotyping Chinese women', *What's on Weibo*, 10 April 2013, online at: https://www.whatsonweibo.com/dangerous-women-the-green-tea-bitch/

9. ibid.

10. Kayla Wong and Tan Min-Wei, 'A "witch" & "unhinged hag" who is "playing with fire": Chinese mock Pelosi for high-profile trip to Taiwan', *Mothership*, [Singapore], 3 August 2022, https://mothership.sg/2022/08/pelosi-china-netizens/

11. Zhang Zhouxiang, 'Don't blame victims. Blame the attackers', *ChinaDaily. com.cn*, 12 June 2022, online at: https://global.chinadaily.com.cn/a/202206/12/WS62a59029a310fd2b29e6229f.html

12. Rachel Cheung, 'Women brutally attacked for turning down man's advances sparks uproar in China', *VICE*, [Brooklyn], 15 June 2022, online at: https://www.vice.com/en/article/k7bqqw/women-china-attack-tangshan-gender-violence

13. Xiaoting Han and Chenjun Yin, 'Mapping the Manosphere. Categorization of Reactionary Masculinity Discourses in Digital Environment', *Feminist Media Studies*, 2022, doi.org/10.1080/14680777.2021.1998185. From my observations, China is witnessing some elements of the 'manosphere', which I call the 'Sino-manosphere'. This, however, is not as radical as that in the West, such as 'men going their own way' (MGTOW), 'involuntary celibates' (incels), or 'pick-up artists' (PUAs). See Jessica Aiston, 'What is the manosphere and why is it a concern?', *internetmatters.org*, [London], 4 October 2021, online at: https://www.internetmatters.org/hub/news-blogs/what-is-the-manosphere-and-why-is-it-a-concern/

14. Laura Bates, *Men Who Hate Women: From Incels to Pickup Artists—The Truth about Extreme Misogyny and How It Affects Us All*, London: Simon & Schuster, 2021.

15. Ellis Gunn, *Rattled*, Sydney: Allen & Unwin, 2022.

16. World Health Organisation, 'Violence against women', *Fact Sheet*, World Health Organisation, Geneva, 9 March 2021, online at: https://www.who.int/news-room/fact-sheets/detail/violence-against-women

17. Huizhong Wu, 'Human trafficking case sparks government response in China', *ABC News*, 9 March 2022, online at: https://www.abc4.com/news/human-trafficking-case-sparks-government-response-in-china/

18. Joel Wing-Lun, 'What Have We Learned From "The Woman in Chains?"', *The China Story*, [Canberra], 9 May 2022, online at: https://www.thechinastory.org/what-have-we-learned-from-the-woman-in-chains/

19. Article 240, Criminal Law of the Peoples' Republic of China, online at: https://www.ilo.org/dyn/natlex/docs/ELECTRONIC/5375/108071/F-78796243/CHN5375%20Eng3.pdf

20. ibid., Article 241.

21. ibid., Article 341; The World Statement, '10 years for buying a panda, 5 years for buying a parrot, and 3 years for buying a woman?' 买熊猫判10年，买鹦鹉判5年，买妇女最重判3年?, *163.com*, 8 February 2022, online at: https://www.163.com/dy/article/GVL49F650551LSF2.html

22. Article 32, Chapter 4: Divorce, Marriage Law of the People's Republic of China, 2001, online at: http://www.npc.gov.cn/zgrdw/englishnpc/Law/2007-12/13/content_1384064.htm

23. Cai Yiwen, 'China's anti–domestic violence law at the five-year mark', *Sixth Tone*, [Shanghai], 1 March 2021, online at: https://www.sixthtone.com/news/1006903/chinas-anti-domestic-violence-law-at-the-five-year-mark

24. ibid.; Standing Committee of the National People's Congress, 'Anti–Domestic Violence Law of the People's Republic of China' 中华人民共和国反家庭暴力法, *gov.cn*, 27 December 2015, online at: http://www.gov.cn/zhengce/2015-12/28/content_5029898.htm

25. Neo Chai Chin, 'Every 7.4 seconds, a woman in China faces domestic violence. Can the tide be turned?', *CNA Insider*, [Singapore], 6 May 2021, online at: https://www.channelnewsasia.com/cnainsider/every-7-4-seconds-women-china-face-domestic-violence-patriarchy-1938081

26. Pan Wang, 'Struggle with Pandemics: Women, the Elderly and Asian Ethnic Minorities during the COVID-19 Pandemic', *Portal Journal of Multidisciplinary International Studies*, vol.17, no. 1–2 (2021): 14–22.

27. Jane Zhang, '#MeToo or not: Controversy lingers after Alibaba fires woman who accused boss of sexual assault', *South China Morning Post*, [Hong Kong], 18 December 2021, online at: https://www.scmp.com/tech/big-tech/article/3159977/metoo-or-not-controversy-lingers-after-alibaba-fires-woman-who; Liu Zhenzhen, 'Chinese TV host accused in #MeToo scandal trumpets return to state broadcaster', *South China Morning Post*, [Hong Kong], 30 December 2022, online at: https://www.scmp.com/news/china/politics/article/3205081/chinese-tv-host-accused-metoo-scandal-trumpets-return-state-broadcaster

28. Associated Press, 'Senior police official sacked in China after attack on group of women in a restaurant', *ABC News*, 22 June 2022, online at: https://www.abc.net.au/news/2022-06-22/police-official-sacked-in-china-after-assault-on-women/101174066; Liu Caiyu, 'China launches a 100-day campaign to crack down on illegal behaviours in wake of brutality at Tangshan restaurant', *Global Times*, [Beijing], 28 June 2022, online at: https://www.globaltimes.cn/page/202206/1269231.shtml

29. Alexandra Stevenson and Zixu Wang, 'China charges 28 people, months after brutal beating of women', *The New York Times*, 29 August 2022, online at: https://www.nytimes.com/2022/08/29/world/asia/china-arrests-beating-women.html

30. Adam Minter, 'In China, don't dare help the elderly', *Bloomberg*, [New York City], 9 September 2011, online at: https://www.bloomberg.com/opinion/articles/2011-09-08/in-china-don-t-dare-help-the-elderly-adam-minter

31. ibid.

32. Megan Levy, '"A seriously ill society": Hit-run case of little Yueyue shocks China — and the world', *Sydney Morning Herald*, 18 October 2011, online at: https://www.smh.com.au/world/a-seriously-ill-society-hitrun-case-of-little-yueyue-shocks-china--and-the-world-20111018-1ltv1.html

33. Yan Yunxiang, 'The Moral Implications of Immorality: The Chinese Case for a New Anthropology of Morality', *Journal of Religious Ethics*, vol.42, no.3 (2014): 460–493.

34. See, for example, Associated Press, 'Illegal food additives still a problem in China', *NBC News*, 26 February 2009, online at: https://www.nbcnews.com/health/health-news/illegal-food-additives-still-problem-china-flna1c9444172; and Rob Schmitz, 'A Chinese woman does a really bad job pretending to be hit by a car', *NPR*, 28 December 2016, online at: https://www.npr.org/sections/goatsandsoda/2016/12/28/507245116/a-chinese-lady-does-a-really-bad-job-pretending-to-be-hit-by-a-car

35. ibid.

The Communist Party of China: Where Are the Women?

1. State Council, *China National Program for Women's Development 2021–2030*, Beijing: State Council of the People's Republic of China, 8 September 2021, online at: http://www.gov.cn/zhengce/content/2021-09/27/content_5639412.htm

2. Minglu Chen, '"Innocent Young Girls": The Search for Female Provincial Leaders in China', *The China Quarterly*, vol.251 (2022): 751–775, at p.756.

3. CPC Central Committee Organisation Department, *Opinions on Further Improving the Work of Training and Selecting Female Cadres and Recruiting Female Party Members* 关于进一步做好培养选拔女干部发展女党员工作的意见, Beijing: CPC Central Committee, 2001.

4. Minglu, '"Innocent Young Girls"', p.753.

5. ibid.

6. Alexandra Stevenson, 'For women in China's Communist Party, it's lonely at the top', *The New York Times*, 19 October 2022, online at: https://www.nytimes.com/2022/10/19/business/china-women-communist-party.html

7. Minglu Chen and Junyi Cai, 'Women's access to political power: An analysis of the life trajectory of Wu Yi', in Cai Shenshen ed., *Contemporary Chinese Female Celebrities*, London: Palgrave Macmillan, 2019, p.171.

8. Murray Scot Tanner, *The Politics of Lawmaking in Post-Mao China: Institutions, Processes, and Democratic Prospects*, Oxford, UK: Clarendon Press, 1999.

9. People's Daily, 'The WF is actively promoting gender evaluation mechanism for laws and policies' 妇联正积极推动法律政策的性平等估评估机制, *People's Daily*, 7 March 2014, online at: http://lianghui.people.com.cn/2014cppcc/n/2014/0307/c382397-24567812.html

10. People's Daily, 'Xi Jinping talks about building traditional family values' 习近平谈家风建设, *People's Daily*, 7 January 2023, online at: http://jhsjk.people.cn/article/31792580

11. Xianlin Song, 'Reconstructing the Confucian ideal in 1980s China: The "cultural craze" and new Confucianism', in John Makeham ed., *New Confucianism: A Critical Examination*, New York, NY: Palgrave Macmillan, 2003.

12. People's Daily, 'Adhere to women's development path of Socialism with Chinese Characteristics, mobilise women to make contribution and walk at the forefront of the era' 坚持中国特色社会主义妇女发展道路组织动员妇女走在时代前列建功立业, *CPC News*, 7 January 2023, online at: http://cpc.people.com.cn/n1/2018/1103/c64094-30379694.html

13. Ministry of Civil Affairs and All-China Women's Federation, *Instructions on Strengthening Educational Work on Coaching in Marriage and Family* 关于加强新时代婚姻家庭辅导教育工作的指导意见, Ministry of Civil Affairs of the People's Republic of China, 9 September 2020, online at: http://www.gov.cn/xinwen/2020-09/09/content_5541839.htm

CHAPTER 3 — Erasing Identities

(Identity) Politics in Command: Xi Jinping in Xinjiang

1. Xinhua News, 'Xi Jinping's tour of Xinjiang' 习近平在新疆考察, *Xinhuanet*, 15 July 2022, online at: http://www.news.cn/politics/leaders/2022-07/15/c_1128836147.htm

2. Joshua Lipes, 'Expert says 1.8 million Uyghurs, Muslim minorities, held in Xinjiang's internment camps', *Radio Free Asia*, [Washington, D.C.], 24 November 2019, online at: https://www.rfa.org/english/news/uyghur/detainees-11232019223242.html

3. Human Rights Watch, 'China: Xinjiang official figures reveal higher prisoner count — half-million prosecuted, imprisoned during crackdown', *Human Rights Watch News* [New York], 14 September 2022, online at: https://www.hrw.org/news/2022/09/14/china-xinjiang-official-figures-reveal-higher-prisoner-count/

4. For a catalogue and assessment of what it determined were likely crimes against humanity in Xinjiang, based on official documents, dozens of firsthand accounts, and investigations by reporters and academics, see Office of the United Nations High Commissioner for Human Rights (OHCHR), *OHCHR Assessment of Human Rights Concerns in the Xinjiang Uyghur Autonomous Region, People's Republic of China*, Geneva: OHCHR, 31 August 2022, online at: https://www.ohchr.org/sites/default/files/documents/countries/2022-08-31/22-08-31-final-assesment.pdf

5. Human Rights Watch, 'China'.

6. Laura T. Murphy, Nyrola Elimä, and David Tobin, *'Until Nothing is Left': China's Settler Corporation and its Human Rights Violations in the Uyghur Region. A Report on the Xinjiang Production and Construction Corps*, Sheffield, UK: The Helena Kennedy Centre for International Justice, Sheffield Hallam University, 2022, online at: https://www.shu.ac.uk/helena-kennedy-centre-international-justice/research-and-projects/all-projects/until-nothing-is-left

7. Xinhua News, 'Xi Jinping's tour of Xinjiang'.

8. Department of Homeland Security, *Strategy to Prevent the Importation of Goods Mined, Produced, or Manufactured with Forced Labor in the People's Republic of China*, Report to Congress, Washington, D.C.: Office of Strategy, Policy, and Plans, US Department of Homeland Security, 17 June 2022, online at: https://www.dhs.gov/sites/default/files/2022-06/22_0617_fletf_uflpa-strategy.pdf

9. The rights supposedly granted non-Han *minzu* at various times and in various documents, including PRC constitutions, comprise a long list of superficially promising but in practice disappointing offers of self-determination, regional autonomy, and cultural and linguistic freedom. One foundational article in the considerable relevant literature is Dawa Norbu, 'Chinese Communist Views on National Self-Determination, 1922–1956: Origins of China's National Minorities Policy', *International Studies*, vol.25, no.4 (1988), online at: https://doi.org/10.1177/0020881788025004001

10. Fei Xiaotong, 'Plurality and unity in the configuration of the Chinese people', The Tanner Lectures on Human Values, delivered at The Chinese University of Hong Kong, 15 and 17 November 1988, online at: https://tannerlectures.utah.edu/_resources/documents/a-to-z/f/fei90.pdf

11. Fei Xiaotong, 'Many origins/one entity pattern of the *Zhonghua* nation' 中华民族多元一体格局, in Fei Xiaotong ed., Many Origins/One Entity Pattern of the *Zhonghua* Nation 中华民族多元一体格局, Beijing: Xinhua shudian, 1989.

12. There is a large and growing literature on the construction of nation and ethnicity in the Qing empire and Chinese republics. These two historical surveys are good starting points: James Leibold, *Reconfiguring Chinese Nationalism: How the Qing Frontier and its Indigenes Became Chinese*, London: Palgrave Macmillan, 2008; and Bill Hayton, *The Invention of China*, New Haven, CT: Yale University Press, 2020.

13. Dru C. Gladney, 'Representing Nationality in China: Refiguring Majority/Minority Identities', *The Journal of Asian Studies*, vol.53, no.1 (1994): 92–123.

14. Sina News, 'From "two inseparables' to "three inseparables"' 从"两个离不开"到"三个离不开", *Ürümqi Evening News*, 4 July 2005, online at: http://news.sina.com.cn/o/2005-07-04/10556344167s.shtml

15. Public Security News, 'Xi Jinping on building a better Xinjiang' 习近平: 建设团结和谐繁荣富裕文明进步安居乐业生态良好的美好新疆, *Public Security News*, [Shanghai], 2 August 2022, online at: https://gaj.sh.gov.cn/shga/wzXxfbGj/detail?pa=f41aa3d5accbfad14fcbf784730c1c7f3246599c78cf0fe472b07090502fe83cd833d49a3b1091867fcb0030fa8a8574f89cd8d0bb43e938

16. ibid.

17. David Brophy, 'Purging Xinjiang's past', in Linda Jaivin, Esther Sunkyung Klein, and Sharon Strange eds, *China Story Yearbook: Contradiction*, Canberra: ANU Press, 2022, p.77.

18. They were replaced with new Uyghur-literature textbooks with readings comprising Chinese literature translated into Uyghur, rather than texts originally written in Uyghur.

19. See also James A. Millward, 'Colonialism, assimilationism and ethnocide', in James A. Millward, *Eurasian Crossroads: A History of Xinjiang*, New York, NY: Columbia University Press, 2021, p.363.

20. Uyghur Tribunal and Adrian Zenz, *The Xinjiang Papers — Document No. 5: Notice of the General Office of the Central Committee of the Communist Party of China on Forwarding the 'Minutes of the Informal Seminar on Several Historical Issues in Xinjiang by the Central Xinjiang Work Coordination Small Group'*, [Transcript, 10 September 2017], London: Uyghur Tribunal, 2021, online at: https://uyghurtribunal.com/wp-content/uploads/2021/11/Transcript-Document-05.pdf

21. National Ethnic Affairs Commission, 'Xi Jinping's speech at the national conference on ethic unity' 习近平: 在全国民族团结进步表彰大会上的讲话, National Ethnic Affairs Commission of the People's Republic of China, 27 September 2019, online at: https://www.neac.gov.cn/seac/xwzx/201909/1136990.shtml

22. National Ethnic Affairs Commission, 'Min Yanping on continuously enhancing the "five identities" of the ethnic groups' 闵言平: 不断增强各族群众的"五个认同", National Ethnic Affairs Commission of the People's Republic of China, 1 December 2020, online at: https://www.neac.gov.cn/seac/xwzx/202012/1143743.shtml

23. 'A nation is a historically constituted, stable community of people, formed on the basis of a common language, territory, economic life, and psychological make-up manifested in a common culture.' Joseph Vissarionovich Stalin, 'Part I: The nation', in *Marxism and the National Question* [Марксизм и национальный вопрос], 1913, translation from Marxists Internet Archive, online at: https://www.marxists.org/reference/archive/stalin/works/1913/03a.htm#s1

24. James Leibold, 'Xinjiang Work Forum Marks New Policy of "Ethnic Mingling"', *China Brief*, vol.14, no.12 (2014): 1–14.

25. Public Security News, 'Xi Jinping on building a better Xinjiang'.

26. Liu Xin, 'Uyghurs not Turk descendants: White paper', *Global Times*, [Beijing], 21 July 2019, online at: https://www.globaltimes.cn/content/1158545.shtml

27. Public Security News, 'Xi Jinping on building a better Xinjiang'.

28. ibid.

29. 'Pictures of party leaders wearing Uyghur hat in meetings with Uyghur compatriots' 盘点历届中央领导戴维族帽接见维族同胞旧照(组图), *Phoenix News*, [Shenzhen], 26 May 2014, online at: https://www.6parknews.com/newspark/view.php?app=news&act=view&nid=31598

30. ibid.

31. ibid.

32. Xinhua News, 'Xi Jinping's tour of Xinjiang'.

33. Ruth Ingram, 'Tourism in Xinjiang: The Disneyfication of Uyghur Culture', *Bitter Winter*, 23 September 2019, online at: https://bitterwinter.org/disneyfication-of-uyghur-culture/

Dispossession and Defiance in Hong Kong

1. For more on this term, see: https://chinaheritage.net/journal/freedom-hi-protesttoo/

CHAPTER 4 — Vive La Résistance

A Year of Protests, Ceremonies, and Surprises

1. Amy Qin and Javier C. Hernández, 'A year after Wuhan, China tells a tale of triumph (and no mistakes)', *The New York Times*, 10 January 2021, online at: https://www.nytimes.com/2021/01/10/world/asia/wuhan-china-coronavirus.html?action=click&module=RelatedLinks&pgtype=Article

2. Christian Shepherd, 'Tales of anguish emerge from China's locked-down Xian, as hospital staffers are fired over woman's treatment', *The Washington Post*, 6 January 2022, online at: https://www.washingtonpost.com/world/2022/01/05/china-covid-xian-lockdown-miscarriage/

3. Bloomberg News, 'Wuhan locks down 1 million residents in echo of pandemic's start', *Bloomberg*, [New York City], 27 July 2022, online at: https://www.bloomberg.com/news/articles/2022-07-27/wuhan-locks-down-1-million-residents-in-echo-of-pandemic-s-start

4. Shawn Yuan, '"Like Wuhan all over again": As Shanghai protests, China censors', *Al Jazeera*, 30 April 2022, online at: https://www.aljazeera.com/news/2022/4/30/like-wuhan-all-over-again-as-shanghai-protests-censors-pounce

5. Key & Peele, 'A man who "really" enjoys a continental breakfast', *YouTube*, 5 May 2021, online at: https://www.youtube.com/shorts/0BJ6O7ThjdM

6. Fefe XZ & WYB, '[ENG SUB] Shanghai Voices of April' 上海四月之声, *YouTube*, 23 April 2022, online at: https://www.youtube.com/watch?v=UtJzvJBZZ4M

7. Lily Kuo and Pei-Lin Wu, 'Chinese university is scene of rare coronavirus lockdown protest', *The Washington Post*, 18 May 2022, online at: https://www.washingtonpost.com/world/2022/05/18/china-peking-university-protest-lockdown/

8. ibid.

9. Ken Moritsugu and David Rising, 'Students protest, discontent grows over China's COVID policy', *AP News*, 17 May 2022, online at: https://apnews.com/article/covid-health-shanghai-china-cbcac582b7d8a92af0ce76e14847b1af

10. Maya Wang, 'Messages of Beijing bridge protester appear in public toilets — the least surveilled places in China. The New Toilet Revolution, the trend is called', @wang_maya, *Twitter*, 20 October 2022, 2.46 am, online at: https://twitter.com/wang_maya/status/1582760079040090120

11. Ji Siqi, 'China coronavirus: Shanghai restrictions caused "more severe economic hit" than previous lockdowns', *South China Morning Post*, [Hong Kong], 1 June 2022, online at: https://www.scmp.com/economy/economic-indicators/article/3180035/china-coronavirus-shanghai-restrictions-caused-more

12. Stephen McDonell, 'I couldn't believe it til I checked but, amidst #ZeroCovid protests here, #China Central Television (CCTV) is editing out close ups of spectators in its coverage of the World Cup so Chinese viewers don't see thousands of fans without masks in the stands. Only crowd wide shots', @StephenMcDonell, *Twitter*, 28 November 2022, 5.45 pm, online at: https://twitter.com/stephenmcdonell/status/1597119441942155264

13. Geremie R. Barmé, 'Fear, fury & protest: Three years of viral alarm — Xi Jinping's Empire of Tedium Chapter XXII', *China Heritage*, [Wairarapa], 2022, online at: https://chinaheritage.net/journal/fear-fury-protest-three-years-of-viral-alarm/

14. Yvette Tan and Emily McGarvey, 'China Covid: Chinese protesters say police seeking them out', *BBC News*, 29 November 2022, online at: https://www.bbc.com/news/world-asia-china-63785351

15. Yang Caini, 'A woman dies in China's COVID lockdown, again', *Sixth Tone*, [Shanghai], 7 November 2022, online at: https://www.sixthtone.com/news/1011588/a-woman-dies-in-chinas-covid-lockdown%2C-again--

Double-Speak as LGBTQI+ Resistance

1. Wei, 'The rise and fall of LGBTQ student groups in China'.

2. Helen Gao, 'China's ban on "sissy men" is bound to backfire', *The New York Times*, 31 December 2021, online at: https://www.nytimes.com/2021/12/31/opinion/china-masculinity.html

3. Nathan Wei, 'The rise and fall of LGBTQ student groups in China', *The China Project*, 27 July 2022, online at: https://thechinaproject.com/2022/07/27/the-rise-and-fall-of-lgbtq-student-groups-in-china/

4. Linda Jaivin and Esther Sunkyung Klein, 'Introduction: From crisis to contradiction — New normals', in Linda Jaivin, Esther Sunkyung Klein, and Sharon Strange eds, *China Story Yearbook 2021: Contradiction*, 2021, pp.x–xxv, online at: https://www.thechinastory.org/yearbooks/yearbook-2021-contradiction/introduction-from-crisis-to-contradiction-new-normals/

5. Josh Chin and Liza Lin, *Surveillance State: Inside China's Quest to Launch a New Era of Social Control*, New York, NY: St Martin's Press, 2022, p.111.

6. Muyi Xiao, Isabelle Qian, Tracy Wen Liu, and Chris Buckley, 'How a Chinese doctor who warned of COVID-19 spent his final days', *The New York Times*, 6 October 2022, online at: https://www.nytimes.com/2022/10/06/world/asia/covid-china-doctor-li-wenliang.html

7. Hui Fang and Shangwei Wu, '"Life and Death" on the Internet: Metaphors and Chinese Users' Experiences of "Account Bombing"', *International Journal of Communication*, vol.16 (2022): 3560–3580.

8. Leta Hong Fincher, 'China's Feminist Five', *Dissent*, [New York], Fall 2016, online at: https://www.dissentmagazine.org/article/china-feminist-five

CHAPTER 5 — Taiwan — Trouble in the First Island Chain

Semiconductors, Supply Chains, and the Fate of Taiwan

1. Author's own translation. For a bilingual version of this speech, see Wang Zichen, 'Xi Jinping's speech on science & tech on May 28, 2021', *Pekingnology*, n.d., 9 June 2021, online at: https://www.pekingnology.com/p/xi-jinpings-speech-on-science-and?s=r

2. Xinhuanet, 'Xi Jinping delivered an important speech at the closing of the Fourteenth National People's Congress in Beijing' 十四届全国人大一次会议在京闭幕习近平发表重要讲话, *Xinhuanet*, 13 March 2023, online at: http://www.news.cn/politics/2023lh/2023-03/13/c_1129430109.htm

3. This article uses the party's translation, 'reunification', for the Chinese term 统一, putting it in quotation marks to signify that Taiwan and mainland China have never been unified under the rule of the CPC.

4. Xinhua, 'The State Council issued the "Outline for Advancing the Development of the Nation's Integrated Circuit Industry"' 国务院印发《国家集成电路产业发展推进纲要》, State Council of the People's Republic of China, 24 June 2014, online at: http://www.gov.cn/xinwen/2014-06/24/content_2707281.htm

5. China Economic Weekly, 'Prism Casts a Pall over China, America's "Eight Guardian Warriors" Seamlessly Infiltrate China' 棱镜笼罩中国美国 "八大金刚" 在中国无缝渗透, *China Economic Weekly*, no.24 (2013), online at: http://paper.people.com.cn/zgjjzk/html/2013-06/24/content_1259850.htm

6. Digichina, 'Full translation: China's "New Generation Artificial Intelligence Development Plan"', *Digichina*, [Stanford], 1 August 2017, online at: https://digichina.stanford.edu/work/full-translation-chinas-new-generation-artificial-intelligence-development-plan-2017/

7. Ausma Bernot and Susan Trevaskes, 'Smart governance, smarter surveillance', in Linda Jaivin, Esther Sunkyung Klein, and Sharon Strange eds, *China Story Yearbook: Contradiction*, Canberra: ANU Press, 2022, pp.18–31, online at: https://www.thechinastory.org/yearbooks/yearbook-2021-contradiction/chapter-1-smart-governance-smarter-surveillance/

8. Xinhuanet, 'Xi Jinping: Control key technology in own hands' 习近平: 把关键技术掌握在自己手里, *Xinhuanet*, 9 June 2014, online at: http://www.xinhuanet.com/politics/2014-06/09/c_1111056694.htm

9. ibid.

10. ibid.

11. ibid.

12. Xinhua News Agency, *Xi Jinping's Report to Twentieth Party Congress* 习近平在中国共产党第二十次全国代表大会上的报告, Beijing: State Council of the People's Republic of China, 25 October 2022, online at: http://www.gov.cn/xinwen/2022-10/25/content_5721685.htm

13. ibid.

14. For an inflection point on the sentiment of US corporations to China's industrial policies, see James McGregor, *China's Drive for 'Indigenous Innovation': A Web of Industrial Policies*, Washington, D.C.: US Chamber of Commerce, 2010, online at: https://www.uschamber.com/assets/archived/images/documents/files/100728chinareport_0_0.pdf

15. Geremie R. Barmé, 'White paper, red menace', *China Heritage*, [Wairarapa], 17 January 2018, online at: https://chinaheritage.net/journal/white-paper-red-menace/

16. Wei Sheng, 'Where China is investing in semiconductors, in charts', *Technode*, [Shanghai], 4 March 2021, online at: https://technode.com/2021/03/04/where-china-is-investing-in-semiconductors-in-charts/

17. Bureau of Industry and Security, 'Addition of Entities to the Entity List', *Federal Register: The Daily Journal of the United States Government*, 21 May 2019, online at: https://www.federalregister.gov/documents/2019/05/21/2019-10616/addition-of-entities-to-the-entity-list; and Bureau of Industry and Security, 'Addition of Entities to the Entity List, Revision of Entry on the Entity List, and Removal of Entities from the Entity List', *Federal Register: The Daily Journal of the United States Government*, 22 December 2020, online at: https://www.federalregister.gov/documents/2020/12/22/2020-28031/addition-of-entities-to-the-entity-list-revision-of-entry-on-the-entity-list-and-removal-of-entities

18. Bureau of Industry and Security, 'Export Administration Regulations: Amendments to General Prohibition Three (Foreign-Produced Direct Product Rule) and the Entity List', *Federal Register: The Daily Journal of the United States Government*, 19 May 2020, online at: https://www.federalregister.gov/documents/2020/05/19/2020-10856/export-administration-regulations-amendments-to-general-prohibition-three-foreign-produced-direct

19. Financial Times, 'Japan to restrict semiconductor equipment exports as China chip war intensifies', *Financial Times*, [London], 31 March 2023, online at: https://www.ft.com/content/768966d0-1082-4db4-b1bc-cca0c1982f9e

20. Cagan Koc, 'China faces more limits on chip-export gear from Netherlands', *Bloomberg*, [New York City], 9 March 2023, online at: https://www.bloomberg.com/news/articles/2023-03-08/netherlands-to-propose-controls-on-chip-gear-exports-to-china

21. Jake Sullivan, 'Remarks by National Security Advisor Jake Sullivan at the Special Competitive Studies Project Global Emerging Technologies Summit', The White House, Washington, D.C., 16 September 2022, online at: https://www.whitehouse.gov/briefing-room/speeches-remarks/2022/09/16/remarks-by-national-security-advisor-jake-sullivan-at-the-special-competitive-studies-project-global-emerging-technologies-summit/

22. Bureau of Industry and Security, 'Implementation of Additional Export Controls: Certain Advanced Computing and Semiconductor Manufacturing Items; Supercomputer and Semiconductor End Use; Entity List Modification', *Federal Register: The Daily Journal of the United States Government*, 13 May 2022, online at: https://www.federalregister.gov/documents/2022/10/13/2022-21658/implementation-of-additional-export-controls-certain-advanced-computing-and-semiconductor

23. Access to advanced NAND and DRAM memory chips is also targeted.

24. Tsai Ing-wen, 'Taiwan and the fight for democracy: A force for good in the changing international order', *Foreign Affairs*, 5 October 2021, online at: https://www.foreignaffairs.com/articles/taiwan/2021-10-05/taiwan-and-fight-democracy

25. See, for example, Ben Thompson's website, *Stratechery*, online at: https://stratechery.com/

26. Angus Grigg, Lesley Robinson, and Meghna Bali, 'US B-52 bombers to head to Australia as tensions with China grow', *Radio New Zealand*, 31 October 2022, online at: https://www.rnz.co.nz/news/world/477764/us-b-52-bombers-to-head-to-australia-as-tensions-with-china-grow

27. Lonnie D. Henley, *China Maritime Report No. 26: Beyond the First Battle — Overcoming a Protracted Blockade of Taiwan*, CMSI China Maritime Reports 3-2023, Newport, RI: China Maritime Studies Institute, US Naval War College, 2023, online at: https://digital-commons.usnwc.edu/cgi/viewcontent.cgi?article=1025&context=cmsi-maritime-reports

28. Xinhuanet, 'PLA Eastern Theater Command fulfills all tasks of joint military operations around Taiwan', *Xinhuanet*, 10 August 2022, online at: https://english.news.cn/20220810/af665e6d544d4aba8fa3d14aa0312f41/c.html

29. Xinhua News Agency, *Xi Jinping's Report to Twentieth Party Congress*.

30. Financial Times, 'US Navy chief warns China could invade Taiwan before 2024', *Financial Times*, [London], 19 October 2022, online at: https://www.ft.com/content/1740a320-5dcb-4424-bfea-c1f22ecb87f7

31. Xinhuanet, 'Xi Jinping emphasises correct guidance for the healthy and high-quality development of the private economy' 习近平强调正确引导民营经济健康发展高质量发展, *Xinhuanet*, 6 March 2023, online at: http://www.news.cn/politics/leaders/2023-03/06/c_1129417096.htm

32. Xinhua News Agency, *Xi Jinping delivered an important speech at the closing of the Fourteenth National People's Congress in Beijing*.

33. Jake Sullivan, 'Remarks'.

34. See the website 'The Spirit of Two Bombs, One Satellite', online at: https://www.12371.cn/special/zgjs/ldyxjs/

35. Wangyi, 'Academic Li Guojie: Decoupling is not scary, Chinese companies not working together is scary' 李国杰院士: 脱钩不可怕, 中国企业不齐心合力才可怕, *Wangyi*, [Hangzhou], 7 January 2021, online at: https://www.163.com/tech/article/FVO27RCJ000999D9.html

36. Mao Zedong, 'Red and expert [31 January 1958]', in *Long Live Mao Zedong Thought*, Beijing: Red Guard Publications, 1969, online at: https://www.marxists.org/reference/archive/mao/selected-works/volume-8/mswv8_04.htm

37. Che Pan, 'China's top chip maker SMIC achieves 7-nm tech breakthrough on par with Intel, TSMC and Samsung, analysts say', *South China Morning Post*, [Hong Kong], 29 August 2022, online at: https://www.scmp.com/tech/big-tech/article/3190590/chinas-top-chip-maker-smic-achieves-7-nm-tech-breakthrough-par-intel

38. Xinhuanet, 'Xi Jinping: Control key technology in own hands' 习近平: 把关键技术掌握在自己手里, *Xinhuanet*, 9 June 2014, online at: http://www.xinhuanet.com/politics/2014-06/09/c_1111056694.htm

Buckle Up: Pelosi's Visit and the Fourth Taiwan Strait Crisis

1. National Human Rights Museum, 'Jing-Mei White Terror Memorial Park', National Human Rights Museum, New Taipei City, 2017, online at: https://www.nhrm.gov.tw/w/nhrmEN/JMParks

2. Shawn Deng, Hannah Ritchie, Yong Xiong, and Eric Cheung, 'China to hold live-fire exercises in waters near Fujian, opposite Taiwan', *CNN*, 30 July 2022, online at: https://edition.cnn.com/2022/07/30/china/china-live-fire-exercises-taiwan-intl-hnk/index.html

3. Joyu Wang, 'China suspends imports of hundreds of Taiwan products', *The Wall Street Journal*, 2 August 2022, online at: https://www.wsj.com/livecoverage/nancy-pelosi-taiwan-visit-china-us-tensions/card/china-suspends-imports-of-hundreds-of-taiwan-products-sK33Qdt5UJpWLguBx0wS

4. Tayfun Ozberk, 'PLA Navy surrounds Taiwan with a massive naval exercise', *Naval News*, [Paris], 4 August 2022, online at: https://www.navalnews.com/naval-news/2022/08/pla-navy-surrounds-taiwan-with-a-massive-naval-exercise/

5. Crystal Hsu, 'Taiwan to weather Chinese reaction', *Taipei Times*, 4 August 2022, online at: https://www.taipeitimes.com/News/biz/archives/2022/08/04/2003782916

6. Mo Jingxi, 'Beijing sanctions seven "Taiwan independence" die-hards', *China Daily*, 17 August 2022, online at: https://www.chinadaily.com.cn/a/202208/17/WS62fc23c8a310fd2b29e72908.html

7. Chen Yu-fu and Jonathan Chin, 'Pelosi's visit: China blacklists non-profits for "secession"', *Taipei Times*, 4 August 2022, online at: https://www.taipeitimes.com/News/taiwan/archives/2022/08/04/2003782954

8. Xinhua News, 'Full text: The Taiwan question and China's reunification in the new era', *Xinhuanet*, 10 August 2022, online at: https://english.news.cn/20220810/df9d3b8702154b34bbf1d451b99bf64a/c.html

9. Stephan Frühling and Guillaume Lasconjarias, 'NATO, A2/AD and the Kaliningrad Challenge', *Survival*, vol.35, no.2 (2016): 95–116.

10. Kyodo News, 'Xi let missiles fall in Japan's EEZ during Taiwan drills, sources say', *The Japan Times*, 11 August 2022, online at: https://www.japantimes.co.jp/news/2022/08/11/national/china-japan-missiles-eez/

11. Deutsche Welle, 'US to conduct "freedom of navigation" transit in Taiwan Strait', *Taiwan News*, 12 August 2022, online at: https://www.taiwannews.com.tw/en/news/4624920

12. Peter Layton, 'Bringing the Grey Zone into Focus', *The Interpreter*, [Sydney], 22 July 2021, online at: https://www.lowyinstitute.org/the-interpreter/bringing-grey-zone-focus

13. Reuters, 'China has "destroyed" tacit agreement on Taiwan Strait — minister', *Reuters*, 5 October 2022, online at: https://www.reuters.com/world/asia-pacific/china-has-destroyed-tacit-agreement-taiwan-strait-minister-2022-10-05/

14. American Institute in Taiwan, *Taiwan Relations Act*, 1 January 1979, online at: https://web-archive-2017.ait.org.tw/en/taiwan-relations-act

Psyops and Cyberwar in Taiwan

1. World Journal, 'Pelosi's visit to Taiwan was hit by cyberattacks' 裴洛西到訪台遭網攻爆, *Yahoo! Kimo*, [Taiwan], 5 August 2022, online at: http://quicklink.anu.edu.au/s8uk

2. Wu Yan, 'Two NTU websites hacked and replaced with "There is only one China in the World"' 台大2網站遭駭「世界上只有一個中國」, *Mirror Media*, [Taipei], 8 August 2022, online at: https://www.mirrormedia.mg/story/20220808edi001/

3. Wang Hau Yu 王浩宇, Facebook page, online at: https://www.facebook.com/WangHauYu/

4. Department of Foreign Affairs and Trade, *Disinformation & Misinformation*, Canberra: Australian Government, 2023, online at: https://www.internationalcybertech.gov.au/our-work/security/disinformation-misinformation

5. Zhuang Yukai, 'Ministry of Foreign Affairs responds to rumour of paying NTD94 million for Pelosi to visit Taiwan' 網傳「9400萬換裴洛西來台」 外交部駁憑空捏造: 美國政府支應, *Mnews*, [Taipei], 4 August 2022, online at: https://www.mnews.tw/story/20220804nm015

6. Arwa Mahdawi, 'Humour over rumour? The world can learn a lot from Taiwan's approach to fake news', *The Guardian*, [London], 17 February 2021, online at: https://www.theguardian.com/commentisfree/2021/feb/17/humour-over-rumour-taiwan-fake-news

CHAPTER 6 — Pacific Links

The China–Solomon Islands Security Agreement: Clear and Present Danger

1. Courtney Gould, '"Little Cuba": Barnaby Joyce makes bizarre Solomon Islands comparison after China deal', *West Australian*, [Perth], 20 April 2022, online at: https://thewest.com.au/business/labor-liberals-trade-blows-over-solomon-islands-security-pact-with-china-c-6504806

2. Georgia Hitch, 'Scott Morrison says Chinese military base in Solomon Islands would be "red line" for Australia, US', *ABC News*, 24 April 2022, online at: https://www.abc.net.au/news/2022-04-24/scott-morrison-china-naval-base-solomon-islands-red-line/101011710

3. Dr Anna Powles, Twitter post, @AnnaPowles, 24 March 2022, 3.10 pm, online at: https://twitter.com/AnnaPowles/status/1506845794728837120/photo/4

4. Reuters, 'China to equip and train Solomon Islands police after anti-China unrest', *The Guardian*, [London], 24 December 2021, online at: https://www.theguardian.com/world/2021/dec/24/china-to-equip-and-train-police-in-solomon-islands-after-unrest

5. Department of Foreign Affairs and Trade, *Agreement between the Government of Australia and the Government of Solomon Islands Concerning the Basis for Deployment of Police, Armed Forces, and other Personnel to Solomon Islands*, 14 August 2017, Canberra: Commonwealth of Australia, Entry into force for Australia 13 June 2018, ATS 14, online at: http://www.austlii.edu.au/au/other/dfat/treaties/ATS/2018/14.html

6. The National, 'PNG and SI seal policing deal', *The National*, [Port Moresby], 10 February 2023, online at: https://www.thenational.com.pg/png-and-si-seal-policing-deal/

7. Powles, Twitter post.

8. Max Walden, Stephen Dziedzic, and Evan Wasuka, 'Here's what's behind the violent protests in the Solomon Islands capital, Honiara', *ABC News*, 25 November 2021, online at: https://www.abc.net.au/news/2021-11-25/solomon-islands-protests-explainer-china-taiwan/100648086

9. Joseph D. Foukona, 'Solomon Islands gets a lesson in Chinese diplomacy', *The Interpreter*, [Sydney], 29 June 2020, online at: https://www.lowyinstitute.org/the-interpreter/solomon-islands-gets-lesson-chinese-diplomacy

10. Emanuel Stoakes, 'Chinese police could crush Solomon Islands opposition', *Foreign Policy*, [Washington, D.C.], 9 August 2022, online at: https://foreignpolicy.com/2022/08/09/solomon-islands-china-security-pact-beijing-policing-democracy/

11. Gregory Raymond, 'Jagged sphere: China's quest for infrastructure and influence in mainland Southeast Asia', *Lowy Institute Analysis*, June 2021, online at: https://papers.ssrn.com/sol3/papers.cfm?abstract_id=3927622

12. Nick Perry, 'Solomon Islands says it will not allow China military base', *The Diplomat*, 1 April 2022, online at: https://thediplomat.com/2022/04/solomon-islands-says-it-will-not-allow-china-military-base/

13. Peter Monte, 'U-boats in Spain: Kriegsmarine U-boats in Spain and Portugal during WWII', Deutsches U-Boot-Museum, Cuxhaven, Germany, online at: https://dubm.de/u-boats-in-spain/?lang=en

14. Agence France-Presse, 'Solomons PM dismisses concerns over China maritime deal', *France24*, 11 May 2022, online at: https://www.france24.com/en/live-news/20220511-solomons-pm-dismisses-concerns-over-china-maritime-deal

15. Simon Denyer, 'How China's fishermen are fighting a covert war in the South China Sea', *The Washington Post*, 12 April 2016, online at: https://www.andrewerickson.com/2016/04/how-chinas-fishermen-are-fighting-a-covert-war-in-the-south-china-sea/

16. Powles, Twitter post.

17. Stephen Dziedzic, Evan Wasuka, and Iris Zhao, 'Leaked documents reveal Chinese company's aviation plans for Solomon Islands to become a "regional hub"', *ABC News*, 29 April 2022, online at: https://www.abc.net.au/news/2022-04-29/avic-solomon-islands-aviation-plan/101022480

18. David W. Panuelo [President, Federated States of Micronesia], 'Letter to Pacific Island leaders', 20 May 2022, online at: https://s3.documentcloud.org/documents/22039750/letter-from-h-e-david-w-panuelo-to-pacific-island-leaders-may-20-2022-signed.pdf

19. *China–Pacific Island Countries Common Development Vision (Draft)*, online at: https://www.documentcloud.org/documents/22037011-china-pacific-island-countries-common-development-vision

20. *China–Pacific Island Countries Five-Year Action Plan on Common Development (2022–2026) (Draft)*, online at: https://s3.documentcloud.org/documents/22039751/china-pacific-island-countries-five-year-action-plan-on-common-development-2022-2026-copy.pdf

21. Kate Lyons and Reuters, 'China's foreign minister tells Pacific leaders "don't be too anxious" after they reject regional security pact', *The Guardian*, [London], 30 May 2022, online at: https://www.theguardian.com/world/2022/may/30/chinas-foreign-minister-to-meet-with-pacific-nations-amid-push-for-sweeping-regional-deal

22. Kirsty Needham, 'Kiribati focuses on trade not security for China visit to remote Pacific island', *Reuters*, 27 May 2022, online at: https://www.reuters.com/world/asia-pacific/australia-warns-against-pacific-security-pact-china-says-interference-will-fail-2022-05-27/

23. Zhang Hui and Hu Yuwei, 'Wang's visit to Kiribati shows devt opportunities, injects firmness to one-China principle', *Global Times*, [Beijing], 27 May 2022, [Updated 28 May], online at: https://www.globaltimes.cn/page/202205/1266745.shtml

24. Tsukasa Hadano and Fumi Matsumoto, 'Kiribati runway project in focus as China's Wang Yi tours region', *Nikkei Asia*, [Tokyo], 29 May 2022, online at: https://asia.nikkei.com/Politics/International-relations/Kiribati-runway-project-in-focus-as-China-s-Wang-Yi-tours-region

25. Phillip Coorey and Andrew Tillett, 'Labor to launch Pacific outreach to counter Chinese influence', *Australian Financial Review*, 25 May 2022, online at: https://www.afr.com/politics/federal/labor-to-launch-pacific-outreach-to-counter-chinese-influence-20220525-p5aodh

26. Penny Wong, 'A new era in Australian engagement in the Pacific', Speech to Pacific Islands Forum Secretariat, Suva, Fiji, 26 May 2022, online at: https://www.foreignminister.gov.au/minister/penny-wong/speech/speech-pacific-islands-forum-secretariat

27. Reuters, 'Fiji PM calls meeting with new Australia foreign minister "wonderful"', *Reuters*, 28 May 2022, online at: https://www.reuters.com/world/asia-pacific/fiji-pm-calls-meeting-with-new-australia-foreign-minister-wonderful-2022-05-28/

28. Daniel Hurst, 'Labor pledges more foreign aid to Pacific with plan "to restore Australia's place as first partner of choice"', *The Guardian*, [London], 26 April 2022, online at: https://www.theguardian.com/australia-news/2022/apr/26/labor-pledges-more-foreign-aid-to-pacific-with-plan-to-restore-australias-place-as-first-partner-of-choice

29. US Department of State, 'Secretary Antony J. Blinken and Acting Fijian Prime Minister Aiyaz Sayed-Khaiyum at a joint press availability', Remarks, Denarau Island, Fiji, 12 February 2022, online at: https://www.state.gov/secretary-antony-j-blinken-and-acting-fijian-prime-minister-aiyaz-sayed-khaiyum-at-a-joint-press-availability/

Beijing Reshapes Its Pacific Strategy

1. Xinhua, 'China, Pacific Island countries vow to strengthen cooperation', *People's Daily*, 15 July 2022, online at: http://en.people.cn/n3/2022/0715/c90000-10123413.html

2. Ministry of Foreign Affairs, 'Wang Yi Talks about China's "Four-pronged Adherence" to Developing Relations with Pacific Island Countries', Press release, Ministry of Foreign Affairs of the People's Republic of China, 27 May 2022, online at: https://www.fmprc.gov.cn/mfa_eng/zxxx_662805/202205/t20220527_10693486.html

3. Denghua Zhang, *A Cautious New Approach: China's Growing Trilateral Aid Cooperation*, Canberra: ANU Press, 2020.

4. Ministry of Foreign Affairs, 'Wang Yi: China's cooperation with South Pacific Island countries having diplomatic relations with China shows a vibrant situation of "two-wheel driving"', Press release, Ministry of Foreign Affairs of the People's Republic of China, 3 June 2022, online at: https://www.fmprc.gov.cn/mfa_eng/zxxx_662805/202206/t20220603_10698495.html

5. Stephen Dziedzic, 'China seeks region-wide Pacific Islands agreement, Federated States of Micronesia decry draft as threatening "regional stability"', *ABC News*, 25 May 2022, [Updated 26 May 2022], online at: https://www.abc.net.au/news/2022-05-25/china-seeks-pacific-islands-policing-security-cooperation/101099978

6. Sean Kelly, 'The China–Solomon Islands Security Agreement: Clear and present danger', *The China Story*, 6 June 2022, online at: https://www.thechinastory.org/the-china-solomon-islands-security-agreement-clear-and-present-danger/

7. ibid.

8. Ben Westcott, 'Pacific leader blasts China's botched attempt to strike pact', *Bloomberg*, [New York City], 15 July 2022, online at: https://www.bloomberg.com/news/articles/2022-07-15/pacific-leader-blasts-china-s-botched-attempt-to-strike-pact?leadSource=uverify%20wall

9. Ministry of Foreign Affairs of the People's Republic of China, 'Wang Yi: China's Cooperation with South Pacific Island Countries Having Diplomatic Relations with China Shows a Vibrant Situation of "Two-Wheel Driving"', Ministry of Foreign Affairs of the People's Republic of China, 3 June 2022, online at: https://www.fmprc.gov.cn/mfa_eng/zxxx_662805/202206/t20220603_10698495.html

10. The White House, *Indo-Pacific Strategy of the United States*, Washington D.C.: Executive Office of The President, National Security Council, February 2022, online at: https://www.whitehouse.gov/wp-content/uploads/2022/02/U.S.-Indo-Pacific-Strategy.pdf

11. Ministry of Foreign Affairs, 'Vice Foreign Minister Xie Feng: What rights do these countries have to make unwarranted comments on the negotiation and conclusion of the Framework Agreement on Security Cooperation between China and Solomon Islands?', Press release, Ministry of Foreign Affairs of the People's Republic of China, 28 April 2022, online at: https://www.fmprc.gov.cn/mfa_eng/wjbxw/202204/t20220429_10675430.html

12. Stephen Dziedzic, 'Chinese Communist Party donates police equipment to Solomon Islands', *ABC News*, 6 July 2022, [Updated 7 July 2022], online at: https://www.abc.net.au/news/2022-07-06/huge-new-donation-from-ccp-police-equipment-for-solomon-islands/101213248

13. Julia Bergin, 'Solomon Islands signs on to China telecom deal — but at what price?', *Crikey*, [Melbourne], 19 August 2022, online at: https://www.crikey.com.au/2022/08/19/solomon-islands-signs-china-telecom-deal/

14. Chen Xiaochen, 'Australia's "Pacific Step-Up" Strategy: Priority Measures, Motivations and Impact' 澳大利亚的"太平洋升级"战略: 重点举措动因与影响, *Contemporary World and Socialism*, no.3 (2022): 167.

15. Pacific Islands Forum, *2050 Strategy for the Blue Pacific Continent*, Suva: Pacific Islands Forum, 2022.

16. Denghua Zhang, 'China's Influence and Local Perceptions: The Case of Pacific Island Countries', *Australian Journal of International Affairs*, vol.76, no.5 (2022): 575–595.

17. China International Development Cooperation Agency (CIDCA), 'Ten major events of the State International Development Cooperation Agency's external work in 2021' 国家国际发展合作署2021年对外工作10件大事, Press release, CIDCA, 20 January 2022, online at: http://www.cidca.gov.cn/2022-01/20/c_1211537297.htm

Building a World-Class Navy: The Story of China's First Aircraft Carrier

1. Sean Kelly, 'The China-Solomon Islands Security Agreement: Clear and Present Danger', *The China Story*, 6 June 2022, online at: https://www.thechinastory.org/the-china-solomon-islands-security-agreement-clear-and-present-danger/

2. Andrew Greene, 'Defence Minister Peter Dutton says a Chinese spy ship has been seen near secretive naval facility off Western Australia', *ABC News*, 13 May 2022, [Updated 14 May 2022], online at: https://www.abc.net.au/news/2022-05-13/chinese-spy-ship-spotted-near-naval-facility-western-australia/101064538

3. Agence France-Presse, 'China launches third aircraft carrier in military advance', *The Guardian*, [London], 17 June 2022, online at: https://www.theguardian.com/world/2022/jun/17/china-launches-third-aircraft-carrier-military-advance-us-fujian-taiwan

4. Nick Childs and Douglas Barrie, 'Catapulting China's carrier capabilities', *Military Balance Blog*, International Institute for Strategic Studies, 10 June 2022, online at: https://www.iiss.org/blogs/military-balance/2022/06/catapulting-chinas-carrier-capabilities; Nadya Yeh, 'China's third aircraft carrier is its most advanced yet', *The China Project*, [New York], 27 June 2022, online at: https://thechinaproject.com/2022/06/27/chinas-third-aircraft-carrier-is-its-most-advanced-yet/

5. Edward Sing Yue Chan, *China's Maritime Security Strategy: The Evolution of a Growing Sea Power*, New York, NY: Routledge, 2022, pp.46–48; Taylor M. Fravel, *Active Defense: China's Military Strategy Since 1949*, Princeton, NJ: Princeton University Press, 2019, pp.162–163.

6. Liu Huaqing 刘华清, *Memoirs of Liu Huaqing* 刘华清回忆录, Beijing: Jiefangjun chubanshe, 2004, p.479.

7. You Xu and You Ji, *In Search of Blue Water Power: The PLA Navy's Maritime Strategy in the 1990s and Beyond*, Canberra: Strategic and Defence Studies Centre, The Australian National University, 1990, pp.11–13.

8. Ian Storey and You Ji, 'China's Aircraft Carrier Ambitions', *Naval War College Review*, vol.57, no.1 (2004): 79.

9. You Xu and You Ji, *In Search of Blue Water Power*, p.12.

10. Vladimir Matyash, 'Minister comments on state of defence industry', *BBC News*, 19 September 1992.

11. Kyodo News, 'China Seeking Aircraft Carrier to Secure South China Sea', *Kyodo News*, [Tokyo], 17 August 1992.

12. Ian Storey and You Ji, 'China's Aircraft Carrier Ambitions'.

13. Sergei Blagov, 'No connection to naval ship, says embassy', *South China Morning Post*, [Hong Kong], 4 April 1998; 'Intelligence', *Far Eastern Economic Review*, 16 April 1998.

14. Ian Storey and You Ji, 'China's Aircraft Carrier Ambitions'.

15. ibid.; 'Macau says waters too shallow for ex-Soviet carrier', *Reuters*, 11 January 2001.

16. John Ward Anderson, 'Turks keep ship going round in circles', *The Washington Post*, 22 July 2001, online at: https://www.washingtonpost.com/archive/politics/2001/07/22/turks-keep-ship-going-round-in-circles/4ae7af0c-3004-43ad-9998-ae2941c01497/

17. Adam Luck and Raymond Ma, 'Beijing claims waters for "floating casino"', *South China Morning Post*, [Hong Kong], 9 September 2001.

18. 'Xu Zengping: The Shangdong man who brought back "Varyag"' 徐增平: 买回"瓦良格"的山东人, *Sina News*, [Beijing], 8 October 2011, online at: http://news.sina.com.cn/o/2011-10-08/031523266045.shtml

19. Ryan D. Martinson, 'Incubators of Sea Power: Vessel Training Centers and the Modernization of the PLAN Surface Fleet' (2022), CMSI China Maritime Reports, 24, online at: https://digital-commons.usnwc.edu/cmsi-maritime-reports/24

20. Xi Jinping, 'Xi Jinping: Building the PLAN into a world-class navy' 习近平: 把人民海军全面建成世界一流海军, *Xinhua*, 12 April 2018, online at: http://www.xinhuanet.com/politics/leaders/2018-04/12/c_1122674567.htm

21. Taylor M. Fravel, *Active Defense: China's Military Strategy Since 1949*, Princeton, NJ: Princeton University Press, 2019, p.232.

22. Edward Sing Yue Chan, *China's Maritime Security Strategy*, pp.149–152.

23. H.I. Sutton, 'Chinese Navy growth: Massive expansion of important shipyard', *Naval News*, [Paris], 15 March 2022, online at: https://www.navalnews.com/naval-news/2022/03/chinese-navy-growth-massive-expansion-of-important-shipyard/

24. Robert S. Ross, 'Nationalism, Geopolitics, and Naval Expansionism: From the Nineteenth Century to the Rise of China', *Naval War College Review*, vol.71, no.4 (2018): 11–44; Robert S. Ross, 'China's Naval Nationalism: Sources, Prospects, and the U.S. Response', *International Security*, vol.34, no.2 (2009): 46–81.

25. See: Arthur Ding, 'Buckle Up: PLA's Military Drills After Pelosi's Taiwan Visit', *The China Story*, 20 October 2022, online at: https://www.thechinastory.org/buckle-up-the-plas-military-drills-after-pelosis-taiwan-visit/

26. 'Strive to comprehensively build the PLAN into a world-class navy' 努力把人民海军全面建设成世界一流海军, *Qiushi*, [Beijing], 31 May 2018, online at: http://www.qstheory.cn/dukan/qs/2018-05/31/c%5F1122897922.htm

27. See Vincent Ni and agencies, 'Chinese navy vessel arrives at Sri Lanka port to security concerns from India', *The Guardian*, [London], 17 August 2022, online at: https://www.theguardian.com/world/2022/aug/16/chinese-navy-vessel-arrives-at-sri-lanka-port-to-security-concerns-from-india

28. Cristina L. Garafola, Stephen Watts, and Kristin J. Leuschner, *China's Global Basing Ambitions: Defense Implications for the United States*, Santa Monica, CA: RAND Corporation, 2022.

29. Conor M. Kennedy, 'Gray forces in blue territory: The grammar of Chinese maritime militia gray zone operations', in Andrew S. Erickson and Ryan D. Martinson eds, *China's Maritime Gray Zone Operations*, Annapolis: Naval Institute Press, 2019, pp.168–185.

30. David D. Chen, 'Lessons of Ukraine Raise Doubts about PLA Modernization', *China Brief*, vol.22, no.7 (2022): 16–21.

31. Sam Roggeveen, 'China's Third Aircraft Carrier Is Aimed at a Post-U.S. Asia', *The Interpreter*, [Sydney], 28 June 2022, Online at: https://www.lowyinstitute.org/publications/china-s-third-aircraft-carrier-aimed-post-us-asia

32. Helen Davidson, 'Chinese military "to have exclusive use of parts of Cambodian naval base"', *The Guardian*, [London], 7 June 2022, online at: https://www.theguardian.com/world/2022/jun/07/chinese-military-to-have-exclusive-use-of-parts-of-cambodian-naval-base-ream-gulf-of-thailand

33. Congressional Research Service, *China Naval Modernization: Implications for U.S. Navy Capabilities — Background and Issues for Congress*, Washington, D.C.: CRS, Updated 1 December 2022, online at: https://news.usni.org/2022/12/06/report-to-congress-on-chinese-naval-modernization-16

CHAPTER 7 — China's Russia Problem

A 'No Limits' Partnership? China–Russia Strategic Cooperation

1. Tony Munroe, Andrew Osborn, and Humeyra Pamuk, 'China, Russia partner up against West at Olympics summit', *Reuters*, 5 February 2022, online at: https://www.reuters.com/world/europe/russia-china-tell-nato-stop-expansion-moscow-backs-beijing-taiwan-2022-02-04/

2. Alexander Korolev, *China–Russia Strategic Alignment in International Politics*, Amsterdam: Amsterdam University Press, 2022, online at: https://www.aup.nl/en/book/9789463725248/china-russia-strategic-alignment-in-international-politics

3. Alexander Korolev and Vladimir Portyakov, 'Reluctant Allies: System-Unit Dynamics and China–Russia Relations', *International Relations*, vol.33, no.1 (2019): 40–66.

4. Xinhua, 'China, Russia agree to upgrade relations for new era', *Xinhuanet*, 6 June 2019, online at: http://www.xinhuanet.com/english/2019-06/06/c_138119879.htm

5. Tony Munroe, Andrew Osborn, and Humeyra Pamuk, 'China, Russia partner up against West at Olympics summit', *Reuters*, 5 February 2022, online at: https://www.reuters.com/world/europe/russia-china-tell-nato-stop-expansion-moscow-backs-beijing-taiwan-2022-02-04/

6. Peter Hoskins, 'Ukraine war: Russia becomes China's biggest oil supplier', *BBC News*, 20 June 2022, online at: https://www.bbc.com/news/business-61861849

7. Reuters, 'South Korea scrambles jets after Chinese and Russian warplanes enter air defence zone', *The Guardian*, [London], 30 November 2022, online at: https://www.theguardian.com/world/2022/nov/30/south-korea-scrambles-jets-after-chinese-and-russian-warplanes-enter-air-defence-zone?ref=upstract.com

8. Amelie Bottollier-Depois, 'China abstains in UN Security Council vote on Russia's annexations of Ukraine', *Hong Kong Free Press*, 1 October 2022, online at: https://hongkongfp.com/2022/10/01/china-abstains-in-un-security-council-vote-on-russias-annexations-of-ukraine/

9. Alexander Korolev, 'On the Verge of an Alliance: Contemporary China–Russia Military Cooperation', *Asian Security*, vol.15, no.3 (2019): 233–252.

10. Vzglyad, 'Russia and China strengthen military rapprochement Россия и Китай усиливают сближение в военной области', *Vzglyad*, [Moscow], 19 November 2014, online at: https://vz.ru/society/2014/11/19/716036.html

11. Korolev, *China–Russia Strategic Alignment in International Politics*.

12. Vasily Kashin, 'Ukraine's losses are China's gains', *East Asia Forum*, [Canberra], 16 June 2022, online at: https://www.eastasiaforum.org/2022/06/16/ukraines-losses-are-chinas-gains/

13. Vasily Kashin, 'Tacit alliance: Russia and China take military partnership to new level', *Commentary*, 22 October 2019, Carnegie Endowment for International Peace, online at: https://carnegiemoscow.org/commentary/80136

14. Ellen Francis, 'China plans to seize Taiwan on "much faster timeline", Blinken says', *The Washington Post*, 18 October 2022, online at: https://www.washingtonpost.com/world/2022/10/18/china-seize-taiwan-plan-blinken/

15. Eric Edelman and Gary Roughead, *Providing for the Common Defense: The Assessment and Recommendations of the National Defense Strategy Commission*, Washington, D.C.: United States Institute of Peace, 2019, online at: https://www.usip.org/sites/default/files/2019-07/providing-for-the-common-defense.pdf

16. Samuel Bendett and Elsa Kania, *A New Sino-Russian High-Tech Partnership*, Canberra: Australian Strategic Policy Institute, 2019, online at: https://www.aspi.org.au/report/new-sino-russian-high-tech-partnership

17. Vzglyad, 'Russia to insure China against US attack Россия застрахует Китай от нападения США', *Vzglyad*, [Moscow], 4 October 2019, online at: https://vz.ru/world/2019/10/4/1001276.html

18. Linda Kay, 'Chinese missile early warning system — with Russian help — may be nearing completion', *Defense World*, [Sioux Falls], 25 June 2020, online at: https://www.defenseworld.net/2020/06/25/chinese-missile-early-warning-system-with-russian-help-may-be-nearing-completion.html#.YULO2SvitPZ

19. Kashin, 'Tacit alliance'.

20. Graham Allison, 'The Thucydides trap: Are the U.S. and China headed for war?', *The Atlantic*, 25 September 2015, online at: https://www.theatlantic.com/international/archive/2015/09/united-states-china-war-thucydides-trap/406756/

21. The World Bank, 'GDP (current US$): China, Russian Federation, United States, India', *Data*, The World Bank, 2021, online at: https://data.worldbank.org/indicator/NY.GDP.MKTP.CD?locations=CN-RU-US-IN&most_recent_year_desc=false

22. Nuno P. Monteiro, *Theory of Unipolar Politics*, Cambridge, UK: Cambridge University Press, 2014.

23. Tai Ming Cheung and Thomas G. Mahnken eds, *The Gathering Pacific Storm: Emerging US–China Strategic Competition in Defense Technological and Industrial Development*, New York, NY: Cambria Press, 2018.

24. Department of Defense, *Indo-Pacific Strategy Report: Preparedness, Partnerships, and Promoting a Networked Region*, Arlington, VA: US Department of Defense, 1 June 2019, online at: https://media.defense.gov/2019/Jul/01/2002152311/-1/-1/1/DEPARTMENT-OF-DEFENSE-INDO-PACIFIC-STRATEGY-REPORT-2019.PDF

25. W.J. Hennigan, 'U.S. unveils strategy for nuclear threats from China and Russia', *TIME*, [New York], 27 October 2022, online at: https://time.com/6225745/biden-nuclear-defense-strategy-china-russia/

26. John J. Mearsheimer, 'US, China heading toward face-off, says Mearsheimer', *Nikkei Asia*, [Tokyo], 26 March 2015, online at: https://asia.nikkei.com/magazine/20150326-Singapore-after-Lee/Viewpoints/US-China-heading-toward-face-off-says-Mearsheimer

27. Korolev, *China–Russia Strategic Alignment in International Politics*.

28. Alexander Korolev, '"Adverse Complementarity" in Russian–Chinese Economic Relations and its Consequences "Неблагоприятная взаимодополняемость" в российско-китайских экономических отношениях и ее последствия', *Problems of Economics and Management of the Oil and Gas Complex* Проблемы экономики и управления нефтегазовым комплексом, no.1 (2018): 44–50.

29. Al Jazeera, 'United States should recognise "free" Taiwan, Mike Pompeo says', *Al Jazeera*, 4 March 2022, online at: https://www.aljazeera.com/news/2022/3/4/us-should-recognise-free-taiwan-pompeo-says

30. Jude Blanchette, Charles Edel, Christopher B. Johnstone, Scott Kennedy, Victor Cha, Ellen Kim, and Gregory B. Poling, *Speaker Pelosi's Taiwan Visit: Implications for the Indo-Pacific*, Center for Strategic and International Studies, 15 August 2022, online at: https://www.csis.org/analysis/speaker-pelosis-taiwan-visit-implications-indo-pacific

31. Arthur Ding, 'Buckle up: PLA's military drills after Pelosi's Taiwan visit', *The China Story*, 20 October 2022, online at: https://www.thechinastory.org/buckle-up-the-plas-military-drills-after-pelosis-taiwan-visit/

32. Nick Whigham, 'Scott Morrison's $10 billion move in face of China threat', *Yahoo! News*, [Australia], 7 March 2022, online at: https://au.news.yahoo.com/scott-morrisons-10-billion-move-in-face-of-china-threat-215231491.html

33. Alexander Korolev, 'The US can't break the Russia–China alliance', *IAI News*, The Institute of Art and Ideas, 29 March 2022, online at: https://iai.tv/articles/the-us-cant-break-the-china-russia-alliance-auid-2088

34. Ravi Buddhavarapu, 'An Indian rupee–ruble trade arrangement with Russia may be ready in a week', *CNBC*, [Singapore], 23 March 2022, online at: https://www.cnbc.com/2022/03/23/fieo-india-rupee-ruble-trade-mechanism-with-russia-may-be-ready-soon.html

35. Suhasini Haidar, 'U.S. deputy NSA warns India of "consequences"', *The Hindu*, [Chennai], 1 April 2022, online at: https://www.thehindu.com/todays-paper/us-deputy-nsa-warns-india-of-consequences/article65279758.ece

Chinese Social Media and the War in Ukraine

1. Carter Center China Focus, 'Chinese public opinion on the war in Ukraine', *US–China Perception Monitor*, The Carter Center, 19 April 2022, online at: https://uscnpm.org/2022/04/19/chinese-public-opinion-war-in-ukraine/

2. Lu Kewen Studio, 'What kind of big power game is hidden behind the strange Russia–Ukraine conflict?' 【卢克文工作室】奇怪的俄乌冲突，背后暗藏怎样的大国博弈?, *Bilibili*, 24 February 2022, online at: https://www.bilibili.com/video/BV1WZ4y1k7aZ

3. 'Emergency deletion, mysterious virus, biochemical experiments … What exactly did the U.S. do in Ukraine?' 紧急删除、神秘病毒, 生化实验 … 美国在乌克兰究竟做了什么?, *Bilibili*, 25 March 2022, online at: https://www.bilibili.com/video/BV1ET4y1i7et

4. Fang Kecheng, 'What is Zimciti? The Commercial Logic of Content Provision on China's Social Media Platforms', *Chinese Journal of Communication*, vol.15, no.1 (2022): 75–94.

5. Vincent Ni, '"They were fooled by Putin": Chinese historians speak out against Russian invasion', *The Guardian*, [London], 28 February 2022, online at: https://www.theguardian.com/world/2022/feb/28/they-were-fooled-by-putin-chinese-historians-speak-out-against-russian-invasion

6. China Daily, 'Exclusive interview with Russia's deputy chief editor of RT' 今日俄罗斯RT副总编辑接受中国日报专访, *China Daily*, 22 March 2022, online at: https://cn.chinadaily.com.cn/a/202203/22/WS62392b59a3101c3ee7accbba.html

7. Yang Tian and Fang Kecheng, 'How Dark Corners Collude: A Study on an Online Chinese Alt-Right Community', *Information, Communication & Society*, vol.26, no.2 (2023): 441–58.

8. Huanqiu Jingrou 寰球镜头, Weibo account, 22 August 2022, online at: https://weibo.com/7188247797/M26KdcVrF

9. Hxotnongd, 'We feel ashamed' 我们感到羞耻, *China Digital Times*, 28 February 2022, online at: https://chinadigitaltimes.net/chinese/677588.html

10. Hxotnongd, Facebook account, online at: https://www.facebook.com/hxotnongd/

11. Jixian Wang, YouTube account, online at: https://www.youtube.com/c/hellojixin/

12. Guyu, 'At Berlin train station, I was struck by the tears of visitors from Ukraine' 在柏林中央火车站, 乌克兰客人的眼泪让我猝不及防, *Weixin*, 29 March 2022, online at: https://mp.weixin.qq.com/s/JNq74Z59TuXeLdR6Y5201w

13. The Weirdo, 'Ukraine on the cliff edge: Past, present and future' 悬崖边上的乌克兰: 过去、现在与未来, *xiaoyuzhou FM*, 26 February 2022, online at: https://www.xiaoyuzhoufm.com/episode/6219840a30fca3133c0f8314; and 'The flames of war have raged for half a year' 战火纷飞这半年, *xiaoyuzhou FM*, 25 August 2022, online at: https://www.xiaoyuzhoufm.com/episode/6306383dea3aed95e5336a8d

14. Story FM, 'The longest night at the Ukraine Museum' 乌克兰博物馆最长的一夜, *Weixin*, 8 June 2022, online at: https://mp.weixin.qq.com/s/lg9z4CaztkQk4eXT62O1NA

15. Ukrainian embassy in Beijing, Weibo account, online at: https://weibo.com/wukelanembassy

CHAPTER 8 — China–Australia at Fifty

Taking Stock at Fifty

1. Australian embassy in China, 'Australia–China relationship overview', Beijing, 2012, online at: https://china.embassy.gov.au/bjng/relations1.html

2. Australian embassy in China, 'Statement at announcement of conclusion of Australia–China FTA negotiations', Beijing, 17 November 2014, online at: https://china.embassy.gov.au/bjng/HOMstatement.html; and Tony Abbott, 'Joint press statement with President Xi, Canberra', [Transcript], Parliament House, Canberra, 17 November 2014, online at: https://pmtranscripts.pmc.gov.au/release/transcript-23977

3. BBC, 'China refuses to apologise to Australia for fake soldier image', *BBC News*, 1 December 2020, online at: https://www.bbc.com/news/world-asia-china-55140848

4. Various reports, plus James Curran, 'Marles' alliance rapture discards Australia's self-reliance', A*ustralian Financial Review*, 24 July 2022, online at: https://www.afr.com/policy/economy/marles-alliance-rapture-discards-australia-s-self-reliance-20220721-p5b3lt

5. Yi Wang, 'Australia–China relations: The larrikin and the rising giant', in *The Far East and Australasia 2022*, London: Routledge, 2021.

6. Kevin Rudd, 'Australia–China joint statement', Media release, Parliament House, Canberra, 30 October 2009, online at: https://pmtranscripts.pmc.gov.au/release/transcript-16883

7. National Museum Australia (NMA), 'Chinese gold miners', Canberra: NMA, n.d., online at: https://www.nma.gov.au/explore/features/harvest-of-endurance/scroll/chinese-gold-miners

8. William Sima, *China & ANU: Diplomats, Adventurers, Scholars*, Canberra: ANU Press, 2015, p.32.

9. Allan Behm, quoted in Laura Tingle, 'Australia deals itself back into the diplomacy game', *Australian Financial Review*, 18 November 2022, online at: https://www.afr.com/politics/federal/australia-deals-itself-back-into-the-diplomacy-game-20221117-p5bz2x

10. Daniel Hurst, '"Actively develop friendship": China's new ambassador strikes softer tone', *The Guardian*, [London], 24 February 2022, online at: https://www.theguardian.com/australia-news/2022/feb/24/actively-develop-friendship-chinas-new-ambassador-to-australia-strikes-softer-tone

11. James Massola and Matthew Knott, 'PM: Meeting with China ambassador would have been a sign of "weakness"', *Sydney Morning Herald*, 26 March 2022, online at: https://www.smh.com.au/politics/federal/pm-meeting-with-china-ambassador-would-have-been-a-sign-of-weakness-20220325-p5a845.html

12. Doug Dingwall, 'Peter Dutton says Defence monitoring Chinese spy ship Haiwangxing off Western Australia', *The Canberra Times*, 13 May 2022, online at: https://www.canberratimes.com.au/story/7736976/aggressive-act-defence-monitoring-chinese-spy-ship-off-wa/

13. Chris Barrett, 'Wong meets Wang as ministers attempt to stabilise Australia–China relations', *Sydney Morning Herald*, 8 July 2022, online at: https://www.smh.com.au/world/asia/wong-meets-wang-as-ministers-attempt-to-stabilise-china-australia-relations-20220708-p5b0a8.html

14. Katharine Murphy, 'Ambassador's fiery speech was the sound of China laying out terms that Australia has already declined', *The Guardian*, [London], 10 August 2022, online at: https://www.theguardian.com/world/2022/aug/10/ambassadors-fiery-speech-was-the-sound-of-china-laying-out-terms-that-australia-has-already-declined

15. Tingle, 'Australia deals itself back into the diplomacy game'.

16. Daniel Hurst, 'Penny Wong raises human rights and trade with Chinese counterpart during historic talks', *The Guardian*, [London], 21 December 2022, online at: https://www.theguardian.com/australia-news/2022/dec/21/penny-wong-raises-human-rights-and-trade-with-chinese-counterpart-during-historic-talks

17. The Foreign Correspondents' Club of China (FCCChina), *Locked Down or Kicked Out: Covering China*, FCCChina, 2021, online at: https://fccchina.org/wp-content/uploads/2022/01/2021-FCCC-final.pdf?x39796

18. See Daniel Hurst, '"A dangerous act": How a Chinese fighter jet intercepted an RAAF aircraft and what happens next', *The Guardian*, [London], 7 June 2022, online at: https://www.theguardian.com/australia-news/2022/jun/07/a-dangerous-act-how-a-chinese-fighter-jet-intercepted-an-raaf-aircraft-and-what-happens-next

19. Lowy Institute, 'Lowy Institute Poll 2022: China', Lowy Institute, 29 June 2022, online at: https://poll.lowyinstitute.org/themes/china/

20. The four points were: 'First, stick to regarding China as a partner rather than a rival. Second, stick to the way we get along with each other, which features seeking common ground while reserving differences. Third, stick to not targeting any third party or being controlled by any third party. Fourth, stick to building positive and pragmatic social foundations and public support.' Ministry of Foreign Affairs of the People's Republic of China, 'Wang Yi meets with Australian Foreign Minister Penny Wong', Press release, Beijing, 9 July 2022, online at: https://www.fmprc.gov.cn/mfa_eng/zxxx_662805/202207/t20220710_10718115.html. For a detailed analysis of Australian media distortion of Wang's four points, see Wanning Sun, 'Misconstruing China's "demands", Australian media beat the drums of war', *Crikey*, 13 July 2022, online at: https://www.crikey.com.au/2022/07/13/australian-media-china-demands/

21. Stephen FitzGerald, 'The Chinese ambassador and our ignorant and hostile media', *Pearls and Irritations*, 12 August 2022, online at: https://johnmenadue.com/the-chinese-ambassador-and-our-ignorant-and-hostile-media/

22. See Australian embassy in China, 'Australian Studies Centres in China', Beijing, n.d., online at: https://china.embassy.gov.au/bjng/studycenter.html; and Chinese Studies Association of Australia (CSAA), 'Chinese Studies in Australia', Sydney: CSAA, n.d., online at: https://www.csaa.org.au/chinese-studies-in-australia/

A Contentious Friendship

1. Geremie R. Barmé, 'Torching the relay', *The China Beat*, 5 April 2008, online at: http://thechinabeat.blogspot.com/2008/05/torching-relay.html

2. Kevin Rudd, 'Beijing University speech by Australian Prime Minister Kevin Rudd', *The Australian*, [Sydney], 9 April 2008, online at: https://www.theaustralian.com.au/news/kevin-rudds-speech-at-beijing-uni/news-story/27376123d50bd47c0334e9e9f6e0f601?sv=bd93bc5ad59e4fc3bfa5dc2cabc9d831

3. Sina News, 'To be an international zhengyou, one needs the magnanimity of pluralism' 认同国际"诤友"要有多元化的雅量, *Sina News*, [Beijing], 10 April 2008, online at: https://news.sina.com.cn/o/2008-04-10/042713712657s.shtml

4. Kevin Rudd, *The Avoidable War: The Dangers of a Catastrophic Conflict between the US and Xi Jinping's China*, New York, NY: Public Affairs, 2022.

CONTRIBUTORS

Geremie R. Barmé was the founding director of the Australian Centre on China in the World at The Australian National University. He is an emeritus professor and the editor of *China Heritage* (https://chinaheritage.net).

Ausma Bernot is a postdoctoral researcher at the Australian Graduate School of Policing and Security, Charles Sturt University. Her current research focuses on the effects that the merging of infotech and biotech triggers in the fields of governance, surveillance, policing, and public safety. Along with Professor Patrick F. Walsh, Ausma is also working to advance the field of health security in Australia. Ausma's doctoral research explored the dynamic interaction between surveillance technologies and social context and questions totalisation of surveillance in China.

Junyi Cai is a sessional lecturer at the University of Sydney. She received her PhD in gender and cultural studies from the University of Sydney. Her thesis considers how the dynamic between the party-state, women and the society in China is shaped, consolidated, re-constituted and reproduced through assorted hegemonic discursive practices. Her research interests include gender and politics, feminist political theory, and discourse analysis.

Dr Edward Sing Yue Chan is a postdoctoral fellow at the Australian Centre on China in the World, The Australian National University. His research focuses on China's foreign policy, security in the Indo-Pacific, maritime security, and the governance of oceans. He is the author of *China's Maritime Security Strategy: The Evolution of a Growing Sea Power*.

Lennon Yao-Chung Chang is an associate professor of cyber risk and policy in the Centre for Cyber Resilience and Trust (CREST) at Deakin University. He is the founder and president of the Australasian Taiwan Studies Association and the vice-chairman of the Asia Pacific Association of Technology and Society. He is currently researching disinformation, co-production of cyber security and internet vigilantism in the Indo-Pacific region. He is also working with governments and NGOs in ASEAN countries on research and training programs to build cyber security capacity and cyber security awareness.

Arthur Ding is a professor emeritus at National Chenghi University. His research focus includes China's security policy, China's defence science and technology system, as well as party-military relations in China. He holds a PhD in government and international studies from the University of Notre Dame.

Kecheng Fang is an assistant professor at the School of Journalism and Communication, The Chinese University of Hong Kong. His research interests include journalism, political communication, and digital media. Before joining academia, he worked as a political journalist at the Chinese newspaper *Southern Weekly* 南方周末.

Sam Chetwin George is a research fellow at *China Heritage* and works as a geopolitical analyst, advisor and Chinese translator. He has over ten years of experience across the private sector, government and leading research institutions. Sam has a master's in East Asian studies from Stanford University and an undergraduate degree in philosophy, politics and economics from the University of Oxford. He is on Twitter at @samchetwin.

Jane Golley is a professor and economist in the Arndt-Corden Department of Economics at the Crawford School of Public Policy at The Australian National University.

Jorrit Gosens received his PhD from RCEES, an institute of the Chinese Academy of Sciences. He is currently a research fellow at the Crawford School of Public Policy at The Australian National University. He researches renewable energy transitions and innovation globally, including in China.

Ben Hillman is the director of the Australian Centre on China in the World and an associate professor at the Crawford School of Public Policy (both at The Australian National University). He is the editor of *The China Journal*.

Linda Jaivin is the author of *The Shortest History of China*, among 11 other books, a literary translator and editorial associate of the Australian Centre on China in the World.

Sean Kelly was previously a policy fellow at the Australian Centre on China in the World. He was a senior diplomat with the Department of Foreign Affairs and Trade, serving inter alia for three postings in greater China (Taipei, Beijing, and as consul-general for Southern China based in Guangzhou) and in a range of key policy positions, including defence and strategic policy director. Sean holds a master's of international law from The Australian National University and a graduate diploma in strategic studies from the Australian Defence Force's Joint Services Staff College.

Alexander Korolev is a senior lecturer in politics and international relations in the School of Social Sciences at the University of New South Wales, Sydney. Before joining UNSW, Alex was a research fellow in the Centre on Asia and Globalisation at the Lee Kuan Yew School of Public Policy, National University of Singapore (2015–2018). His research interests include international relations theory and comparative politics, with special reference to China and Russia, great-power politics, and China–Russia–US relations. He is currently working on a research project which explores how small and middle powers can survive and secure their national interests amidst intensifying great-power rivalry.

Louisa Lim is a senior lecturer in audiovisual journalism at the Centre for Advancing Journalism at the University of Melbourne. A former BBC and NPR correspondent, she is the author of *Indelible City: Dispossession and Defiance in Hong Kong* and *The People's Republic of Amnesia*. She co-hosts *The Little Red Podcast*.

Adam Y. Liu is an assistant professor at the Lee Kuan Yew School of Public Policy, National University of Singapore. His main research interests include Chinese politics and political economy. He is currently working on a book project that explores how central-local politics drove the formation, expansion, and operation of what he calls a 'state-owned market' in China's banking sector. The project is based on his dissertation, which won the 2020 BRICS Economic Research Award.

Annie Luman Ren is a literary scholar and postdoctoral fellow at the Australian Centre on China in the World, The Australian National University. Her research focuses on the poetics of the mid-Qing novel *Hongloumeng* 紅樓夢 (also known as *The Story of the Stone*) and, by extension, the poetic world of the Bannerman (*qiren* 旗人) that underpins this literary masterpiece.

James A. Millward is a professor of inter-societal history at the Walsh School of Foreign Service, Georgetown University, where he teaches Qing, Chinese, Central Asian, and world history. Millward is the academic editor for the 'Silk Roads' book series published by the University of Chicago Press, and a former president of the Central Eurasian Studies Society.

Neil Thomas is a fellow on Chinese politics at Asia Society Policy Institute's Center for China Analysis. He was previously a Morrison Scholar at the Australian Centre on China in the World. He is based in Washington, DC, and is on Twitter: @neilthomas123.

Pan Wang is a senior lecturer in Chinese and Asian studies at the University of New South Wales. She is the author of *Love and Marriage in Globalizing China* (Routledge, 2015 and 2018). Her research areas include love, marriage, and gender in China and Chinese media and communication. You can find her on Twitter: @panwang119

Yi Wang is a political scientist at Griffith University and a former media executive and diplomat. His book *Australia-China Relations post 1949: Sixty Years of Trade and Politics* remains the only sole-authored, systematic account of Australia–China relations, covering the entire span of bilateral history from the immediate postwar years to the present era.

Jeffrey Wasserstrom is a chancellor's professor of history at UC Irvine, where he also holds courtesy appointments in law, literary journalism and political science. He often writes for newspapers and magazines as well as scholarly journals, and his books include, as author, *Vigil: Hong Kong on the Brink* (2020) and, as editor, *The Oxford History of Modern China* (2022).

Joel Wing-Lun is a lecturer in history and Asian studies at the University of New South Wales.

His research uses fieldwork and village documents to examine the social, economic, and environmental impact of imperial expansion on communities in South-west China from the seventeenth through to the twentieth century. He is currently researching marriage practices and networks in Guizhou province at the turn of the twentieth century.

Barry van Wyk is a business editor at *The China Project*, and a research associate at the Africa–China Reporting Project at the Centre for Journalism, University of the Witwatersrand, Johannesburg.

Hongzhang Xu is a researcher, and an advocate of transdisciplinary research and cross cultural communication. Hong's research considers how our societies can adapt to and benefit from changes based on the underlying power relations and cultural values that are integral to social change and to the institutional dynamics that mediate human–environment and human–human relations. His current studies focus on investigating Aboriginal and Torres Strait Islander mathematics and sciences. Hong is also interested in global Indigenous sciences, sustainable natural resource management, and trade-off issues between conservation and development, as well as just transitions to carbon neutral and sustainable development.

Peishan Yann, educated in Singapore, Australia, and China, is fascinated with cultures and languages. She is pursuing her master's in translation and interpreting at the University of Melbourne.

William Yang is the East Asia correspondent for Germany's international broadcaster Deutsche Welle. He writes about social and political issues in China, Hong Kong, and Taiwan, as well as China's growing influence around the world.

Denghua Zhang is a research fellow at the Department of Pacific Affairs, The Australian National University. His research focuses on Chinese foreign aid, foreign policy, and China in the Pacific.

PREVIOUS *CHINA STORY YEARBOOKS*

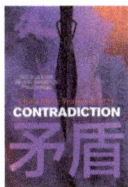

2021: *Contradiction*

In the second year of the COVID-19 pandemic, the many facets of crisis — the theme of last year's *China Story Yearbook* — fractured into pictures of contradiction throughout Chinese society and the Chinese sphere of influence.

Contradiction: the ancient Chinese word for the concept holds within it the image of an unstoppable spear meeting an impenetrable shield. It describes a wide range of phenomena that English might express with words like conflict, clash, paradox, incongruity, disagreement, rebuttal, opposition, and negation. This year's *Yearbook* presents stories of action and reaction, of motion and resistance.

The theme of contradiction plays out in different ways across the different realms of society, culture, environment, labour, politics, and international relations. Great powers do not necessarily succeed in dominating smaller ones. The seemingly irresistible forces of authoritarianism, patriarchy, and technological control come up against energised and surprisingly resilient means of resistance or cooptation. Efforts by various authorities to establish monolithic narrative control over the past and present meet a powerful insistence on telling the story from an opposite angle. The *China Story Yearbook 2021: Contradiction* offers an accessible take on this complex and contradictory moment in the history of China and of the world.

2020: *Crisis*

The *China Story Yearbook 2020: Crisis* surveys the multiple crises of the year of the Metal Rat, including the catastrophic mid-year floods that sparked fears about the stability of the Three Gorges Dam. It looks at how Chinese women fared through the pandemic, from the rise in domestic violence to portraits of female sacrifice on the medical front line to the trolling of a famous dancer for being childless. It also examines the downward-spiralling Sino-Australian relationship, the difficult 'co-morbidities' of China's relations with the United States, the end of 'One Country, Two Systems' in Hong Kong, the simmering border conflict with India, and the rise of pandemic-related anti-Chinese racism. The *Yearbook* also explores the responses to crisis of, among others, Daoists, Buddhists, and humourists — because when all else fails, there's always philosophy, prayer, and laughter.

2019: *China Dreams*

The year 2019 marked a number of significant anniversaries for the People's Republic of China (PRC), each representing different 'Chinese dreams'. There was the centennial of the May Fourth Movement — a dream of patriotism and cultural renewal. The PRC celebrated its seventieth anniversary — a dream of revolution and national strength. It was also thirty years since the student-led protest movement of 1989 — dreams of democracy and free expression crushed by party-state dreams of unity and stability. Many of these 'dreams' recurred in new guises in 2019. Xi Jinping tightened his grip on power at home while calling for all citizens to 'defend China's honour abroad'. Escalating violence in Hong Kong, the ongoing suppression of Uyghurs in Xinjiang and deteriorating Sino-US relations dominated the headlines. Alongside stories about China's advances in artificial intelligence and genetically modified babies, and its ambitions in the Antarctic and outer space, these issues fuelled discussion about what Xi's own 'China Dream' of national rejuvenation means for Chinese citizens and the rest of the world.

2018: *Power*

In 2018, the People's Republic of China (PRC) was, by most measures, more powerful than at any other time in its history and had become one of the most powerful countries in the world. Its economy faced serious challenges, including from the ongoing 'trade war' with the United States, but still ranked as the world's second largest. Its Belt and Road Initiative, meanwhile, continued to carve paths of influence and economic integration across several continents. A deft combination of policy, investment, and entrepreneurship has also turned the PRC into a global 'techno-power'. It aims, with a good chance of success, at becoming a global science and technology leader by 2049 — one hundred years from the founding of the PRC.

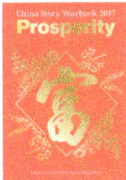

2017: *Prosperity*

A 'moderately prosperous society' with no Chinese individual left behind — that's the vision for China set out by CPC general secretary Xi Jinping in a number of important speeches in 2017. 'Moderate' prosperity may seem like a modest goal for a country with more billionaires (609 at last count) than the United States. But the 'China Story' is a complex one. The *China Story Yearbook 2017: Prosperity* surveys the important events, pronouncements, and personalities that defined 2017. It also presents a range of perspectives, from the global to the individual, the official to the unofficial, from mainland China to Hong Kong and Taiwan. Together, the stories present a richly textured portrait of a nation that

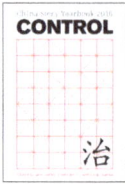

in just forty years has lifted itself from universal poverty to (unequally distributed) wealth, changing itself and the world in the process.

2016: *Control*

'More cosmopolitan, more lively, more global' is how the *China Daily* summed up the year 2016 in China. It was also a year of more control. The Communist Party of China laid down strict new rules of conduct for its members, continued to assert its dominance over everything from the internet to the South China Sea and announced a new Five-Year Plan that Greenpeace called 'quite possibly the most important document in the world in setting the pace of acting on climate change'.

2015: *Pollution*

This *Yearbook* explores the broader ramifications of pollution in the People's Republic for culture, society law and social activism, as well as the internet, language, thought, and approaches to history. It looks at how it affects economic and political developments, urban change, and China's regional and global posture. The Communist Party of China, led by 'Chairman of Everything' Xi Jinping, meanwhile, has subjected mainland society to increasingly repressive control in its new determination to rid the country of Western 'spiritual pollutants' while achieving cultural purification through 'propaganda and ideological work'.

2014: *Shared Destiny*

The People's Republic of China under the leadership of the Communist Party of China and Xi Jinping, has declared that it shares in the destiny of the countries of the Asia and Pacific region, as well as of nations that are part of an intertwined national self-interest. The *China Story Yearbook 2014* takes the theme of Shared Destiny 共同命运 and considers it in the context of China's current and future potential.

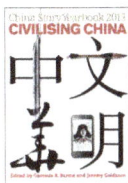

2013: *Civilising China*

As China becomes wealthier and more confident on the global stage, it also expects to be respected and accommodated as a major global force — and as a formidable civilisation. Through a survey and analysis of China's regional posture, urban change, social activism and law, mores, the internet, history, and thought — in which the concept of 'civilising' plays a prominent role — *China Story Yearbook 2013* offers insights into the country today and its dreams for the future.

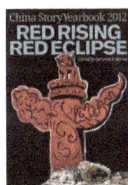

2012: *Red Rising, Red Eclipse*

The authors of *Red Rising, Red Eclipse* survey China's regional posture, urban change, social activism and law, human rights and economics, the internet, history, and thought. This inaugural *China Story Yearbook* offers an informed perspective on recent developments in China and provides a context for understanding ongoing issues that will resonate far beyond the Dragon Year of 2012–2013.

www.ingramcontent.com/pod-product-compliance
Lightning Source LLC
Chambersburg PA
CBHW050806270326
41926CB00026B/4578